Keeping Them Out of the Hands of Satan

Critical Social Thought

Series editor: Michael W. Apple
Professor of Curriculum and Instruction and Educational Policy
Studies, University of Wisconsin-Madison

Already published

Keeping Them Out of the Hands of Satan

Evangelical Schooling in America
SUSAN D. ROSE

Routledge
New York London

First published in 1988 by

Routledge
An imprint of Routledge, Chapman and Hall, Inc.
29 West 35 Street
New York, NY 10001

Published in Great Britain by

Routledge
11 New Fetter Lane
London EC4P 4EE

Copyright © 1988 by Routledge, Chapman and Hall, Inc.

Printed in the United States of America

Library of Congress Cataloging-in-Publication Data

Rose, Susan D., 1955–
    Keeping them out of the hands of Satan : evangelical schooling in
America/Susan D. Rose.
        p.   cm. —(Critical social thought)
    Bibliography: p.
    Includes index.
    ISBN 0–415–90004–2
    1. Fundamentalist churches—Education—United
        States. 2. Church schools—United
        States. I. Title. II. Series
    LC586.F85R67 1988   377.8–dc19 87–30679

British Library Cataloguing in Publication Data

Rose, Susan D.
    Keeping them out of the hands of satan :
    evangelical schooling in America.—
    (Critical social thought).
    1. Church and education—United States
    I. Title II. Series
    261   LC427
    ISBN 0–415–90004–2

To my family
and those special others who have shared with me their belief in
the power of human potential and their faith in a spirit that
transcends human possibility.

Contents

Series Editor's Introduction

The dislocations of the 1960s and 1970s—the struggles for racial and sexual equality, military and political adventures such as Vietnam and Watergate, the resilience of economic crisis—produced both shock and fear. "Mainstream culture" was shaken to its very roots in many ways. Widely shared notions of family, community, and nation were dramatically altered. Just as important, no new principle of cohesion emerged that was sufficiently compelling to create a cultural center. As economic, political, and valuative stability (and military supremacy) seemed to disappear, the polity was itself "balkanized." Social movements based on difference—regional, racial, sexual, religious—became more visible.[1] The sense of what Marcus Raskin has called "the common good" was fractured.[2]

For many, traditional social democratic "statist" solutions were seen as being part of the problem not part of the solution. Traditional conservative positions were more easily dismissed as well by critics. After all, the society on which they were based was clearly being dramatically altered. The cultural center could be *built* (and it had to be built by well-funded and well-organized political and cultural action), certain right-wing critics of traditional conservatism claimed, around the principles of the New Right. The New Right confronts the "moral, existential, [and economic] chaos of the preceding decades" with a network of exceedingly well-organized and financially secure conservative organizations incorporating "an aggressive political style, an outspoken religious and cultural traditionalism, and a clear political commitment."[3]

Since its inception, the New Right project has been aimed at constructing a "new majority" that will "dismantle the welfare state, legislate a return to 'traditional morality,' and stem the tide of political and cultural dislocation which the 1960s and 1970s represented." Using a populist political strategy, it marshals an assault on "liberalism and secular humanism" and links this with what some observers have argued is "an obsession with individual guilt and responsibility where social questions are concerned (crime, sex, education, poverty) and a fierce anti-statism."[4]

The New Right has been able to rearticulate traditional political and cultural themes and in so doing has effectively mobilized a mass base of adherents. Among its most powerful causes and effects has been the growing feeling of disaffection about public schooling among conservative groups. Large numbers of parents and other people simply no longer trust either the institutions of education or the teachers and administrators in them to make "correct" decisions about what should be taught or how to teach it. The rapid growth of evangelical schooling and the emerging tendency of many parents to teach their children at home rather than send them to publicly supported schools are clear indications of the state's loss of legitimacy.[5] Susan Rose's book provides us with a remarkably lucid account of what the choice to send one's children to an evangelical school means in this context. Why do parents make such a choice? What happens within such schools? What do the curricula, teaching, and social relations look like? What social visions guide their policies and practices? What are the possible social results of such schooling? *Keeping Them Out of the Hands of Satan* helps us answer these questions in insightful ways.

Because of the dislocations of the 1960s and 1970s and because of the complicated social agenda behind it, the growth of phenomena such as the Christian schooling movement cannot be fully explained as the result of these parents being child-centered. As Allen Hunter has argued, such action may come "less from a direct concern with children than from a New Right conviction that children bind men and women to identities as fathers and mothers within the 'traditional' family." For many people within this movement "proper" relations between parents and children serve to "enforce clear gender roles," teach traditional values, and usually provide an "anti-welfare state defense of pro-capitalist economics."[6]

We cannot understand why parents and others would establish schools of this type unless we place them in a larger framework of assumptions about human nature, religion, sexuality, gender, work, play, and authority. The movement is situated within a complicated set of dynamics including the backlash against feminism and social protest movements, fears of the disintegration of the family, and an increasingly hard world of economic uncertainty.

"Since the mid-1970s losing control over one's children and the environment within which they grow up has itself been a real fear and has also symbolized a more diffuse fear that social and cultural change is out of control or controlled by undemocratic elites" (Hunter, p. 1).

A considerable number of individuals believe that "the family has been debased because motherhood has been culturally demeaned." In their view, urban elites have caused discipline, restraint, and propriety to be scoffed at. For them, the protection of their children from these forces is caught up in a set of gender and class relations in which the ultimate role for women is that of mother and fatherhood embodies the ethics of breadwinner and legitimate authority who "enforces moral behavior on those in his charge." At its broadest level, their sense of the need for social and cultural restoration is often coupled with a larger set of political affiliations in which patriotism and a commitment to unrestrained capitalist growth play an important part (Hunter, pp. 3-4).

This is not the first time that these fears and their accompanying politics have entered the American landscape, a point nicely made in *Keeping Them Out of the Hands of Satan*. As Rose documents, periods of revivalism, of "great awakenings," are recurring tendencies in our past. The New Right's "authoritarian populism" has extensive roots in the history of the United States. The political culture here has always been influenced by the values of the dissenting Protestantism of the seventeenth century. Such roots become even more evident in periods of intense social change and crisis.[7] Walter Dean Burnham has stated it in the following manner:

Whenever and wherever the pressures of modernization—secularity, urbanization, the growing importance of science—have become unusually intense, episodes of revivalism and culture-issue politics have swept over the social landscape. In all such cases since at least the end of the Civil War, such movements have been more or less explicitly reactionary, and have frequently been linked with other kinds of reaction in explicitly political ways.[8]

All of these points do serve to place the evangelical schooling movement in its larger social context, a context we ignore at our own risk. At the same time, however, we must not ignore how it is that real groups of people make decisions in their day-to-day lives. The parents, church groups, and others who have established evangelical schools do so out of genuine commitments that are not simply negative. These people are not merely puppets of larger structural forces. They are not simply manipulated by the well-financed and well-organized New Right agenda. These influences *are* very visibly there, of course. However, the persons involved in such schooling are searching for things that are missing in all too many of our institutions—a sense of control and community, an education that responds to the wishes of local actors and is not highly bureaucratized or dominated by top-down mandates, a need for a system of ethics that could guide our conduct.

These hopes and dreams may be part of a larger ideological movement and, indeed, may result in social and educational policies and practices that many of us would find more than a little unwise. However, with the help of Rose's book, we can begin to gain a better understanding of the motives, beliefs, and personal struggles behind the decisions by many people to establish evangelical schools. When these beliefs become embodied in real people, it is harder for us to stereotype, harder for us not to recognize the partly positive moments in what some of the parents are striving for. This does not mean that everyone should agree with the social and educational policies avowed by many of the evangelical educators who are represented in this book. Indeed, there will be a whole array of issues raised that may cause substantial worry for democratically inclined readers. But Rose has succeeded in presenting us with a much more balanced picture than what our usual stereotypes allow for. The Christian school movement is *not* monolithic. Not all schools are alike. Not all groups of parents want the same things for their children. And, not all visions of culture, appropriate educational experiences, and teaching and learning are the same. The two schools Susan Rose focuses on are strikingly different in important ways. Both are avowedly Christian and evangelical. However, one is organized around openness in teacher/student interaction and prides itself on its flexibility and on the personal interactions between teachers, students, and curricula. The other is characterized by a totally prepackaged curriculum that is purchased from a for-profit centralized curriculum development house. This latter school, an academy based on the principles of A.C.E. (Accelerated Christian Education), prides itself on having few formal teachers and having students proceed through standardized lessons at individual student "offices."

Both groups of parents want the very best for their children. Both communities are willing to sacrifice to get it. What sets them apart for Rose is the specific class configuration of each of the groups. The first, more open school links its children to the flexible dispositions and skills required for middle-class occupations. The A.C.E. school, whose parents tend to be more working class, culturally and economically, provides an education suited for positions in the low paying, increasingly de-skilled service and military sectors of our economy. Thus, for Rose, each of these schools may be linked to the reproduction of unequal class and gender relations and each needs to be understood in the context of the class culture it serves.

One of the most interesting parts of *Keeping Them Out of the Hands of Satan* is its description and analysis of the standardized methods of Accelerated Christian Education. The growing significance of A.C.E. schools should not be underestimated. A.C.E. programs are completely pre-packaged and are similar to corporate franchises in many ways. Rose describes its growth and enrollment aims as:

> A.C.E. is a for-profit corporation operating out of Texas with a nationwide network of approximately 5,000 entrepreneurs who pay for the use of the A.C.E. system. A.C.E. began in 1970 with forty-five students. By 1972,

there were 4,000; by 1974, 30,000; by 1976, 80,000; by 1978, 160,000; by 1980, 275,000 students. As of 1986, A.C.E. operates from 5,900 schools throughout the United States and in eighty-six foreign countries. The average school size is thirty-five to seventy students. Moreover, they provide curriculum to 1,600 families in the United States and 300 families in foreign countries who are educating their children at home. . . . Their goal [is to have] ten thousand schools with one million children by 1989.

Even with her evident sensitivity to the complicated motives behind the parents' choice to establish an A.C.E. school, Rose rightly raises a number of fears. As she says, among the ultimate effects of such educational practices is the separation of working-class children into isolated small schools, the further class stratification that will then emerge, and the inability of such students to question what they are receiving. In essence, "they may be getting the best preparation for the army, the factory, or the automated office."

This said, however, we need again to remember that there are a number of contradictory tendencies at work here. Schools established by evangelical groups are often the result of genuinely populist tendencies. As I noted and as Rose demonstrates, many of the people involved in them are in fact attempting to win back control over the institutions which affect their lives and the lives of their children from what they perceive to be anonymous and elite forces in society. As I have argued in *Education and Power*, there are partly progressive tendencies in this, ones that should not be dismissed out of hand.[9] Yet very often this is a right-wing populism. It can be less than sympathetic to the needs of oppressed and poor people and is often coupled with political and economic ideologies that have significant anti-democratic elements as well.

There is yet another contradictory tendency at work here. Since such Christian schools overtly sidestep state control—they are not public but private institutions—they often teach a curriculum that itself embodies extremely conservative elements. This fact is obvious, but it deserves comment. Many individuals on the left side of the political spectrum have argued that the government is often simply a tool of domination. Schools only teach the ideology of the powerful. That this is an overstatement is made clear when we have a case in which the state is *removed*. The A.C.E. schools offer a paradigm case here. Without the partly progressive messages embodied in the curriculum in public schools, some children will be taught only a very conservative view of international affairs, of gender and race relations, of our economy, and so on.

This presents something of a dilemma for educators and others who are interested in democratizing curricula and teaching policies and practices in schools. To what extent can we empower parents, the community, dispossessed groups, teachers, students, and others, and at the same time ensure that the knowledge that is taught does not embody a truncated vision of justice, does not destroy our sense of the common good? Some policymakers have proposed voucher plans that would be guided by a form of state regulation to deal with this dilemma. The dangers of such a policy are too numerous to note here.[10] Though not overtly about such policy decisions, Rose's insightful portrayal of education in two distinct kinds of evangelical schools can certainly help us see the implications, both positive and negative, of such policies.

The author's ability to demonstrate sympathetically yet critically the kinds of education going on in these two schools and her honesty in pointing out where some of this education may lead makes her book significant. Her recognition of the history of these kinds of movements, the linkages she makes between evangelical schooling and class and gender relations in the larger society, and her ability to present her information clearly and sensitively, all combine to make *Keeping Them Out of the Hands of Satan* a volume that should be read by people in education, government, religious studies, sociology—and anyone who is interested in a movement that will have a growing impact on our society for decades to come.

Michael W. Apple
The University of Wisconsin, Madison

Preface

The Bible clearly states that the wife is to submit to her
husband's leadership and help him fulfill God's will for his
life (cf. Eph. 5:22–24; Cor. 1. 3:18). There can be no doubt
as to the meaning of these passages. She is to submit to
him, just as she would submit to Christ her Lord. This
places the responsibility of leadership upon the husband,
where it belongs. In a sense, submission is the wife learning
to duck, so God can hit the husband. He will never realize
his responsibility to the family as long as she takes it. If the
wife wants her husband to be more of a leader, she must let
go of the reins. Most men do not enjoy fighting their wife
for control over the family, so they sit back and do nothing.
In time, the wife has a nervous breakdown trying to run
something God did not call her to run. (Dr. Edward
Hindson, former Director of Counseling at Jerry Falwell's
Thomas Road Baptist Ministries)[1]

The man's attraction is to a woman, not to a "professional
person," and certainly not to a competitor whose success
makes him feel inadequate in his God-given role as a
provider. (James Robison, Evangelist)[2]

These passages reflect the struggles of power, control, and
constraint that have characterized the latest Evangelical
Awakening in the United States. They attracted my attention and
stimulated my adrenalin flow—not because they were unfamiliar
but because they enjoyed fresh and renewed currency in the late
1970s and early 1980s. Evangelicals viewed the attempt to bring

men and women closer together as an attack on the "God-given and natural rights" of men. The struggle for greater egalitarianism was defined as an adversarial struggle between men and women, rather than a struggle of all people for a more just and liberating set of roles, experiences, and life chances.

I became interested in the Evangelical Movement and the rise of the new Religious Right in the early 1980s as I was doing research on domestic violence and the sources of stress and support for families in America. I was intrigued by groups who proclaimed themselves "pro-family," yet simultaneously protested against mandatory child abuse reporting, shelters for battered women, and the International Year of the Child, declaring it "one of the most demonic things to have come along in the past decade." How did they arrive at such conclusions? How did they reconcile these positions? The Family Protection Acts initially aroused outrage and anger in me that then became somewhat tempered by genuine puzzlement, serious curiosity, and legitimate concern.

The politics of the contemporary Evangelical Movement center on issues of control and commitment. "Man" is supposed to submit to Christ, wives to their husbands, and children to their parents. Any questioning of the "God-given" lines of authority is considered an act of ungodly defiance. Furthermore, in equating godliness with Americanism such resistance to tradition is considered a sign of not only un-Christian but also unpatriotic behavior. Evangelicals are concerned that the country is being lost to communism, that free enterprise is being overpowered by big government, and that Christianity is being seduced by secular humanism.

The evangelical cry went out. In the words of Reverend Jerry Falwell, "What America needs is a return to the old time values that made America great." That means, in the mainstream of evangelical thought, to go back to the days of patriarchal, parental, and Protestant supremacy. Contemporary evangelicals would like to roll back the advances made by the women's and civil rights movements which have challenged not only the legitimacy of patriarchal authority, but also its very desirability for women, children, and men of any color, creed, or class.

The women's, civil rights, and ecumenical movements, affirmative action, secular humanism, and global education are all perceived as threats to traditional American values and the "historic" and "natural" stratification of authority, power, and status. But the political aspirations of the new evangelicals do not stop at saving souls or strengthening the traditional American family. The belief in America's manifest destiny is still strong; evangelicals hope to carry out America's holy mission to Christianize the rest of the world. Their involvement in the politics of Third-World nations is a telling example.

Whether the issue is suppressing popular unrest in Latin America or South Africa or pacifying labor unrest and dissatisfaction with the economy in the United States, evangelicalism tends to be aligned with elite economic interests and conservative, right-wing governments. Although some exceptions exist (for example, Evangelicals for Social Action), a close alliance between the military and "God's army" of evangelicals is well established.

But this book does not focus on the political and economic activities of evangelicals; rather it focuses on the meaning systems, organizational structures, and daily lives of evangelicals. The in-depth ethnographies of two evangelical communities should help, however, to make the economic and political phenomena more comprehensible. By exploring the evangelical institutions of church, home, and school at the grass-roots level, we can come to understand better the appeal and practice of evangelicalism. And, I would argue, to understand the appeal of Ronald Reagan, his White House administration (which includes other notable born-agains, including the Attorney General, Edwin Meese), and the elevation of Lieutenant-Colonel Oliver North to heroic status as a man of conviction—no matter how illegal behavior—one needs to understand the history and power of conservative evangelical religion in America.

Why have so many working- and middle-class people embraced elitist economic arguments and policies? Many evangelicals preach that the civil government is ordained by God and therefore must be obeyed. Evangelical preachers stress obedience, order, and discipline and at the same time offer a theology of prosperity. Why did Jim and Tammy Baker's "You can make it happen today!" or Oral Roberts's "Something good is going to happen to you today" hold so powerful a message for so many people? People are searching for a sense of coherence, for order in their personal and public lives. What kinds of compromises are they making?

In the two communities I studied, I found many of the people much more genuine and consistent than their more vocal and prominent spokesmen. As Jim and Tammy Baker siphon off millions of dollars and Oral Roberts bargains for money with sensational suicide threats, the people of Covenant and Lakehaven are still trying to live the Word as faithfully as they can. Why is it that they turned and remain faithful to evangelicalism? What do they believe and how do they practice their beliefs?

The research

In order to understand the evangelical resistance to more egalitarian relationships between rich and poor and men and women, I needed to come to a better understanding of who evangelicals were as institutional actors and as individuals. I wanted to explore the meaning systems of evangelicals who were increasingly becoming an important political force in contemporary American society. Why was evangelicalism appealing to so many people, in fact, to approximately 22% of Americans (eighteen years and older). How did they make sense of their lives and their world? What was the history of the evangelical movement and how did contemporary evangelicals fit into this history and into the complexities of American life? And a question central to this book, how were they educating the next generation?

Much has been written about the demographic characteristics and the political views and mobilization of evangelicals, but few studies have gone beneath the structural surface to examine what evangelicals believe and how they act on those beliefs. Exceptions to this include Alan Peshkin's ethnography of a fundamentalist Baptist school (*In God's Choice*, 1986) and Nancy Ammerman's insightful work on a fundamentalist fellowship in New England ("The Fundamentalist Worldview," 1985). Also Pat McNamara's work on Christian families and their worldviews ("The New Christian Right's View of the Family and its Social

Science Critics," 1985) represents the kind of in-depth interviewing and observation that are needed to reveal the meaning of evangelical culture in contemporary American society. All of us faced the same challenge: to delve deeper and understand better. Spending time with people and participating in the daily activities of school, family, and church life over a period of two years helped me to understand better both the rhetoric and the reality of the lives of people in the Covenant and Lakehaven communities. My fieldnotes recorded the daily interactions and routines. By observing the form, content, and style of people's interactions, I became better aware of the consistencies and contradictions of their lives.

From the spring of 1982 through the spring of 1984 I carried out in-depth ethnographies of two evangelical fellowships, both located in upstate New York within thirty miles of one another. Each had approximately the same size fellowship, and had established schools in 1974. The middle-class, independent, charismatic Covenant community is very different, however, from the predominantly working-class, fundamentalist Baptist Lakehaven community.

These two communities were selected from a survey of Christian schools that I conducted in Lynchburg, Virginia and in three contiguous counties in upstate New York. I approached each fellowship by attending church services. This gave me an hour or two orientation to the church before introducing myself and the interests I had in Christian education. I wanted to know who had initiated these schools, who conceived and organized the curriculum and the fund-raising, and whom the schools served. Did this grass-roots movement which began to grow dramatically in the 1970s empower parents?

I communicated my interests in the following way:

I am doing a study of Christian schools. Very little is known about Christian schools in general, and individual schools in particular. It is evident that you and other people involved in this school feel strongly enough about wanting to educate your children in an environment you feel comfortable with and believe in, that you have put your efforts into establishing and/or supporting this school. I am studying Christian schools in this area and in New York/Virginia as a beginning attempt to provide a profile of Christian schools. Such a study will not be able to fully capture the "essence" of your school, but it will provide useful and interesting information to other Christian schools and to the general public.

Through this general approach, I visited and surveyed eighteen schools. As I had anticipated, just walking into the school proved much more effective than writing a formal letter of introduction or calling in advance on the phone. Value is placed on personal contacts rather than on more formal introductions. Also, once I was on the scene, dressed appropriately and seeming respectable enough, I had a much greater chance of engaging people who otherwise had little or no interest in "being studied."

Although a number of communities were resistant to academic research, their emphasis on evangelicalism meant that I was seen as a potential convert; therefore, people tended to see this as an opportunity to witness to me, to share their life stories in an attempt to win me over to Christ. Once they had decided I was not an evil person, "although one has to be careful because the devil can be disguised as an angel—particularly in the latter days," they were willing to consider the possibilities of being part of a study.

The difficulty in gaining entree is not the only reason why many academics may shy away from doing research on evangelical communities. Evangelicals are not the only ones who share a sense of distrust of and distaste for the "other"; the non-evangelical or the "unsaved" is also likely to be suspicious of and threatened by the values, beliefs, and actions of the "saved." Each group is likely to be uncomfortable in the presence of the other, to feel hostility and, perhaps, pity for the other who from their perspective is entrapped in a "false consciousness."

Christian education presents a paradox to contemporary critics. While it contributes to religious and educational pluralism by establishing alternative institutions, its commitment to a monolithic doctrine threatens that very pluralism.[3] The conflict for some of us may lie in our commitment to diversity and pluralism and in our contrary desire to curtail any ideology that proclaims that there is "One and Only One Truth." The conflict arises between those who see the world in absolutist terms and those who see it in relativist terms. There may be no way to bridge such fundamental differences, but what is often ignored—by all sides—is the large common ground of concerns and desires shared by Americans of many persuasions. Contemporary Americans are working their way through a period of cultural disorientation; the various mazeways we create and negotiate will all help define our future—some will be more effective than others in leading the way to tomorrow.

This book attempts to explore both the common and the divergent ground by examining the values, commitments, and actions of contemporary evangelicals. I focus on the lives and interactions of a group of working-class, fundamentalist Baptists and a group of middle-class independent charismatics, both of whom are negotiating their way in the modern world.

The first three chapters introduce the socio-historical context of contemporary American evangelicalism and the dramatic growth of Christian schools in the latter half of the twentieth century. Given some understanding of the fertile ground for evangelical education, the next four chapters provide a descriptive ethnography of the Covenant and Lakehaven communities, and the schools they sponsor. The book concludes with a comparative analysis of the two communities and the processes of socialization. In presenting the ethnographies, I have tried not to distort the story of the Covenant and Lakehaven people. But inevitably their stories are told through me, and thus carry with them my selective bias. As much as possible, the themes that I have chosen to explore and the parts of the story I have chosen to tell are grounded in the values, orientations, and concerns of each group. Because different issues are more salient for one group than the other, the presentation of each group varies somewhat.

I resisted interspersing comparative and critical material with the earlier chapters for two reasons. First, I did not want to distract the reader—who likely lives outside the world of the Christian schools—from the explication of evangelicals' beliefs and practices in their own terms. Second, my critique of Christian education that finds expression in the last chapter is only partially developed; it has not been able to explicate all the psychological, social, and economic factors that tie religious belief to the earthly project of creating and maintaining a system of education. But that does not release any of us from the responsibility of asking hard questions and speculating about the possible consequences of such education. There are numerous issues that merit serious consideration as we contemplate the future of education and the future of American society.

In the end, when I speculate about the connection between Christian education, socio-economic classes, and the current development of the American economy, I want to give the reader some food for thought rather than an economistic reading of history. I do not believe that one can point to a strict "correspondence" between the needs of late-capitalist society in the United States and the purposes of these Christian schools. But I do think we need to ponder the parallels of educational and corporate development, which suggest that we ought to be concerned about a future that is likely to offer diminishing expectations to many, perhaps most, Americans.

The rise of evangelicalism as a conservative political force comes at a time when liberalism is not coping well with the problems of American society and the elite are organized to maximize their own economic self-interests. Evangelicalism, the folk religion of Americans, once again spreads to fill the emptiness. In the Fourth Great Awakening (1960–the present), as in previous awakenings (see Chapter 1), the predominantly grass-roots movement of evangelicalism has given voice to a popular expression that supports the conservative economic message coming from the top. Today, the complex of conservative political and social attitudes that are associated with evangelicalism serves as the handmaiden to this conservative economic argument. More egalitarian ideals and ideas are considered a threat—be they the more equal redistribution of resources (money, jobs, health care, education) or of power among people of different classes, colors, creeds, and genders.

In the discussion that follows, I hope that I can illuminate the concerns of two groups of evangelicals and how these people are coping with the realities of daily life. This may begin to explain why evangelicalism is appealing to them, what forms of resistance and accommodation they are engaged in, and what desires and hopes they hold for their children.

Acknowledgments

This book is a result of over two years of field work in evangelical communities. I want to again thank the people of Covenant and Lakehaven, and the numerous other principals, preachers, teachers, students and laypeople who have willingly given of their time and their commitment in order to share with me their beliefs and their faith. Raised as a p.k. (preacher's kid) in a liberal Methodist home, I was familiar with certain Christian traditions but was very much a foreigner to evangelical culture. In many ways, I was entering a new culture and it held for me the same kind of excitement that any adventure holds when one is not sure what one will find and how one will be affected by the experience. I had much to learn and the people of Covenant and Lakehaven had much to teach. This they did very patiently, eager to communicate and to bring me along in their understanding. For this, I am very grateful. The people of both fellowships were extremely generous with their time and their caring which is what made this study possible and as rewarding as it has been. This is not to say that they withheld judgment or warning but that they often tried to express them with equanimity; this I attempt in return.

In reflecting upon the people's lives and choices within these communities and how they are similar to and different from those of other people and communities I have come to know, a number of friends contributed considerably. A special thanks goes to Jonathan Plotkin, Julia Rose, Ron Keith and Donna Fish for their continual support.

Relationships have been known to be strained in the process of writing dissertations and books. But they can also be stimulated, and indeed, initiated. My husband, Steve Brouwer, and I met over a conversation about evangelicalism. That conversation has continued and expanded. Steve became and remains my most critical and patient editor. His insight and encouragement have contributed greatly to the book and beyond.

I especially want to thank my dissertation committee, from whence this all began. Glen Elder, Jr., Robin Williams, Jr., Carol Greenhouse, and Joan Brumberg provided the kind of guidance and support through my doctoral program at Cornell that kept me asking questions and digging deeper. It was a pleasure and privilege to have been directed by such fine scholars. Finally, I want to thank Michael Apple. His writings helped to sharpen my thinking and his cogent comments as series editor helped to strengthen the writing of this manuscript.

Thanks also to the Lehman Foundation for the fellowship support throughout the four years of graduate school that made this initial inquiry possible, and the Sage Graduate Fellowships and the Sigma Xi Dissertation Research Grant for additional financial support. Dickinson College also provided support for the costs of preparing the manuscript and continuing research on North American evangelical activity in Guatemala for which I am very grateful. Thanks also to Brenda Bretz and Elaine Mellen for help with the typing.

And the family—I want to thank my families, the Roses and the Brouwers, for their love and support. Over the past five years, they somehow managed to sustain their interest and their willingness to put up with someone who is obsessed with ekeing out a manuscript on weekends, evenings and holidays.

Keeping Them Out of the Hands of Satan

Introduction

Over the past twenty years, we have been witnessing the resurgence of evangelicalism. Today, the Christian School Movement is the fastest growing sector of private education, representing one of the most important mobilization efforts of evangelicals to regain influence in our society. In an attempt to exercise greater control over the socialization of the young, parents of approximately one million children—20% of the total private school population—have enrolled their offspring in private, evangelical Christian schools. Attempting to enclose their children within the trinity of family–church–school, evangelicals hope to win their children over to Christ before they are "seduced" by the secular world. Many evangelicals believe that Christian education is critical to the fight they want to win:

> The battle for the Christian school is thus the battle for the faith. We are in the most important and crucial war of religion in all history, the struggle between Christianity and humanism.[1]

What is this enemy called secular humanism? Television evangelist James Robison explains:

> Although it [secular humanism] ostensibly champions the dignity of man, it denies he has a soul or is capable of salvation, and it leads inexorably to his degradation and a level of existence barely superior to that of animals. Its "creed book," the *Humanist Manifesto*, favors freedom of sexual choice, equality between men and women, abortion on demand, suicide, euthanasia, and one-world

1

government. It is ultimately responsible for crime,
disarmament, declining SAT scores, "values clarification,"
and the new math. And it seeks to limit free enterprise,
distribute wealth to achieve greater equality, and place
controls on the uses of energy and the environment. What is
the origin of such consummate evil? It is spawned by
demonism and liberalism, and that's a fact.[2]

We are left here with quite a political and social bundle. And
this bundle is being carried into the courtroom as well as the
classroom: the recent Tennessee court decision (Mozert v.
Hawkins County Bd. of Education, 827 Fed. 2d 1058 [6th Cir.
1987]) settled in favor of Christian parents who want to censor
educational materials used in public schools; the Alabama case
(Smith v. Bd. of School Commissioners of Mobile County, 827
Fed. 2d 684 [11th Cir. 1987]) that was initiated into the court
system in order to decide whether secular humanism is a religion,
and if so, what its role is in the public school system.

Much litigation and legislation have accompanied the growth of
Christian schools, for the significance of these schools lies in the
challenge they present to contemporary American culture in
general, and education and parenting in particular. The controversy over parents' and states' rights continues to rage; the
challenging question of how we should educate our children
continues to be debated. Few studies, however, have examined
the organization of Christian schools; the processes that characterize school life; or the effect they may have on the lives of
students, their families, and their communities.

Parents serve as mediators between society and the individual.
Their repertoire as socializers comes from their own upbringing
and experiences, as well as from their anticipation of their
children's future roles and experiences. But parents are not alone
in this task; other sources compete for influence over the young.
The structure and requisites of our society powerfully frame our
possibilities and desires for action in ways that may often
transcend our awareness. Therefore, in investigating the processes
of socialization and education, it is important to consider the
interaction of social, psychological, cultural, and historical
factors. One needs to consider the "person, process, and
context."[3]

Who are evangelicals and why are they enrolling their children in Christian schools? How are they socializing their children? How might Christian education serve the young as they enter adulthood and the workforce of the 1990s? How might it serve the capitalist political economy of contemporary American society?

Evangelicals are engaged in cultural production, in creating new forms of educational experience for themselves and their children. The establishment of Christian schools in the midst of a society that values educational conformity requires energy, confidence, and resourcefulness. But while evangelicals are challenging the established order of American public education, they are also reproducing the social structure of American society. The movement is both innovative in its educational methods and reactionary in its attempt to restore traditional values and re-establish Protestant education in American society.

This book tells a story about people's lives, about the search for coherence, the struggle for control, and the building of community. The book focuses on two groups of evangelicals, a working-class, fundamentalist Baptist congregation that I will refer to as Lakehaven; and a middle-class, independent charismatic fellowship that I will refer to as Covenant. Counted among the 22% of Americans (eighteen years and older) who identify themselves as born-again Christians, they share a fundamental belief in the necessity of personal faith in Jesus Christ as their personal Savior and Lord; the full authority of the Scriptures in matters of faith and practice; and the urgency of winning others over to Christ.[4]

According to Gallup polls, about one in five Americans share these three beliefs, although many others share a commitment to one or two of these affirmations. While the definition of the term "evangelical" has been slippery and varied, I find Richard Quebedeaux's classification scheme to be the most useful. When I refer to evangelicals, I will use it as an umbrella term to include both fundamentalists and charismatics who share core evangelical beliefs.

The fundamentalists, emerging at the turn of the twentieth century, took on recognizable form after World War I. They became an opposition movement against the modernists who, in accepting biblical criticism, evolutionary theory, and the Social Gospel, departed from orthodox belief. Believing that the secular world is sinful and corrupting, they took, in Reinhold Niebuhr's words, a *Christ against culture* position. As fundamentalists, the Lakehaven Baptists are inclined to be separatists, politically and socially conservative, holding anti-communist and pre-millennial apocalyptic beliefs.

The charismatics, on the other hand, tend to be less separatist, believing in the potential of *Christ transforming culture*. The movement itself is a more middle-class expression of the older "classical" Pentecostalism that, like fundamentalism, was also very exclusive and separatist. The major theological differences find expression in the charismatic emphasis on religious experience and testimony rather than on the defense of doctrine and the letter of the law that is central to the fundamentalist tradition. While the charismatics believe in the "baptism of the Holy Spirit," divine healing, prophecy, and speaking in tongues, the Baptists condemn these practices as the work of the devil. The Lakehaven Baptists would see the Covenant charismatics' "insistence" on using their "gifts" as divisive to the Christian community.

It is important to recognize that neither the Evangelical Movement nor the Christian School Movement is monolithic. The fact that much diversity exists is important to the identity of the groups themselves; to our understanding of their meaning and significance; and to the political power they wield in contemporary American society.

For example, while Lakehaven and Covenant share a mono-lithic doctrine common to evangelical Christianity, they differ substantially in how they conceive of human nature. The Baptists emphasize man's voluntary transgression into sin and his depraved nature; they attempt to repress vice by constraining the individual. The charismatics, on the other hand, emphasize man's temptation by the environment and satanic forces, which they consider partly to blame for man's sinfulness; they seek to develop virtue and perfect the individual by building a strong community that can combat evil forces.

While both communities define the secular world as evil, their ways of dealing with that world differ. Like the Covenant people, the Lakehaven Baptists support the free-enterprise system and the privacy of the family, and feel very threatened by government intervention, affirmative action, and the women's movement. In response to progressive legislation and changing social norms, the Baptists tend to withdrawn from the world and do the best they can within their own community. The Covenant people, on the other hand, feel they are responsible for countering what is going on in society. They see themselves on the offensive:

> In folk religion, people were told to "close the windows and keep out the devil." We, however, are on the offensive.
> The blows we receive are from a retreating enemy (Col. 2).
> This does not mean that the blows are not serious—they are, for the enemy is trying to recapture lost ground. The devil's advantage is that he moves among human affairs undetected. If we are aware, then his strategies have much less power. (Excerpt from a Covenant sermon)

These orientations, in turn, affect how they are socializing their children. The Baptists seek to protect their children from the world by sheltering them:

> Some people say we are protecting them from the world, sheltering them. Well, that's right. I don't want them in the world. I want them to go into Christian service. It's like tomatoes in a greenhouse; you have to protect them and nourish them until they grow strong before you put them in the garden. (Academy mother)

The Lakehaven Baptists pray that their children will be able to preserve their individual faith in the midst of a contaminating secular world. Good citizenship is defined as taking care of oneself rather than becoming actively involved in social or political change.

But while the Baptists emphasize the ability of the individual to withstand, the Covenant people emphasize the power of the collective to change. They are preparing their students to act on the world:

> We do not want to keep them from the world but from the

5

evil one (John 17:15–16). We want them to be able to
discern right from wrong, good from bad. . . . Kingdom
education comes to its fullest when the home–church–school
community surrounds the student with a consistent
environment where Jesus Christ is the center. . . . The
children who can weave in and out of these three
institutions and find life and abundance will be able to form
a well-equipped army of mature individuals ready to go out
into a deteriorating world and conquer every domain for the
King. (Covenant handbook)

The process of socialization reflects the interaction of the
theological and class orientations of these communities. The
orientation towards pessimism vs. optimism, externalization vs.
internalization, supervision vs. autonomy, routinization vs. complexity, conformity vs. self-direction distinguishes the working-
class, fundamentalist Baptists from the middle-class charismatics.

The predominantly middle-class charismatic parents and educators rely on intensive interaction with students in an attempt to
instill their values and beliefs. They are communicating their view
of the world as a place in which individuals are actors who, in
relation to one another, can change the world. Discussion and
joint activities are used as a form of interactive learning whereby
ideologies are explored and explanations are given. Their
organizations are characterized by a high degree of complexity
and experimentation and a low degree of supervision and
routinization.

The working-class Baptists rely on rules to regulate students'
behavior. They have chosen a highly standardized and individualized system of instruction which encourages privacy and
reinforces conformity to external demands. They are transmitting
their view of the world as a place in which individuals need to
conform to certain prescribed behaviors and expectations in
order to preserve themselves as good Christians. Their organizations are characterized by a high degree of supervision,
formalization, centralization, routinization, and tradition.

Are Christian schools the vanguard of a new educational
structure or will they continue to present only alternatives to

America's mainstream educational system? Are evangelicals recreating an earlier kind of Christian/civic education, or are they creating a unique, innovative blend of Christian education that adapts to the needs of people living in contemporary society? Is Christian education antagonistic towards or supportive of modern society?

Based on value consensus rather than political consensus, the Christian schools are relatively free from political constraints. They are unencumbered by a large bureaucratic system, and therefore, have a much greater degree of flexibility. Furthermore, they are able to select their students. But while they have been constructed as fortresses to protect their children from worldly influences, their unintended effects may be far different. By recruiting students from homogeneous backgrounds and training them along class lines, they may be even more effective in reproducing a stratified society than their public school counterparts.

Covenant and the Academy

These two schools were selected because they represented very different traditions within evangelicalism. At the beginning of my research, I attended a conference of 350 Christian school administrators from forty-seven states. Throughout the week of workshops, lectures, prayer meetings, and socializing I learned much about the philosophy, rhetoric, goals, concerns, and problems of school administrators and the schools they run. This helped direct me in selecting two schools for in-depth ethnographic studies. Both the Academy, a fundamentalist Baptist school which uses the Accelerated Christian Education (A.C.E.) curriculum, and Covenant, an independent charismatic school which uses secular texts, are located in upstate New York; both were founded in 1974; and both have the same size student body.

Established in 1974, the Academy is sponsored and run by the Lakehaven church and draws its constituency primarily from Lakehaven and two other Baptist churches in neighboring towns; 15% of its students are "unchurched." The Academy enrolls seventy-six students from kindergarten through 12th grade. These students represent forty-five families, and half of the school-age children of the Lakehaven congregation.

The Academy is an A.C.E. school. Begun in 1970, A.C.E. now operates 5,000 schools throughout the United States and an additional 600 schools in eighty-six foreign countries. It is estimated that two-thirds of all Christian schools that open and 10% of the private school population use A.C.E. (for more detail on this, see Chapter 2). A highly standardized system of education, it provides all the information, materials, and equipment necessary to set up a school quickly and inexpensively. Christian curricula, furniture manuals, procedural guides, administrator and teacher training, even uniforms, although few schools choose to use the latter, are included. Given the high degree of standardization and formalization of A.C.E. and the Academy's identification as fundamentalist Baptist, this school can be considered highly representative of a significant number of evangelical Christian schools. Furthermore, both A.C.E. and secular critics have recognized A.C.E. as innovative and potentially influential in providing leadership for educational reform.

The Covenant school provides an interesting and important contrast to the Academy. The comparison of the two schools highlights the diversity of Christian education and the significance of class to the socialization and education process. It is more difficult, however, to assess how representative the Covenant school may be. Established in 1974 by an independent, charismatic fellowship, Covenant school is also church-run. All of the children of the Covenant community attend the school; a few other children from neighboring fellowships and 5% unchurched children also attend. Covenant enrolls seventy-two children in grades kindergarten through 8.

In terms of size, grade range, and sponsorship, it is similar to other Christian schools. A home-grown system of education based on a Montessori model, how representative Covenant is in organization and style is open to question. Covenant school spawned four schools in surrounding areas, not an uncommon pattern. While these satellite schools are similar in organization and style, each is unique. For example, the mother school uses fairy tales in teaching and decorating rooms and emphasizes the arts. One of the satellite schools denounces any reference to fairies, elves, or witches and concentrates on the basic academic and agricultural subjects. According to the administrators, the schools reflect the occupational orientations, educational experiences, and talents of their associated fellowships. The leaders of all of the schools and associated fellowships are in close and frequent contact. Many of them were trained at Covenant, and likewise, they are training other members of the fellowship to go out and start Christian schools in other communities.

Covenant too is innovative—in ways quite different from the Academy. Teachers and parents are much more involved in developing their own curriculum and in "teaching all knowledge from a Christian perspective." While both the Academy and Covenant agree that Christians must struggle to free themselves from a secular mind-set in order to approach all things from a godly perspective, they hold very different interpretations of what this should mean. The Covenant people believe that

> all knowledge belongs to God. . . . Therefore, there is no distinction made between sacred and secular subjects or curriculum within the school. It is not the text itself, but rather the context in which a text is placed that determines its value. To the degree it is man-centered, it is secular and humanistic; to the degree it is seen from God's perspective, it has eternal value. (Covenant Handbook)

People at Covenant are critical of A.C.E. methods. Likewise, A.C.E. and the Lakehaven Baptists would challenge the approach that Covenant takes. They believe that it is essential to limit materials and censor readings. Unlike at Covenant where different versions of the Bible are read and discussed, the Academy and A.C.E. materials use only the King James edition. They are striving to present a "pure" Christian curriculum, and argue that, "Adding Bible to secular texts is like trying to neutralize poison with good food."

Covenant and the Academy are both Christian schools, but they differ radically in how they educate their children. The differences between the schools reflect the differences in world view, ethos, and class of the two sponsoring fellowships. Just as the "world" holds different meanings and experiences for people (depending on ideology, class, personality, and life histories), so

9

do people have different notions about how to bring their children up in the world.

The recent proliferation of Christian schools represents, in part, the efforts of evangelicals to proclaim themselves as guardians of American culture. Caught in a world whose complexity tends to render people impotent, evangelicals have chosen to delimit their world in order to gain control over it. By establishing a coherent network among the primary socializing institutions of church, home, and school, evangelicals can exercise greater control over the definition and transmission of values and norms. It enables them to achieve, within their world, a greater degree of consistency and consensus. They have created an environment in which they feel more at home.

Evangelicals are not the only ones who feel that the social fabric is disintegrating, that they are being assailed by forces beyond their control. What is distinctive is how they identify and cope with these forces. Evangelicals identify them as satanic; therefore, their response is framed differently from some other Americans who may blame the hegemony of a corporate elite or mass, commercialized culture as the culprit. The varied definitions of the contemporary situation are indicators that Americans of many persuasions are searching for a sense of meaning and belonging. Americans are in a period of cultural disorientation and are searching for a way through the maze.

1

A Search for Coherence

> Believing with Max Weber, that man is an animal
> suspended in webs of significance he himself has spun, I
> take culture to be those webs, and the analysis of it to be
> therefore not an experimental science in search of law but
> an interpretive one in search of meaning.[1]

> The tool-making, laughing, or lying animal, man is also the
> incomplete animal—or, more accurately, self-completing
> animal. [He is] the agent of his own realization.[2]

People often turn to religion in their search for coherence, feeling
the need to make sense of the world and their relationship to it.
As discriminating creatures, we strive to feel at home in a world
that becomes ours through definition.

As parents and educators, our search for coherence becomes
an even more complicated and imperative task as we attempt to
prepare our children for the world and fashion the world for our
children. In socializing our children, we are helping them to
construct a meaningful world, "a world in which rules, discipline,
and ordinary activities make sense."[3] An important part of that
socialization process is helping our children to "become at home
in the world," however we may define the parameters.

Socialization is the process by which people and institutions
transmit the values, beliefs, and behaviors necessary for appropriate functioning in their particular culture to others. It is a
recruitment process—whether recruiting children into adult
worlds or resocializing adults into different roles or a new
subculture. Socialization involves "the whole process by which an

individual born with behavioral potentialities of enormously wide range is confined within a much narrower range—the range of what is customary and acceptable for him according to the standards of his group."[4]

When the culture is relatively clear in its expectations, the task of socializing agents is more straightforward and less self-conscious. When consensus about standards and roles, and therefore, about what should be transmitted does not exist, the integration of the individual and the cultural system becomes more problematic. Both lack of clarity at the cultural level and competition among socializing agents tend to cloud definitions of socialization goals and processes. As society becomes more complex, the desire to become more "at home" with oneself as a *social and cultural being* becomes all the more salient, for the sense of self is intimately connected to one's sense of coherence about the world.[5]

During the life course of individuals and societies, some periods are characterized by smooth progressions; other times are disrupted by crisis and turmoil.[6] Periods of cultural discontinuity reflect the gap between normative expectations and reality. They both threaten and reflect individual crises:

> We can think of culture in its most abstract and mythical
> level as a paradigm that selects, interprets, and powerfully
> affects our impression and feelings and desires. When
> culture begins to leave many questions unanswered and
> many needs unfilled, then individuals suspect that their own
> emotions and experience are only a blurred identity, and
> the cultural system may be pushed aside.[7]

Many people today feel as though they are caught in "a world turned upside down."[8] The rapid rate of social change and the competing demands of families, work, church, education, and peers take their toll on individuals who are trying to find their way in the world. Furthermore, the weakening of extensive ties among neighbors and kin has weakened many people's sense of belonging and identity.

Numerous books, including *The Lonely Crowd* by David

Riesman, *The Pursuit of Loneliness* by Philip Slater, and *Habits of the Heart* by Robert Bellah et al., tangle with the contemporary problems of loneliness, meaninglessness, and anomie. *Habits of the Heart*, for instance, deals with the malaise of middle-class moral limbo and the loss of a coherent moral language through which people can express themselves and communicate effectively with one another. Indeed, the apathy that so many decry may result more from people feeling overwhelmed and impotent than from disinterest. The paradox of too many decisions but too few real choices can entrap as well as exhaust us. For example, a recent commercial for Wendy's (a fast food restaurant) proclaimed the glories of American society wherein people have the freedom of choice (hamburgers with or without cheese, with or without onions, with or without pickles, and so on). In the background, they used a Russian fashion show to present a stark and humorous contrast. Displaying the latest fashions of evening, sports, and housewear, the Russian model wore the same dress for each occasion. Such commercialized and celebrated "freedom of choice" parodies the very values of freedom and individualism in our culture. We are a people caught between a strong ethic of individualism and a culture of conformity. Not only are we encumbered by many trivial choices, but as individuals and communities, we are often left with no real decision-making power.

Today, the family, school, church, peer group, and media contend with one another for influence over the adult as well as the child. The degree of coordination, consensus, and consistency, as well as the relative influence among socializing agents, is open to question and investigation. Moreover, the mass homogenization of culture confuses the issues. While people blame the media, especially television, for corrupting young people and exposing them to adult secrets too early, the American populace continues to turn to the media for advice. As "cultural reality" becomes increasingly defined at a corporate, consumer level, the ability of family, educational, and religious groups to define cultural meaning and direction becomes all the more difficult.

As cultural pluralism becomes more diffuse in American society, the more numerous and varied the reference points in the socialization process become.[9] People are often unsure of what their goals are or "should be" for themselves and their children. For some whose goals are clear, the process of how to secure them is uncertain.

But while people respond in a variety of ways—from avoidance to rebellion—they do not give up the search for coherence. They continue to struggle to find some relief, some understanding of the cosmos, the world, the self—and their intermingling relationships. This quest is primarily philosophical and religious, for these are existential endeavors. Therefore, it is no surprise that in the midst of cultural disorientation, we are witnessing a resurgence of religious interest.

Today, evangelical churches have increased in number as mainstream Protestant churches have lost members; the New Religious Right exercises a major political influence; the Christian Broadcasting Network (CBN) is one of the largest television networks; and the Christian School Movement is the fastest growing sector of private education. Why?

For a significant number of Americans, evangelicalism provides a perspective that makes sense of their world, as well as provides role models and guidelines for living in it. For many who have converted, it offers a greater sense of social and personal coherence.[10] It offers people assurance that their lives will be meaningful and that things will "turn out O.K." One need only trust in the Lord. As Aaron Antonovsky defines it, a sense of coherence is

> a global orientation that expresses the extent to which one
> has a pervasive, enduring though dynamic feeling of
> confidence that one's internal and external environments
> are predictable and that there is a high probability that
> things will work out as well as can be expected.[11]

Antonovsky emphasizes that this does not mean that things always work out well, but that given the circumstances, they work out as well as possible. In evangelical terms, "the road may not be all smooth but the bumps provide good testing grounds." One's world is reasonable in the sense of being comprehensible— through reason, faith, and/or intuition. Furthermore, people do not need to feel as though they are personally in control, as traditional Western measures of locus of control have stressed.[12] They may be willing to relinquish control to the expert, or the Ultimate Authority, without feeling that their sense of coherence is being threatened.[13] The sense of coherence is generalized; it is a fundamental part of one's personality and the cultural ambience. The search for coherence, then, is both personal and communal.

The rate of technological and social change has contributed to people's sense of uncertainty and uneasiness, for it makes it more difficult to anticipate future roles. This diminishes parents' power and confidence since their primary purpose is to socialize children into society, that is, to prepare them to conform adequately to accepted standards and perform anticipated roles. When standards are ambiguous and the projection of roles untenable, parents will experience frustration in trying to fulfill a role that places impossible demands upon them.

Likewise, other socializing institutions will be caught in a net of contradictory and often ambiguous expectations that render them impotent. Consequently, it is not surprising that the socializing institutions, originally designed to serve complementary roles, blame each other for their incompetency: schools blame the family, families blame the schools, and the community and church struggle with each other to arrive at a more satisfying consensus regarding relevant goals and guidelines.

The situation becomes all the more debilitating for parents when one considers that increasing ambiguity about the goals and means of institutional socialization is concomitant with a greater emphasis on socialization as the primary task of the family. Given the greater insulation of the nuclear family, parents are more isolated in their parenting roles; less likely to have had opportunities to observe and help their own parents bring up siblings; and more often confronted by contradictory advice on how to raise their children.

Responses to feelings of parenting inadequacy vary from abdication of responsibility to a redefinition of the task. It is no coincidence that the proliferation of Christian schools with their emphasis on character building rather than vocational training, and on complementary relationships among the primary socializing institutions of church, family, and school has occurred during a time of cultural ambiguity about socialization goals and means. Rather than focusing on specific roles, evangelicals stress general, "universal," timeless qualities that represent to them the "good man," that is, the "Christian man." Dependent upon a high degree of ideological consensus, the church, family, and schools join together to clarify and reinforce one another in their socializing roles. Their responsibility is to "bring their children up in the Lord"; the heavenly Father will direct their children's lives: what job they will hold, whom and when they will marry, how many and what kind of children they will have.

Such a belief and reliance on a Superior Being who is willing and able to take the responsibility not only for their own lives but also for the lives of their children can reassure and encourage parents and teachers in their socializing roles. Many of these parents and educators, especially in the charismatic fellowship, speak of a time, before conversion, when they were confused, uncertain, and lost. They are now quick to tell you that they do not have all the answers, but they have the essential one. *By surrendering their lives to Christ and faithfully following the Scriptures, they find themselves much more secure in their parenting.*

This reported change in perceptions of their ability to parent raises the issue of control. Built into evangelical ideology is the sanction to admit weakness and failure. It is acceptable to be confused and to make mistakes, for man is acknowledged as weak; he can "do all things only by the grace and power of God." Furthermore, much of man's failure can be attributed to the work of the devil. Therefore, elders can "call up a person" (confront them) on parenting techniques or their relationships with their children, while allowing both parties to save face. They agree to join together against the evil forces that are trying to tear them asunder.[14]

In this sense, evangelicalism offers absolution for those who believe in absolutes; it provides a way for people to free themselves of rigid, immobilizing standards without sacrificing their belief in those standards. Cognitive dissonance is reduced because the gap between beliefs, values, and behavior is acknowledged, explained, and dealt with in two crucial ways: 1) through the radical conversion experience which makes "the old man new," and 2) through the recognition of change and development as a gradual process whose ultimate goal is perfection—either in this life or the after-life. Those who view themselves in dichotomous terms as being good or bad, as successes or failures are encouraged to view development from a different perspective.

For these evangelicals, the belief that God will work things out does not absolve them of responsibility. To the contrary, if a person enters into the "Covenant," establishing a personal relationship and alliance with God, then he or she is expected to "pay a price." Being "chosen" by God and accepting Him implies a system of reciprocity whereby parents, teachers, and elders agree to bring their children up under guidelines which are specified in the Scriptures. Believing that Christianity is only one generation away from extinction, since each individual must *choose* salvation, the adult leadership is desperate for their children to understand the importance of the decision and desire to follow Christ: "it is a matter of life or death—eternal life or death."

The relevance of religion

The power of religion stems from its ability to offer a sense of coherence; it presents a particular worldview complete with characters, plot, theme, setting, and history. The power of religion, as Clifford Geertz puts it,

> lies in its capacity to serve, for an individual or for a group, as a source of general, yet distinctive, conceptions of the world, the self, and the relations between them. . . . The religious perspective . . . moves beyond the realities of everyday life to wider ones which correct and complete them, and its defining concern is not action upon those wider realities but acceptance of them, faith in them. Rather than detachment, its watchword is commitment; rather than analysis, encounter.[15]

17

Religion is a system of nonempirical beliefs, rituals, and organizations that deals with the ultimate concerns of human existence. Some people, unable to explain the troublesome daily occurrences of ill health, death, misfortune, and injustice turn to transcendent explanations. By offering ultimate explanations and meaningful interpretations, religion makes suffering sufferable—not by eliminating it, but by imbuing it with meaning.[16]

Specific events or situations—be they economic deprivation, migration, or urbanization—do not necessarily inspire periods of heightened religiosity. Rather, it is "persistent . . . difficulty in grasping certain aspects of culture, self, and society . . . that [eventually] renders one chronically uneasy."[17] Religion provides guidance and support to those who are at their breaking points because of analytical, emotional, or moral impotence. When people have reached the limits of their analytical capacity to explain events, of their power of endurance, or of their ability to work through an ethical paradox, religion can be efficacious in helping them to understand their world from a new perspective and to accept the "human" limits of their understanding. People who submit to the guidance of the Ultimate through faith are granted a freedom from responsibility for that which they cannot comprehend, control, or resolve.

Religion, as a cultural system, has helped shape the configuration of social institutions as well as the lives of individuals by helping them to define cultural values that in turn regulate normative behavior. The focusing of local and national attention on matters of religious import during particular periods in American history suggests the societal need for a reorientation of beliefs and values, behavioral patterns, and institutional structures. William McLoughlin has labeled these periods of heightened religiosity in America the Four Great Awakenings.

Both Anthony Wallace and William McLoughlin argue that revitalistic movements or Awakenings begin in periods of major social upheaval,

> in periods of cultural distortion and grave personal stress, when we lose faith in the legitimacy of our norms, the viability of our institutions, and the authority of leaders in church and state.[18]

Furthermore, they are periods of revitalization that eventuate in "profound cultural transformations." Each of the American Awakenings was preceded by periods of cultural disorientation and succeeded by periods of renewed national unity, direction, and purpose. The First Great Awakening (1730–1760) occurred in the years preceding the American Revolution; the Second Great Awakening (1790–1840), in the years preceding the Civil War; the Third Great Awakening (1890–1920), in the years preceding the two world wars, during a period of massive industrialization and urbanization; and the Fourth Great Awakening (1960–the present) began in the years preceding the Vietnam War and the social revolutions of the 1960s. Whether or not America emerges from the Fourth Great Awakening with a greater sense of national unity and purpose remains to be seen. The notion of manifest destiny, however, may well have become obsolete as America redefines her role and responsibility in the global arena of the late twentieth century. In order to place the contemporary evangelical movement in perspective, it is important to have a sense of the change and continuity throughout America's four major awakenings.[19]

The First Great Awakening (1730–1760)

Revivals of the First Great Awakening challenged the established church hierarchy. Instead of formalized church ritual, the new revivalism emphasized the need for a personal relationship with Christ and individual readings and interpretations of the Scriptures. Just as in the sixteenth century when the printing press placed the Scriptures in the hands of the laity, so did the First Great Awakening witness a transfer of authority from clergy to laity as the written and spoken word became more accessible to the common man. Characteristic of all the awakenings, a new form of spiritual elitism transcended class, ethnic, and denominational lines: one was either "saved" or "unsaved." The status of "being saved" was no longer ascribed or determined by the church hierarchy. Rather, people were saved by grace, by asking Christ into their lives.

Furthermore, in order to protect their right to practice their own religion, people rejected the notion of a national church. Rather, the process of disestablishment (whereby no church would be sanctioned by the state or dominated by any other church) led to the development of a new organizational form: the "denomination." In practice, this meant that religious groups would have to persuade voluntarily rather than coerce people to believe in the "true" Christianity. This emphasis on persuasion has had a great deal to do with the shaping of Protestant Christianity since the eighteenth century. Recruitment became a priority of denominations, and numbers of converts and the size of the treasury became important signs of success.

McLoughlin argues that the greater authority and responsibility given individuals in their spiritual lives influenced the new consensus that emerged from the First Great Awakening. The new ideology was more democratic and optimistic than the Calvinist doctrines of predestination and election and found expression in the American War for Independence and the unique sense of American identity that followed the First Great Awakening.

The Second Great Awakening (1790–1840)

The new ideology evolving out of the Second Great Awakening centered on America's mission to Christianize not only her own territory but the whole world. Nathaniel Taylor, a leading theologian and pastor of the time, no longer equated self-love with Calvinistic selfishness but with love and benevolence for the whole universe. He explained that Christ had suffered out of a willingness to sacrifice himself for the love of God and man, not as a punishment for the sin of Adam. The belief in the personal conversion experience, which implied the freedom of individuals to change, encouraged post-millennial optimism and perfectionism. If individuals could change, then the world was no longer bound by tradition, history, or environment. Consequently, in the Second Great Awakening, American evangelicalism would reach out to new populations: to non-Christians (or heathens) and, domestically, to women.[20]

The rapid growth and changing configuration of the relative

size of American religious groups took place during the period 1787–1850.[21] The free market encouraged the competition that stimulated church growth. The various, although consistently impressive estimates of church growth help to explain why the revivalists of the Second Great Awakening thought they were well on their way to bringing God's kingdom on earth.[22]

This ideological reformulation in turn helped shape and legitimate new organizational forms. The development of denominations spawned a collection of benevolent societies and educational institutions. New converts were organized into reform and missionary societies that worked for temperance, aid to the poor, Sabbath observance, the abolition of slavery, and the evangelization of the world. Sunday schools, academies, and colleges were established for the purposes of recruitment, socialization, and ministerial training. Evangelicalism in the Second Great Awakening extended beyond the churches to the building of community and welfare services; many women became involved in this process.[23]

The Third Great Awakening (1890–1920)

The intervening years between the Second and Third Great Awakenings were divisive ones. The Civil War shattered national and evangelical unity. The same religious symbols—the Bible, God, Heaven and Hell—were used by both sides to defend their conflicting positions on slavery and on the direction the national economy should take. With increasing industrialization, person-to-person transactions evolved into more impersonal, corporate contacts. Increasing mobility uprooted community ties. But while foreign missionary enterprises continued to gain momentum, the domestic reform program turned increasingly to social work and away from evangelical conversions.

The Young Men's Christian Association (YMCA) is a case in point. Established during the Second Great Awakening to evangelize young men, it built rooming facilities and libraries, and sponsored recreational activities. As evangelizing declined, the facilities themselves became the primary appeal of the YMCA.[24]

Social reform efforts had been tried and found failing; they could not match the problems that advancing industrialization, urbanization, and massive immigration introduced. Public schools, heralded as the secular means by which the "coming of the Kingdom on earth" would be ushered in, had not been able to obliterate poverty or crime, nor had reform schools or prisons. The Civil War did not erase prejudice and discrimination; temperance laws did not stop drinking. The "Righteous Empire" had not been realized either at home or abroad.[25]

German rationalism, higher biblical criticism, and Darwinism were challenging the basic doctrines of Christian faith and traditional notions about how the world was ordered. If, according to Darwinism, man was not free from hereditary and environmental constraint, what role did God and conversion play? How far could man go in reforming society?

Confusion over the present and desperation over man's condition and future prospects led people in the Fundamentalist, Pentecostal, and Holiness Movements to hold "prophetic conferences." Like the Millerites of the Second Great Awakening,[26] they discussed the coming of holocaust and claimed rebirth as the only means to salvation. When rational means failed, people turned to more magical solutions; faith healing revived.

Whereas the First Great Awakening helped to usher in the new democracy and the Second helped to further America's manifest destiny and facilitate the building of many new institutions, the Third Great Awakening was socially and politically conservative. Rather than forging ahead to gain new ground by altering ideologies or establishing new institutional forms, fundamentalists in the Third Great Awakening struggled to maintain their ground by turning society back to an earlier religious orientation. This was perhaps most dramatically demonstrated in the Scopes Trial of 1925. The debate between Clarence Darrow, arguing for evolution, and William Jennings Bryan, defending creationism, is often referred to as the event that declared fundamentalism obsolete. However, as witnessed in the Fourth Great Awakening, it did not become a dead issue; controversy over creationism and evolution continues to rage in the courtroom and the classroom.

As fundamentalists retreated to prayer, the institutions they established in the nineteenth century were reorganized, and in the process, secularized. Overlapping voluntary and charity associations became local, state, and national "welfare" bureaucracies; schools became age-graded and coordinated into elementary, junior, and senior high schools; competing regional businesses merged into national corporations. The Progressive Era reform promoted increased centralization, formalization, and professionalization. Control shifted from voluntary, denominational associations to government bureaucracies. No longer was government to play a laissez-faire role; rather, its new role entailed a positive responsibility to regulate business, labor, and family.[27]

This shift reflected an increasing societal emphasis on "this-worldly" activity. The new faith was placed in social engineering rather than in individual regeneration through conversion. More and more the Bible was considered to be divinely inspired (instead of divinely written), and historically specific. The absolutes no longer held; relativism had taken over.

The Third Great Awakening largely involved young, rural, middle-class Americans who had immigrated to the cities.[28] The more liberal Social Gospel Movement and Christian Socialists who concentrated on the needs of the lowest immigrant classes, failed to reach "a vast, undigested middle class transplanted from the farm."[29] Evangelicalism responded and reinforced for these people the traditional values associated with the Protestant work ethic, respect for authority, patriotism, and the supremacy of Protestantism. Again, evangelicalism stressed individual salvation, independent of the state of society and the sins of other men; the focus was on individual character, not social conditions. Denominational ties associated with ethnicity (evident during the Second Great Awakening) became all the more sharply delineated during the Third Great Awakening as different ethnic-religious groups competed with one another for jobs, housing, and influence.[30]

The consensus derived from the Third Great Awakening helped prepare America for the crusades that would "make the world safe for democracy." The nation once again united to engage in war in 1917 and 1941.

The Fourth Great Awakening (1960–the present)

By the 1960s, the legitimacy of the old consensus and institutional structures designed to build a better world were thrown into question. Science, once heralded as the new hope for revealing God's laws and leading the world to millennial perfection, proved to be a disappointment, and at times even a threat. The continued testing of atomic and nuclear weapons threatened future wars and genetic defects.

The launching of Sputnik by the Russians in 1957 threatened America's technological, scientific, and educational supremacy and hastened the reorganization of school curricula.[31] The rise of Third-World nations, most of whom chose to remain neutral rather than accept the leadership of the United States, and the controversy over the Vietnam War challenged America's position and role. The Supreme Court decision to no longer accept "separate but equal status" for black Americans and the Women's Movement challenged the traditional stratification system of United States society.

Americans began reporting a loss of faith in political, religious, and educational institutions.[32] From Watergate to the Iran-Contra arms affair, the legitimacy of the United States government has been seriously questioned. Americans are left questioning what to believe in.

What unites evangelicals, across time and place, is the belief in the full authority of the Scriptures, a personal relationship with Christ as Savior, and the urgency of converting others to Christ. Evangelicals have consistently de-emphasized the institutional side of religion, valued religion of the heart over that of the head, and equated patriotism with Christianity, overlapping the symbols of flag and cross.

The internal organization of the contemporary evangelical movement, however, has paralleled the increasing specialization of American society. According to Richard Quebedeaux's analysis, evangelicals of the Fourth Great Awakening can be divided into groups of fundamentalists, charismatics, and neo-evangelicals.[33] While many evangelicals work within the Southern

Baptist Convention and other mainline denominations, many local evangelical groups have extricated themselves from any denominational affiliation and thus have followed the organizational pattern typical of sects.[34] Wanting to be independent, they often identify themselves as "Covenant fellowships" and as "Christians." As earlier in American religious history, the "Covenant" once again defines the primary social classification of "saved" versus "unsaved."

While religious beliefs and rhetoric have persisted across the Awakenings, the social and political positions of evangelicals have fluctuated. Once the sponsors and regulators of mainstream social institutions, they are now the initiators of alternative religious, political, and educational institutions. Having lost control of the dominant culture during the early twentieth century, by the 1940s they prided themselves on sectarianism and preserving their identity in the midst of secular society.[35] By the late twentieth century, evangelicals became engaged in a struggle to regain social and political influence in a culture they once defined and directed.

The struggle and character of evangelicalism in the Fourth Great Awakening results from social, political, economic, and technological factors which for many have contributed to the spread of a sense of chronic uneasiness and cultural disorientation. The redistribution of power strained the limits of evangelical tolerance, as the "doctrine of entitlement" seemed to entitle everyone to everything. Protests in the 1960s by blacks, women, gays, and the poor threatened to undo such "fundamental" arrangements as sex roles and racial and class relations. These protests, likewise, disturbed the elite who feared "too much democracy" and egalitarian sentiment. As in previous awakenings,[36] alliances were made between wealthy industrialists and evangelists. While big business feared the loss of control and power, many conservative, white, working- and middle-class Americans feared the loss of status and jobs. Their fears were not unfounded, for the threat of material decline was and continues to be real, as statistics on the increase in the cost of living and the shrinking middle-class indicate.[37]

The evangelical response of the Fourth Great Awakening was

to call again for a return to the values of "old time religion that had made America great."[38] A core of evangelicals are again acting out the Americanism of the late nineteenth and early twentieth century. The increasingly middle-class constituency of evangelicals, who identify themselves as "self-made, hard-working, and too easily preyed upon by big government, labor, minorities, and inflation,"[39] have taken primarily a defensive stance in contemporary society. Some segments of the evangelical movement, however, have shifted to an aggressive political position on a number of social issues related to the family and the role of women. Evangelicals tend to advocate a "pro-family platform" which stands against women's rights (the Equal Rights Amendment [E.R.A.], affirmative action, birth control, abortion, shelters for battered women); children's rights (including mandatory child abuse reporting and the International Year of the Child); and progressive educational materials that in any way "diminish, deny or denigrate the traditional sex role norms as historically understood in the United States" (Family Protection Acts of 1981). The new Christian schools represent just one thrust of a multi-pronged attempt to exercise influence on social morality through legislation, political campaigning, television evangelism, and other social institutions.

By reuniting the three major socializing institutions of family, church, and school, evangelicals hope to achieve a greater coherence in their own lives, bring their children up in the faith, and bring morality back to the United States. At the same time, they rally to support the political and economic supremacy of America, for they are concerned with protecting or improving their economic position in a society where it is eroding away.[40]

By exercising greater influence over the media and integrating the institutions of family, school, and church, many evangelical parents and educators are not only gaining greater control over the socialization of their young—and thereby, greater influence over society—but are also integrating many aspects of their own lives. Having felt dispossessed or uprooted throughout much of the twentieth century, contemporary evangelicals have mobilized in an attempt to reclaim control. At a personal level, their faith has helped to explain, and thereby resolve, some of the conflict between disparate beliefs, expectations, and behavior. The greater consistency and support at both the individual and institutional levels have helped to reduce role strain and to offer a greater sense of empowerment to individuals and groups who may have doubted their ability to act upon the world. In fact, my observations suggest that Christian schools may make as great a difference in the lives of parents, teachers, and religious leaders as in the lives of their students.

2

Morals and Quarrels: Christian Schools and Social Change

Education is preparation for the good life—Aristotle

Schools, as socializing institutions, are invested with the responsibility of articulating social values and goals. But the question of what should be taught and by whom continues to be debated; and the controversy over parental versus states' rights continues to rage. Just as people differ in their notions of the "good life," so do they differ in their notions of education. Such disagreements, rooted in conflicting value and ideological orientations, have found expression in the United States in varying forms of educational organization and experience.

Much controversy has accompanied the growth of Christian schools in secular society. The controversy reflects the tension between the interests of dominant and minority groups, and between expert and lay control of education. The schools also reflect the tension between prevailing and alternative configurations of educational values and forms. In opposition to the dominant culture, they criticize contemporary society by relying on more fundamental elements of the culture that have become outdated.[1] Thus, the Christian schools criticize secular humanism and values clarification in public education, and rally around the teaching of "the basics" and moral education that once represented both Protestant and patriotic sentiments.

Here again, the schools are serving as "battlefields for social change."[2] As one among many diverse interest groups, evangelicals have tried to claim control over the education of their children in order to inculcate their values and prepare the young for roles that conform to their notions of the good society. As Barbara Finkelstein writes:

> The multifarious events and occurrences that define the history of education in urban America can be understood as attempts by one or another group to preserve, protect, nurture, rebuild, and/or transform community. It is a history of conflict between increasingly diverse groups for control over the network of relationships enclosing the young, and for the power to censor, filter, and define significance.[3]

The presence of conflict in an institution that is as important and central as education and that is embedded in a heterogeneous society is not surprising. Most surprising is the absence of an ideology that legitimates conflict in the educational arena, particularly in a society that celebrates competition in the political and economic arenas.[4] But because struggles within education—among religious, immigrant, ethnic, and ideological groupings—were defined as divisive, they were rendered unacceptable. The mission of the schools was to rise "above politics."

The Protestant majority rallied in the mid-nineteenth century to establish a common school that would socialize all children, especially immigrant children in need of Americanization. America's manifest destiny began at home—in the schools. Thus, while the churches operated on the basis of voluntarism and competed with one another to recruit members, the schools became an arena where all Protestants worked together. The public school, an important socializing institution, became the substitute for the American national church.

Catholics were acutely aware of this. In reaction to Protestant control of the common school, replete with the use of Protestant hymns, prayers, and the King James Bible, Catholics established their own parochial school system in 1874.[5] In the early twentieth century, with the enactment of child labor laws, stricter enforcement of compulsory education laws, the extension of the upper-age limit for students, and increasing secularization, other groups such as the Amish began to withdraw from the public schools and begin their own schools.

The Amish felt that the increasing consolidation of schools undermined their parental and community authority over the education, and thus, the minds and souls of their children. Educational reports confirmed their suspicions:

One of the greatest factors in favor of the consolidation of schools is that it enlarges the neighborhood. . . . By means of this larger unit the petty jealousies and narrow prejudices of the old smaller unit are broken down. All the children of this larger unit become acquainted and thus enlarge their horizons.[6]

The Amish, however, had no desire to dismantle their primary unit nor to enlarge their children's horizons; on the contrary, they were trying desperately to preserve their traditional, religious lifestyle. Skeptical of education that teaches critical questioning, the Amish continued to favor rote learning and teaching "the basics," including obedience and respect for authority and tradition.

During most of the twentieth century, evangelicals tended to be separatists. While they established a number of independent post-secondary educational institutions and bible colleges, it was not until Protestant control of public education gave way to secularization in the mid-twentieth century that they became interested in establishing their own primary and secondary schools.

They called their schools the "Christian" schools. In contrast to other religious schools (the established Catholic, Lutheran, Episcopal, Quaker, Amish, and other parochial schools), the term "Christian" represents the distinction contemporary evangelicals draw between themselves as "saved" and others who are "unsaved." By dividing the world into two camps of Christian and non-Christian, of sacred versus secular, evangelicals attempt to clarify their own identity. Social classification is based on inclusion versus exclusion; yet success for evangelicals is dependent upon winning over the "unsaved."

The tension between exclusion and recruitment is related to the historical fact of disestablishment, a gradual process which resulted in the protection of religious freedom by preventing state sanction of any church. Secured by 1833, disestablishment was a self-protective device to prevent domination by any one religious group rather than an expression of broad religious tolerance or acceptance of the religious values and beliefs of others.[7] In practice, it meant that religious groups would have to persuade voluntarily rather than coerce people to believe in the "true" Christianity. Based on voluntarism, American Protestant denominations, in particular, compete with one another for members and for influence.

One outcome of disestablishment was that schools in the mid-nineteenth century, rather than churches per se, became the new arena in which to exercise control and extend religious influence.[8] By the twentieth century, however, civil religion had taken hold and schools had become increasingly secularized. As control slipped out of the hands of more orthodox Protestants, evangelicals became increasingly dissatisfied with public education.

Marianne Brown, writing for the *Gospel Herald*, states the concern of many conservative religious groups who have chosen to maintain their own separate schools in order to retain parental control and educate their children in accordance with their religious beliefs:

> The nation would consider utterly ridiculous the idea of sending its soldiers to Russia to be trained in order to later fight that nation. Just so, it is ridiculous to have children trained in the world to combat the forces of evil.

Christian schools in secular society

Evangelicals are engaged in a symbolic crusade. For them, the "common ground" that once belonged to white, Anglo-Saxon Protestants who professed a common core Christianity and patriotism and glorified the virtues of a departed rural tradition has been lost.[9] It destroyed itself when it expanded to include the interests of other religious, racial, ethnic, and special-interest groups. From the mid-1950s, as America shifted from a Protestant nation to a three-religion country,[10] Catholics became less inclined, and evangelical Protestants more inclined to enroll their children in private schools.

Dr. Paul Kienel, Executive Director of the Association of Christian Schools International, represents the views of many Christian school promoters when he writes that

> the unofficial partnership between the Protestant Church and the public school is in serious decline. Therefore, we are taking the initiative to reestablish quality, protestant education in our country.[11]

Evangelical Protestants, at one time the sponsors and regulators of the mainsteam educational system, are now turning to alternative forms to exercise control over the education of their children. Their actions are motivated by their desire to restore religious authority in American society; to reinforce parental authority; and to provide quality education for their children while protecting them from drugs, sex, violence, and the lack of discipline in the public schools.

Evangelicals had been displaced. By the 1960s, they had begun to establish their own network of institutions in an attempt to reclaim lost territory:

> We have to reclaim America. . . . I believe that Americans want to see this country come back to basics, back to values, back to biblical morality, back to sensibility, and back to patriotism.[12]

Evangelicals act in response to a series of perceived threats, the most serious of these being the general secularization of life and the legislatively mandated secularization of public schools. Court decisions prohibiting prayer (*Engel v. Vitale*, 360 U.S. 421, 1962) and Bible readings and devotions in public schools (*School District of Abington v. Schempp*, 374 U.S. 203, 1963) offended evangelicals because these actions excluded God. As the Vietnam War and the Watergate scandal challenged the notion of America as the "Righteous Empire"[13] and chipped away at the glorious image of flag intertwined with cross, evangelicals were becoming convinced that even the best of civil religion had been lost; a righteous patriotism had been excluded from the public schools.

Furthermore, court decisions desegregating schools (*Topeka v.*

Brown, 1954), an increasing divorce rate and single parenting, as well as the civil rights, womens rights and child rights movements of the 1960s and 1970s challenged the "supremacy" and "legitimacy" of the traditional, white Protestant, middle-class, patriarchal family. Indeed, the "traditional" American family with father as the primary breadwinner, and mother at home with the children is a minority among American families. The majority of married women and mothers, including many evangelical women, now engage in paid work outside the home.[14]

Many parents are looking for allies in their children's upbringing rather than for adversaries. The professionalization of teachers distanced parents from the schools and created suspicions about parental competence and the wisdom of parental involvement in the educational process. Evangelicals began withdrawing from the public schools in the 1950s (with the largest exodus being in the 1970s); they established their own schools where they could hire teachers on the basis of personal character and religious commitment. In the Christian schools, character continued to count more than academic credentials or pedagogical expertise. These teachers, usually members of one of the sponsoring churches, could teach about the Bible and Christ and reinforce the religious beliefs and values of parents and religious leaders.

In a study of fifty-six Christian schools operating in twenty-six states, George Ballweg found that religious conviction was not the primary factor motivating parents to enroll their children in Christian school.[15] Rather, social and moral concerns (exposure to drugs, sex, violence, lack of discipline) were more salient. Administrators that I interviewed in Virginia, New York, and at Grace Theological Seminary likewise estimated that only 10–15% of parents initially enrolled their children primarily for religious reasons. Concern over the content of the curriculum may be used more as a way of legitimizing rather than explaining the decision to enroll children in Christian school. But from an evangelical perspective, the school atmosphere, the way in which students are taught, and the whole matrix of social relations is as important as the specific information that is taught.

Nonetheless, a major concern of some Christian school administrators is the lack of understanding of Christian education among their constituency. They are concerned that parents may talk about the decline in the quality of public education in a way that rationalizes their own experiment, instead of focusing on the quality of Christian education. Still, the findings of Gallup polls and educational reports that point to declining S.A.T. scores, rising illiteracy rates among high school graduates, and violence in the schools are used as calling cards for potential recruits.

Thus, while administrators/pastors may start schools primarily to promote religious ideals—salvation and moral development— and to bolster the church's ministries, parents tend to send their children for social and moral reasons. Leading educators of the Christian School Movement stress concern over the national decline in academic achievement and the need to "return to the basics" as a primary reason for the growth of Christian schools.[16] These three major reasons for establishing and enrolling students—religious, social-moral, and academic—emerge from the literature, interviews, and questionnaires. Consistent with their roles, evangelical pastors and administrators, parents, and educators tend to emphasize, respectively, the salience of each of these three factors.

Contemporary Christian School Movement

The Christian School Movement is the fastest growing sector of private education in the United States. Estimates indicate that schools have been established at a rate of two per day since 1960.[17] Enrollment numbers some one million students, approximately 20% of the total private school population.[18] However, Christian school students represent only 2–3% of the national school population. Thus, while the rate of growth is impressive, the real significance lies not so much in its numbers as in the challenge and alternatives that the Christian School Movement offers the dominant culture.

A brief history of school enrollments will help to place the Christian schools in context. During the 1930s–1940s, public schools were relatively quiet and stable. Enrollments had decreased; dissidents had started their own schools; immigration had attenuated; and the number of births had decreased as a result of the Great Depression. Not until after World War II, when new "immigrant" groups (such as the southern Blacks and Puerto Ricans) began to flood into the cities, did school populations begin to significantly change.[19] As Otto Kraushaar reports:

> A ground swell of private school growth began soon after the Great Depression; private school enrollment accelerated after World War II, cresting in the mid-sixties. . . . Since then, a decline in Catholic school enrollment has evidently more than offset the increase in small, but growing groups of Protestant, Jewish, black, experimental, free, and segregationist schools.[20]

Between 1960–1975, both public and non-public school enrollments declined by 40%, while Christian school enrollments increased by a factor of 4 or 5.[21] Private school enrollment peaked at 6.25 million in 1964, according to the data of the Census Bureau. By 1979, it had declined to 4.23 million. While Christian and independent schools were growing, enrollments in Roman Catholic schools plummeted by 2.5 million. Between 1965–1975, Christian schools showed a 202% increase in enrollments; Hebrew schools showed a modest increase of 37%; and Catholic schools showed a decrease of 38%.[22] Thus, as George Ballweg points out,

> during a period of reported high unemployment when there existed a very real threat of a national economic recession, with reports of declining enrollments in both public and non-public schools, and increased educational budgets being submitted by all levels of government, the Christian School Movement grew [dramatically].[23]

The Christian School Movement represents the second largest group in private education. The first is the Roman Catholic schools with an enrollment of 3.2 million students. On the conservative side, Robert Smith, Executive Director of the Council for American Private Education (CAPE), a consortium of religiously affiliated and independent school associations representing 90% of the private school population, estimates Christian school enrollment to be about seven hundred thousand students. After rounding off figures, CAPE estimates the numbers of students being educated by major private school groups in the United States as of 1982 to be as follows:

Friends	Lutheran
15,000	220,000
Episcopals	Nais[24]
60,000	315,000
Seventh Day Adventists	Christian
90,000	600,000–700,000
Jewish	Roman Catholic
100,000	3.2 million

Paul Kienel, Executive Director of the Association of Christian Schools International (ACSI) estimates that one million children in the United States are enrolled in Christian schools. According to Bruce Cooper, this figure represents approximately a 630% increase in Christian school enrollments since 1965.[25]

It is difficult to determine how many Christian schools exist because in many states they do not need and generally do not choose to be accredited. Furthermore, as with many small-scale organizations, many that are started close down within the first three years. However, estimates indicate that between fifteen thousand and eighteen thousand Christian schools exist with an average enrollment of between 100 and 150 students, but ranging from five to 2,500 students.[26]

According to Dennis Brown's study of fifty Christian schools in Southern California, the majority of schools range from kindergarten to 6th grade; some range from kindergarten to 12th grade, and several from 9th to 12th grade.[27] In my sample of Christian schools in Lynchburg, Virginia and three counties in upper New York State, two-thirds of the eighteen schools had intermediate grade ranges, that is, from kindergarten through 4th or 8th grade. Because of the organic growth of many of these schools, the grade range is determined by the longevity of the organization and its age constituency; the type of curriculum; financial stability; the existence of alternative high school education; and philosophy. The most common pattern is for schools to open initially with kindergarten and 1st grade. The next year, as students move on to a higher grade, they will add on a 2nd grade, and so on. This is partially dependent on the age distribution of the fellowship which primarily determines the grade structure of the school, although most schools accept students whose parents are not members of the associated fellowship.

In short, the greater the degree of isolationism, the greater the likelihood that schools would extend through 12th grade. Likewise, the older the school, the greater the age range of children in the fellowship *or* the greater the use of the A.C.E. curriculum (which is designed to allow for a low teacher–student ratio and limited physical and financial resources). Further, the greater the perceived unavailability of alternative high school education (either public or Christian), the greater the likelihood that the school will extend into the higher grades.

Whether or not to accept non-Christian students or students from outside the fellowship has been an issue for debate. The controversy involves the tension between evangelism as the primary mission of the church and the desire to build a community that protects their children from the contamination of the world and the "unsaved." Most schools have decided on a policy which accepts a minority of "non-Christians." Certainly a two-way process of selection is at work; all of the Christian schools I visited explicitly stated their educational philosophy and policy as a Christian school. If parents were to enroll their children, they had to agree to the policies (e.g., chapel, Bible studies, spanking, dress codes, and so forth).

The Christian school movement is inter-denominational and Protestant. Its constituency consists primarily of American Baptists, Assemblies of God, the Brethren, Free Will Methodists, Nazarenes, Southern Baptists, and many independent Bible churches. Many of these denominations have sponsored post-secondary education for some time, but their venture into elementary and secondary education is a relatively new phenomenon. Although its constituency is drawn from all socio-economic classes, it is primarily a white, middle-class, grass-roots movement that took root in the 1950s and soared in the late 1960s and 1970s.[28]

Until the 1970s, however, Christian schools were islands unto themselves, scattered and powerless. In 1972, the American Association of Christian Schools was founded. As of 1982, it numbered 1,080 schools with 175,000 students. In 1978, a merger of several small associations took place, forming a second major school group, the Association of Christian Schools International. The largest Christian school association, it numbers 1,728 schools including 126 colleges with 320,950 students. The third major association (started in 1920 by Dutch Calvinists), Christian Schools International, is now expanding its membership to include new Christian schools. It numbers 400 schools with 70,000 students; however, a total of 1,600 use their services. Schools that do not agree with the association's Calvinistic theology are admitted as Associate Members, with access to all services but no voting rights or board representation.

These three associations offer a variety of services including monitoring legislation at the state and federal levels; legal assistance; school and teacher accreditation; professional training; teacher placement; insurance packages; and national competitions in athletics, academic debates, music, and Bible. They serve primarily as lobbying organizations which monitor legislation and defend individual cases at the local, state, and federal levels. Between its founding in 1978 and 1982, the Association of Christian Schools International spent $374,260 in legal defense of Christian schools. As Robert Liebman and Robert Wuthnow observed, in the 1970s evangelicals began to re-emerge in the political arena with "many of their leaders cutting their political teeth defending Christian schools they had helped to organize."[29]

The nature of alternative education has been diverse, and its goals and constituencies have been continually redefined throughout American history. During the late 1960s and the early 1970s, middle-class liberals supported "free schools" which emphasized individual creativity and freedom from constraints. Today, middle- and working-class evangelicals support Christian schools that stress discipline and respect for authority. Both movements, however, wanted schools that reinforce parental values and beliefs; the major difference is that the rhetoric of the free-school movement never advocated making the family and school congruent. Rather, it pushed for critical politics, encouraging children to challenge traditionalism, including aspects of family roles and ritual.

Today, evangelical Protestant schools argue that public schools neither represent "common ground" nor Protestant principles. In an attempt to preserve their right to religious expression and to educate their children according to their values, a significant number of evangelical Protestants have turned to Christian schools. Some schools were established as segregationist academies; others have never discriminated on the basis of race and have been open to a racially and ethnically diverse population.[30] But they do justify their existence and tax-exempt status on the basis that they are extensions of religious ministries.

The tables have turned. The contemporary evangelical stands in opposition to public education precisely because it is not Christian enough. Once considered a just and functional response to the demands of a heterogeneous society, public education has come to be regarded with contempt by contemporary evangelicals. Other interest groups—professional public educators and main-line Protestants, Jews, and, increasingly, Catholics who support public education—accuse the Christian schools of being divisive, narrow-minded, authoritarian, and bigoted.

The educational philosophy of Christian schools

> Education is not preparation for life; it is life itself. (John Dewey)

The above statement by John Dewey is one of the few that evangelicals would accept. In general, they reject him as an atheist, evolutionist, and secular humanist (moreover, a board member of the American Humanist Association when the first "Humanist Manifesto" was published in 1933). They reject his "progressive" philosophy of education for being child-centered rather than God-centered. The following passage by Dewey is often cited in the Christian school literature:

> Faith in the prayer-hearing God is an unproved and
> outmoded faith. There is no God and there is no soul.
> Hence, there are no needs for the props of traditional
> religion. With dogma and creed excluded, then immutable
> truth is also dead and buried. There is no room for fixed,
> natural law or moral absolutes.

A. A. Baker, vice president of Pensacola Christian Schools and A Beka Book Publications (a major publisher for Christian school materials) outlines what he considers to be the philosophical foundations of "God-denying progressive, pragmatic education":

1. Express yourself.
2. Do your own thing.
3. Get rid of your inhibitions.
4. The individual is no longer important; it is the group that counts.
5. Knowledge for the sake of knowledge is useless.
6. You learn only by experience.
7. Competition in any form is taboo.
8. Nationalism is a dirty word.
9. The American way is not the best way.
10. If it satisfies a want, it must be right.[31]

What Baker does not address is the essential tension between the individual and the collective expressed in both his own thinking and that of progressive and Christian education. He criticizes secular education in points 1–3 for being too individualistic, and in points 4–5 for being too socialistic (concerned with the group and downplaying competition). This paradox reflects the dualism in American society between the values of individualism and egalitarianism, and liberty and equality. As their alternative to public education, Christian schools are proposing holistic, authoritative, disciplined, and God-centered education that emphasizes character development and spiritual training. Affective and moral domains are considered at least as important as cognitive domains. Moreover, school is considered just as real and important for children as work is for adults. Concerned with personal salvation rather than good works, evangelicals value personal character and relationships over activities and accomplishments. When people at Covenant and the Baptist school were asked what they are preparing their children for, they responded

we want to introduce our students to certain disciplines of knowledge that will cause them to develop their God-given intelligence, gifts and abilities to their potential and cause their true identities as God created them to develop. (Founder of Covenant)

we want the individual child to find their identity and salvation in Jesus. (Covenant teacher)

to teach them to love the Lord. Academics will pass away. (Academy teacher)

we want to guide and influence character growth. It is more important that they learn not to be selfish and not to lie; they'll eventually learn that 2+2=4. (Covenant teacher)

Given these orientations, how have they chosen to structure their schools? The Christian School Movement, like the evangelical movement, is not monolithic. Rather, variations among schools reflect ideological, organizational, and demographic characteristics, as well as the talents and personal styles of those who establish and operate them. But general organizational types can be identified; schools tend to be either church-run or parent-sponsored and to be organized around one of the following curricula:

- A.C.E. that supplies standardized, individualized packets of Christian materials renders teachers unnecessary; little opportunity for group work; students work in their own cubicles.
- A Beka Christian materials that encourage rote learning and drills; used in a traditional classroom style.
- Secular materials that are placed within a Christian perspective, involving more class discussion; used in a traditional classroom style.

In each case, Bible readings, worship, and prayer times accompany regular instruction.

Much of their general educational philosophy is similar; the following excerpts taken from the Covenant handbook represent the pedagogical orientations of Covenant School as well as those of the Baptist school and the Christian School Movement in general:

Mathematics: In light of the order God has produced in the material universe and its set relationships in space and time, we cannot overlook Mathematics as being an instrument for teaching our students concepts of order and logic that Creation itself portrays as a very attribute of God. Mathematics is an exact science and in this present age of "relative truth," it affords the Christian school an excellent opportunity to teach each student how to comprehend the orderly world around him, created by God who presents Himself as Absolute Truth (John 14:6).

Science: Students should come to view Science not as a discipline that destroys the traditional values of Christian faith, but as a secondary interpretive aid to the Biblical revelation [i.e., understanding how creation works]. Because the Biblical perspective is far deeper and more inclusive than the scientific viewpoint, reaching to the area of ultimate meaning, the Biblical revelation has the final priority.

English: In the Kingdom of God our communications skills are a prerequisite for our walk, for to know God is to understand Him as He is revealed through the Word (John 1:1, 14 and 2 Timothy 3:16). We receive this revelation through listening or reading. Once we come to know Christ, that knowledge of Him must flow through us to others as we speak and write (Matthew 28:19–20). The Word is manifest in language. . . . Kingdom people must become skillful craftsmen in communication, language artists. Ineffective and unclear communicative endeavors hinder unity and one-mindedness (Genesis 11:6–7).

Social Studies: Genesis 1 tells us that God created the heavens and the earth as well as every living and non-living thing in them. In light of this revealed fact, we need to accumulate and transmit to our children what God has created and how it may affect us who are a part of that Creation. We need a working knowledge of the world, its geography, and its people that will enable us to better be "in this world but not of it." We learn in our study of

Scripture that the Lord God acted upon and in the world's history to shape and mold it according to His plan. He raised up kings and nations and tore them down always with a purpose in mind that was not at times clear to those participating.

In general, Christian schools stress the Christian history of America, the fight for religious freedom, the integral relationship between patriotism and Christianity, the religious foundation of the polity and educational system, and the religious character of traditional American leaders such as George Washington and Abraham Lincoln. Proponents of Christian schools point to studies that show the decline in the religious and moral content of commonly used schoolbooks. The McGuffey Readers, once commonly used in public schools, sold an estimated 120 million copies between 1836 and 1920. They were filled with stories with a moral and even included Bible stories. Paul Kienel, Director of the Association of Christian Schools International, writes

> while William McGuffey pointed children toward God in the first half century of public education, another American educator in the second half century turned them away from God. His name was John Dewey.[32]

A content analysis of children's readers by Richard DeCharms and Gerald Moeller found that moral teaching declined from 1830, and had practically disappeared by 1959.[33] Likewise, Ruth Elson found that

> nineteenth-century schoolbooks were designed to train the child's character rather than his powers of critical thought. . . . Their authors freely express fervent faith in religion, patriotism, honesty, and hard work as well as in temperance.[34]

Christian school advocates want to remedy what they consider to be ungodly and un-American progressivism in the schools. But how to construct a Christian curriculum is not immediately clear. Much debate among Christian educators concerns the "true" integration of Christian beliefs and values with academic subjects, and the development of a "truly Christian curriculum." Clearly recognizing that one does not yet exist, James Bidwell and Ronald Chadwick, two of the leading proponents of the Christian School Movement suggest that evangelicals must struggle with what it means "for Christians to free themselves of a secular mind-set in order to approach all things from a godly perspective."

The two schools that I have studied, Covenant and the Academy, are good examples of how divergent curricular methods for producing "true Christians" can be. By describing the fellowships and schools in detail in the following chapters, I hope to give the reader an understanding of how the communities attempt to educate their children in ways that will integrate their beliefs and practices.

3

To Live in Fellowship: Covenant Community

The Covenant community defines itself as "a people separate from the world." They talk of themselves as pioneers, as pilgrims who are journeying through a foreign land. One of the distinctive features of this fellowship is its music. Folk songs, written primarily by the head elder and other members of the fellowship, reflect the ideology of the group. Through these songs, they relate their goals, hopes, fears, and praises to one another, their God, and their children:

> We are only pilgrims on this earth,
> Searching for the city of our birth.
> No more looking back on where we've come;
> Following the footsteps of the Son.
>
> We are not afraid to trust Your love,
> Strengthened by Your power from above.
> We will love according to Your plan
> While we travel through a foreign land.
>
> Faithful was the Son when He was sent;
> And faithful are the men of covenant.
> If we never know all we have seen
> You will keep Your promise to our seed.
> (Ted Standquist and M. Hillenbrand)

Their desire to create and transmit not only a community but a culture is explicitly stated:

> We are the pilgrims who climb the mountains high
> Who cross the plains watching the sky

We ford the rivers and know the desert's way
We chart the seas day to day, today
We are the people who choose the narrow gate
That leads to life. The way is straight—
Just like the runner who runs to win the race
Just like a flint we set our face.

We are sons of the Most High God
All that we are and have is laud
Some will die and some will sing
We are all praises to the King.

We are a nation though in a foreign land
Who have a King, who takes a stand
We fight the good fight.
We raise the standard high
Declare the truth, unveil the lie.

I have used samples of folk songs to illustrate the worldview of the Covenant people. In so doing, I have started where they would start and with what they most highly value—their music. These people have written their own folk songs that chart their journeys and teach their children, who are kept in separate schools until early adolescence. A strong oral tradition exists; songs that have been taught to fellowship members and school children over the years have only recently been recorded by them. This oral tradition reflects, in part, the importance placed on spontaneity and learning through interaction with people and resistance to standardization.

In order to convey most effectively the ethos of the Covenant community, I will attempt to portray these people in the fellowship as they see and talk about themselves. Since this is their story told through me, it has its biases, grounded in time and in my particular experiences and perceptions.

The Covenant Fellowship is a people who have set themselves apart. In part, they have rejected a culture they inherited. In part, they have struggled to create a new society out of the old. They once lived in a barn. They now have grown as a people and occupy houses around the barn. They speak a common language with those around them, and yet, they each have their own tongue that informs the way they think and the way others think about them. They are a peace-loving people, and yet, continually speak of the need to prepare for military warfare—in the spiritual realm. In the earthly realm, red ribbons adorn their trees, protesting against shedding the blood of fetuses.

The story has many beginnings, for the people had many and varied beginnings. John was a rock-and-roll musician and ex-drug addict. Joe came from the country, a farmer by trade and inheritance. Sam was an electrician, divorced and in debt. Sally sped by one day on her boyfriend's motorcycle, traveling fast to nowhere and even faster away from her middle-class background; both decided to stay. Linda was a biology student from Long Island. Peter was a professor of animal science. In those early years of the late 1960s, most were young, single, and searching for meaning in their lives. The majority came from so-called Christian homes, but they didn't believe in their parents' views of or commitments to Christianity. In fact, many were soon to claim first-generation Christian status: born-again to Christ.

Some were straight, others had experimented with "everything." It appears that the majority who had "dropped-in" to Covenant had "dropped-out" of society. Although they attempted to separate themselves from the world, they redefined the meaning of separation. Separation no longer was perceived as alienation or as rebellion against a cold, unjust world, but rather as submission to a higher authority. In attempting to build a Christian community, they concentrated on building one another up, affirming the best in one another while acknowledging the worst.

> He's building a building with men as the stones,
> Where love is the cement, it will be His home.
>
> We are a building made up of living stones
> To house our God upon His throne.
> We're built together—designed to stand and stay
> In covenant day to day, today.

Not all of the people were countercultural youth; they came from both experimental and traditional backgrounds. But when one asks them about what distinguishes their fellowship, they respond that it is not their differences but rather their common commitments and values. In the process of building a community, they say that they have given up some of their identity and independence as individuals. By joining hands with one another, each individual is less free to pull him or herself up or to leave the circle. People originally came to the barn in search of themselves; finding themselves in relation to one another, they were bound not to leave.

Sensitive to the promise of God's continual revelation, the Covenent Fellowship continues to experiment. Skeptical about tradition, which is often described as a "trapping," they have embraced change almost as ritual. While this encourages spontaneity, it can prove strenuous since satisfaction is considered deadly. They cannot settle; they must move on—together —through this foreign land, ever approaching the Kingdom of God.

Covenant people see themselves as pilgrims who are traveling through a foreign, "worldly" (hostile, unclean) land in search of the city and Kingdom of God. They recognize that they might not realize their dreams of God's promise in their own life, but they believe that their children or their children's children will. Believing that the extinction of Christianity is only one generation away (a sentiment commonly expressed by evangelicals), it is vital that they socialize their children "into the ways of the Lord." Although children cannot claim Christian status through their parents but must individually decide to accept Christ as Savior, adults do believe that appropriate role models and Christian environments will render children more susceptible to the Holy Spirit. Therefore, socialization is crucial—not only for children, but for people of all ages. Although it is not labeled as such, a life span perspective that addresses the processes of acculturation as well as enculturation is incorporated into their theory of human development. These people worship a "King" and are willing subjects who pay the price for "eternal life." They stress their worship of Christ as *King* as being distinctive:

> Before his majesty the King . . .
> We have seen the revelation,
> He's enthroned on exaltation;
> So we come in jubilation,
> To celebrate before the King!

Bow down to the Lord in the splendor of holiness,
Dance in His honor, all men on earth . . .
Declare among the nations: "The Lord is King . . ."
The Lord is King.
He is King of Kings.

Let us dance, let us sing, and
Come to the courts of the King.
Come along, sing His song,
Bring your praises and thanksgiving.

The Covenant people consider their worship of Christ as King as important because it implies that there is a ruler, and therefore, a government. Government implies authority and order. The degree to which authority is a common theme in discussions, prayers, and sermons indicates that it is a central issue. One couple, discussing the influence of the 1960s counterculture on the development of the fellowship, stressed that "the positive influence was the emphasis on loving relationships; however, we've run into a lot of problems when it comes to obeying authority. Many of us are used to rebelling and fighting for independence." Obedience to authority, then, is considered a central struggle for people at Covenant.

The challenge for many of the leaders and members of the fellowship was to submit *willingly* to authority. Since many of these people were countercultural youth who spent years questioning all authority, finding one they accepted as legitimate was revolutionary. For a new community with a young leadership, evangelical Christianity supported individual experimentation and interpretation while providing a sense of tradition and authority which had stood the test of time. The "authority of the Scriptures" gave them a sense of history and legitimacy that normally takes a long time to develop.[1]

The Covenant people talk and sing about worshipping Christ as King, not in fear but in the joy of celebration. Choice rather than coercion defines their submission to God; order is secured rather than imposed. The relationship between Master and subject is considered more affective than instrumental. Rather than stressing the Calvinist image of God as a stern, distant Father who judges His children or the image of Christ as the

49

Mediator between God and man, the charismatics emphasize the Holy Spirit who lives *within* man. Furthermore, Christ is defined less often as the go-between and more intimately as man's friend. After friend, the next most common description of Christ is as bridegroom. This implies, for evangelicals, a loving, conjugal relationship with Christ, who as *bridegroom* is the protector of and provider for the bride—in short, the bride's Lord. Some men in the fellowship discuss the fact that they struggle to relate to Christ as a bridegroom: "It's easier for the women because of their natural roles. It's a real challenge for me to think about switching the roles and seeing myself as the bride."[2]

For women in this community, the idea of being a loving and submissive bride is accepted as being natural. The notion complements much of the socialization they received as females growing up in American society during the 1950s and 1960s. But for the men, the idea was a radical one. In the conversion experience and identifying themselves as Christ's bride, men were asked to develop "feminine" traits (submissiveness, humbleness, meekness, faithfulness) and to de-emphasize their "masculine" traits (aggressiveness, toughness, being-in-control).[3]

The Covenant women, in other respects as well, have adopted traditional roles for themselves while they tried to make of their men "modern" men, that is, men who are both "strong" and "sensitive" and invested in both work and family. One Covenant woman expressed it this way:

> We are looking for strong, sensitive men. In the early days
> of the community, we had a lot of emasculated men who
> joined the kingdom. It seemed that a lot of the men who
> joined the Kingdom community were weak—it was a result
> of the families they were coming from. If we wanted strong
> men, we had to build them up.

The fellowship encouraged men to be both strong and expressive. They want them to express their feelings, to cry when they are hurt and when they are joyful.[4]

In their emphasis on Christ as a just King and *Friend* (rather than on God as a judgmental Father whom one fears), and in their description of man as being tempted by satanic forces rather than being inherently evil, the Covenant people draw more heavily from the New Testament than the Old Testament. They emphasize that Christ suffered out of a willingness to sacrifice Himself for the love of God and man, not as a punishment for the sin of Adam. Similar to Reinhold Niebuhr's formulation, they define self-love not as a narcissistic but rather as a positive love which needs to orient itself to other people in order to fulfill itself. Thus, self-esteem is important so that people can enter into positive relations with others and carry out God's work in the most effective manner. Pride is still considered a deadly sin.

Both the common ideology that unites the group, and their comparison by negation to those who are "unsaved" and therefore spiritually dead, reinforce the cohesiveness of the group. Within the group, joy prevails over fear, love over punishment, challenge over comfort. Celebration is a means of building solidarity, cohesiveness, and commitment. By celebrating the Covenant, they remind themselves of it; by continually reaffirming it, they reconfirm its promise to them as a body and as individuals. By repeatedly emphasizing their *willingness* to submit their lives to Christ, bondage is recast into freedom and Christian duties and responsibilities into privileges of the chosen people. A personal relationship with Christ requires sacrifices, but reciprocity is recognized *and* expected.

The word "charismata" comes from the Greek meaning "gifts." As a charismatic fellowship, Covenant believes in the Baptism of the Holy Spirit and the gift of tongues. A series of baptisms can take place in the life of an individual. While members have similar descriptions of the process of being born-again, all emphasize that it is different for different people. One woman in her mid-twenties from a fundamentalist background explained, "For some it's a momentous occasion—a real break. For me, it was the next step in obedience." But however the conversion is experienced, "having the Holy Spirit in you is the most powerful weapon you can have—it helps you battle the enemy."

Speaking in tongues is considered a gift from the Holy Spirit, an individual's own special prayer language that is understood only by God and the individual.

It's a matter of letting go of control, especially the intellect. It's the intellect that gets in the way for most people. A lot of people are skeptical about it at first, they think it's a little crazy. But you've got to let yourself suspend belief and have faith, and really be receptive to the Holy Spirit. (Teacher)

Receiving the gift of tongues (i.e., beginning to speak in tongues), seems to be most difficult for those from fundamentalist backgrounds and for intellectuals.

The verses and melody of the following song communicate the sense of joy that people equate with being born-again—a joy so great that it cannot be contained, even though it may not (in fact, cannot) be understood by unbelievers:

> The joy is bubbling, bubbling, bubbling deep down inside.
> Others may not understand it, but I can't hide it.

The "gifts" are one symbol of the reciprocity that defines their relationship with God. An alliance or covenant is entered into. In return, man must fight on God's side—not only to ward off temptation at the individual level, but also to fight *for* God. "We need to be a strong and prepared army of God." The following excerpt, from "The Armor of God" illustrates this theme of the Christian Soldier:

> Take up the full armor of God
> Gird your loins with truth
> Put on the breastplate of righteousness
> To cover your heart, to cover your heart
> Stand firm.
>
> On your feet the gospel of peace
> Take the shield of faith
> To extinguish the flaming missiles
> Of the enemy, of the enemy.
> Stand firm.
>
> Take the helmet of salvation
> And the word of God
> Which is the sharp sword of the Spirit
> And pray at all times, and pray at all times.
> Stand firm.

These are not songs which are sung by rote with little attention paid to the words or the meaning. Rather, these symbols are discussed in informal conversations and followed up in sermons. A sample from one sermon illustrates:

> Tonight's sermon is Intelligence Briefing #2. . . . Now some of you may be saying, "Not again." But it is very important. We must be aware and ready; if not, the attack can be fatal. There are demonic and serious enemy attacks in our midst. . . . We must be strong in the Lord and in the strength of His might. "Put on the whole armor of God, that you may be able to stand against the wiles of the devil [Eph. 6:10]."

In their Statement of Faith, a separate section clarifies their beliefs about spiritual warfare:

> We believe that God and His people are opposed by supernatural foes in the persons of Satan and his principalities, powers, and demons. . . . We believe Satan to be a liar and thief. As God's people we have been commissioned and given authority to expose Satan's lies and to take from him all that he has stolen.

The symbolic crusade is fought out at both social and spiritual levels.

A majority of the original group identified themselves with the counterculture, having had experimented freely with drugs, sex, and spiritual forms, and tended towards political liberalism and egalitarian relationships. These individuals transformed themselves in the process of shifting from an identification with the counterculture to an affiliation with an alternative culture. The conversion experience of "dying to oneself" transformed them into "new men," whose previous ideological orientations had changed considerably.[5] The evangelical emphasis on "gemeinschaft" relations, love, individualism, and experimentation, however, represent strong threads of continuity with their countercultural background.

Although at first glance, the counterculture seems a strange bedfellow for fundamentalist religion, both actually share some striking ideological and value commitments. A vocal group of youth in the 1960s questioned the legitimacy of the "establishment." The size and concentration of their cohorts on college campuses and the accompanying socio-political factors—primarily the Vietnam War, racial unrest, and the ongoing threat of nuclear war—contributed to the power of their protest. Rejecting materialism, the mechanization of human beings, and instrumentalism in relationships, the counterculture emphasized love, tolerance, expressiveness, creativity, and the power of the individual to affect personal and societal change.

When secular means failed to provide meaningful explanations and resolutions, people sought other means for fulfilment. Presented with an abundance of choices but disillusioned with their previous experiences, some of the countercultural youth turned to evangelical religion.[6] In many cases, this was a natural transition, for evangelicalism offered a meaningful, albeit authoritative, normative system, one which retained an emphasis on individualized religious experience and interpretation. Evangelicalism stressed personal relationships with God and with people; love was to be shared within the framework of a communal ethic.

The convergence of psychological and religious terminology helps explain why transition from a secular to a religious mode was negotiated with relative frequency and ease. Countercultural youth who were used to meditating or "getting their heads together" could easily identify with evangelicals' concept of taking "time-off" in order to talk with God. Listening to the "inner voice" or the "inner dialogue" could be readily translated into listening or talking with the Holy Spirit. The Eastern mystic who "walks the Path" would understand the evangelical who "walks the Way." "Doing your own thing" finds expression in evangelicalism's emphasis on individual interpretations of Scriptures. Furthermore, prayer could be identified as self-administered therapy as well as a spiritual dialogue.[7] Evangelicalism legitimates individual experience and values affective relationships within the "family of God," and at the same time, provides guidelines for living. Furthermore, by stressing values associated with the Protestant work ethic, it resocializes people to function in society.[8] Evangelicalism gave those who "dropped-out" a way to justify their re-entry into mainstream society; they could be reborn to being "in this world but not of this world."

Social organization

Believing in the active working of the Holy Spirit, the Covenant people are quick to point out that the growth and development of their fellowship and school are organic, not organizational. In fact, they do not call themselves a church and laugh about a time a few years ago when the county installed a road sign labeled "church" to control traffic. "We laughed and said, 'Oh, so that's what we are!' Other people around here wondered; we didn't look like a church—there were no crosses or steeple or anything. Just a barn and with a sign like 'Love Inn,' it really made them wonder! A lot of people stopped by thinking we were a restaurant or free-love commune."

Founded in 1969 by a disk jockey and ex-drug addict from New York City, the fellowship was an outgrowth of a radio ministry. A woman, listening to the Christian broadcast found herself healed of arthritis and called in to offer her barn. Eventually the barn was cleaned up and turned into a coffeehouse and gathering area for young people. If people needed a place "to crash," they could stay there. In the early years, a theater company, national newspaper, and coffeehouse ministry were key features of the fellowship.

By the mid-1970s, the leaders felt that they had become so involved in the outreach ministries, that they had lost sight of who they were and what their primary mission was—salvation and nurturing a Christian sense of community. They decided to close down the theater, newspaper, and coffeehouse; discontinue the Sunday evening services that were open to anyone; and break up into inclusive, small family groups. Through a process of networking, they distinguished a core membership from visitors and hangers-on. Initially, four groups of six to ten families met once a week in each other's homes for worship. Because of the seclusion of these meetings, some people (mainly parents of young people who had joined and were planning to marry someone from the fellowship) accused the group of being a cult. An investigation—conducted by area clergy and university staff—cleared Covenant of the charge, reporting that coercion was not involved in recruiting or keeping members (Fellowship members; *Ithaca Journal*, 1983).

A year later, with a more solidified theology and sense of direction, they reinitiated Sunday evening services to which everyone was welcome. The more inclusive family groups continued as well. Thus, when the need arose, they turned from outreach programs designed to recruit new people to "in-reach" programs designed to foster a sense of community and commitment among those already involved. At this point, rather than reestablishing the ministries they once supported, they decided to focus on "in-house" socialization—the most important mission was to bring their children up in the way of the Lord. They began a school.

The charismatic emphasis on being open to the direction of the Holy Spirit continues to caution them against being too structured in organizational affairs. No bulletins prescribe the content or order of the service. Instead, a high value is placed on "letting the Holy Spirit move among us and direct the service. The Holy Spirit, not man, should guide the service. Man's role is to be sensitive and responsive to the desires of the Holy Spirit." Nonetheless, a structure does exist, although it is not as readily apparent to an outsider.

People generally gather around 5:30 p.m. on Sunday evenings and soon thereafter, the service begins. Sometimes an elder (there is no appointed minister, but rather a hierarchy of between seven to nine men, all married and in their early to mid-thirties) will call people to worship. Generally however, as though by tacit agreement, the group quiets down and someone begins a song. The band will pick up the song and those who know the words will sing along. One song flows into another: some are accompanied by the beat of a band of guitars, electric cello, drums, and tambourine; others are sung a capella, sounding like an ethereal choir; others remind one more of a pep rally cheer, replete with chanting, clapping, and jumping up and down. When someone "feels moved to prayer," they will pray so that all can hear; otherwise, between songs, one can hear numerous people muttering, moaning, or exclaiming: "Thank you Jesus, thank you Lord," "Praise you, Lord," "Oh, Jesus," "Oh, Lord," "Thank you, Jesus," "Bless you, Lord." People sit and stand freely during the worship part of the service. Hands are often uplifted during prayer. Faces, too, are lifted upwards; eyes may be open or closed, and people usually wear an expression of either ectasy or deep concern. Often people will sway and clap to the music or move to the center where room for dancing is cleared. Typically, men and women dance separately. Women express their feelings through "spontaneous" artistic solos and collective circle dances. The dances can be best described as graceful. The majority of women who dance are young, single women; mothers also dance with their older daughters. Men tend to dance singly—either alone or with a number of other men; every now and then they will join together in a circle dance or dance with their infants in their arms.

Infrequently, an elder will interrupt this relatively free-flowing worship service and direct people's attention to the content and tone of what they are singing. He engages the fellowship in *dialogue*, teaching through interaction. He asks what is appropriate, pointing out the discontinuity in the theme of the songs that were initiated or the appropriateness or inappropriateness of dancing. For example, one elder interrupted the singing, questioning people for lifting their hands to God rather than directing their attention to one another:

> The song is about the city of God and our love for one another—we should be singing to each other. Start the song again, this time singing to the person next to you of your love for them.

From week to week, the atmosphere changes to some extent. People comment on the fact that this week is filled with greater fervor than last week, or this week seemed more subdued. At times, the worship will spill over and fill the entire two hours. At others, more time will be spent on the sermon. Typically, the singing and prayers last about an hour and the sermon that follows will last for about forty-five minutes. Then, the service will conclude with some singing and the passing of the collection plates. People linger afterwards to talk with one another, to collect farm produce that they have ordered, to arrange social and church activities for the following week, etc.

Compared with mainstream Protestant and Catholic churches,

services are loosely structured; no hymnals, choirs, robes, crosses, religious symbols, or altars are to be found. The meeting hall is located in the old loft of the barn. Chairs, not pews, line up in rows on three sides. On the fourth side sits a slight platform upon which the elders sit; a lecturn stands in the center of the platform. To one side of the platform, the band of musicians sit. In the center of the room is an area that is used for dancing and sitting during the sermon.

An active, hierarchical counseling system operates, with "older brothers and sisters in Christ disciplining those who are younger in the Lord." Spiritual and emotional support are primary, and people often refer to the fellowship as their extended family. One man, upon announcing the birth of his son earlier that day (Sunday), said that he was happy to share the good news "with my family here before we shared it with our own families." Another mother declared,

> We're not afraid of difficulty. God uses it to test us. We will confront it. Furthermore, our greatest strength is that we are a people, a community—we're not alone—we're a family!

Leadership

The leadership is shared among seven to nine men. The mean age of the leadership, thirty-five, reflects the youth of the congregation. A hierarchy does exist, with one head elder, three elders at the second rank, and then the others following. However, the number of positions at each rank is not fixed; it is dependent upon the experience, maturity, and tenure of the men involved.

Each of the elders is married. After faithfulness and commitment as a Christian, the most important criteria for whether or not a man is ready to assume a leadership position is his family life. Is his family in order? Is his wife happy? Are his children orderly? People at Covenant believe that the family is a microcosm of God's family and kingdom. In order for a man to serve God and lead men, he must first be able to lead his own family. The most important commitment a person has is to his God, then to his family, and finally to his work. The Covenant fellowship considers itself a training ground for "men of God" who will move into leadership positions; some will stay at Covenant, others will spread out to other communities. Therefore, if a man is deemed ready by his mentor or "shepherd," he will be encouraged to assume more responsibilities. The training process involves potential leaders sitting in on important meetings, learning through observation and participation.

The organizational style of Covenant fits, in many respects, the classification of a sect. The sect is a voluntary association of people committed to an ethico-religious ideal. In tension with the world, it takes an uncompromising stance towards the secular world. Members must go through a conversion experience and adhere to rules that are very strict. No professional clergy exists, and subsequent leaders are drawn from within the ranks of the fellowship. The "clergy" are charismatics who tend to be perceived by the more established churches as eccentrics. The fellowship is an exclusive moral community charged with intimacy. Theology is characterized as strict and literalistic. Services are informal and highly emotional.

Although Covenant still retains these original sect-like qualities, it has grown more conservative and structured over the years. "We used to do some really crazy things. Things are a little tamer now, a little more predictable." This is a pattern common to the development of sects which over time either tend to die out or become more church-like. As Bryan Wilson (1967) points out, the recruitment by conversionist sects of new members who do not have the same commitment and investment as the older, original members is likely to make the group more accommodating; they become more like denominations. For this particular group, age is also an important factor. Fifteen years ago, the founding members were in their late teens and early twenties. Since then, they have grown older and have taken on the responsibilities of starting and supporting their own families. Since that time also, the social and political climate of the United States has become more conservative and less experimental. Covenant incorporated as a church in 1983; but members still argue that they resist the institutionalization of religion.

Authority in relation to gender is central to Covenant's notion of government, family, and God's natural order. Many of the women who considered themselves quite strong and at one time, "political," recognized that they had relinquished their independence and authority to men. Many of the Covenant women were consciously aware of the compromises they had made to build fulfilling relationships with their men:

> The women are aware they have sacrificed. We had to step down in order to let them [men] step up to their "God-appointed" positions. We had to relinquish some of our power. We value it because it's part of God's order and government.

The Bible legitimated their reasoning: "according to Scriptures, this was the way things should be." The husband is believed to be the spiritual head of the community and family. He is "Lord of the household" and is responsible for protecting and loving his wife who is his helper; assisted by her, he is responsible for leading, training, and disciplining his children. Wives are to submit to their husbands who, in turn, submit themselves to God.

But this does not mean that women do not feel resentment or frustration. Mary, a middle-aged woman and wife of an elder, says

> we also get frustrated at times. If we have a concern, we'd go to [one of the elders]. Well, there's nothing that's more of a slap in the face to a Kingdom woman, than to be told to: "Pray about it."

For her, telling women to pray is like relegating them to the back seat, or more specifically in the holy war against evil forces, to behind-the-line combat. While this is important because it supports men on the front lines and is consistent with the explicit ideology of female roles exposed by the fellowship, Mary expresses resentment.

How does she deal with her anger? At times it erupts into confrontation and/or crying; more often it is suppressed or dealt with through rationalization or prayer.

There are a lot of strong women here; we have some "run

through the flowers ladies," but a lot of us had to step down in order for our husbands to rise to their God-given responsibilities and positions. We're still strong, but in different ways. For instance, we might not preach or make the major decisions in church, but we're there talking to our husbands and they listen. We're prayer warriors.

Anger does exist, but it is suppressed as this woman falls back to the standard discussion of men's and women's roles.

I've seen visions of battlelines drawn and women are on the frontlines with men. . . I am a prayer warrior for my husband who is an educator. But we are a team and when he becomes a pastor, then I will be an equal as a pastor's wife. Until then I pray. He is my Lord. He's not perfect, but he's my Lord. He is the priest of this household, I the priestess.

Mary goes on to reiterate that the sexes are by nature different; that women are ruled by the heart and men by the head. Therefore, they must play different roles. Men are better suited to leadership positions for they hold up better under stress. "Studies have been done by the Air Force to show this."

.Rationalization, then, may be interpreted as people's attempts to explain and soften compromised decisions made under difficult circumstances. For example, another woman describes her nervous breakdown and attributes it to her working and not fulfilling her rightful responsibilities as wife and mother to her three children. She talks about the days after she had committed herself to Christ but had not yet fully submitted herself to her husband. (Both she and her husband grew up in fundamentalist homes.)

He was tending the farm and I had finished school and had a good administrative job. I really felt good about what I was doing and moving ahead. I was realizing how competent I was. But he felt threatened. He thought I should be at home more with the kids, and helping out on the farm. Well, I really resisted—I can be very stubborn! I'm also a strong, dominant woman. I could do things more easily and often better than my husband, but then I'd be

upset because he wasn't stronger. I didn't listen to him or to
what Christ was trying to tell me. The elders talked to us,
and told me that in order for things to work out I would
have to give in and be willing to accept the leadership of my
husband. Well, God hit me hard. I guess when you have a
hard head, you need to be knocked down hard in order to
get you to pay attention. [In short], I went through a
nervous breakdown. It was awful for about a year—I was so
depressed; I'd just cry and cry. I couldn't get out of bed.
But I learned—the hard way. I finally submitted and things
are much better now.

She left her job and stayed home with her children and helped
her husband out on the farm. She and many others in the
fellowship would agree with Edward Hindson's judgment and
warning:

If the wife wants her husband to be more of a leader, she
must let go of the reins. Most men do not enjoy fighting
their wife for control of the family, so they sit back and do
nothing. In time, the wife has a nervous breakdown trying
to run something God did not call her to run.[9]

Rather than interpreting illness as a form of both surrender
and rebellion against the prescribed roles for women in this
particular social context (as contemporary feminist theories
would suggest),[10] these women interpret it as a sign of women
"stepping out of their place," and thereby disrupting God's
natural order. As in many circles in previous historical times,
conflict within the family was attributed to the "restless woman."
Many of the Covenant women, however, believe that the
compromises were worth the gains they made in attracting a
husband who was committed to his family. Many of them talked
about the rough times they had while they were single,
"liberated" women or single mothers trying to support a family.
A mother-to-be in her early thirties, who described herself as
once having been *very* political and feminist, commented:

Our feminist fight had failed us. Oh, there was a time [while
in college] when I swore I'd never get married or have

children. Even after I started coming to services here and
Milk Meetings,[11] I questioned a lot. Mr. ____ who led the
meetings [for new people interested in the fellowship] didn't
like flaky women—and many of the women in the
fellowship were flaky. Well, I came in my army fatigues,
didn't wear make-up, and would ask a lot of questions
about things I didn't know. I've always been outspoken.
Well, Mr. ____ took me under his wing. That's where I met
my husband. So God had different things in mind and He
has brought me much happiness.

For some of these women, the fellowship did not necessarily
offer them strong, sensitive husbands, but rather support as
single mothers. After struggling to be independent women who
had to work and support their children on their own, the
fellowship offered them a support system and community. People
regularly baby-sat for one another; older boys and men served as
big brothers and fathers to their children, modeling in this sense,
the role of Christ. Furthermore, Christ and God provided a
substitute for their husbands and the fathers of their children:

Christ serves all my needs. He is my bridegroom—literally.
If it's God's will and the right man comes along, I would
like to get married again. If that happens, then Christ will
step aside and that man can fulfill the role of bridegroom.
But until that time, I am content. (Divorced woman and
mother of three children in her early forties)

Sometimes I think it would be good if the children had a
father around. We talk about that. It's hard being a single
parent. But I tell them—"you have a Father in heaven who
loves you very much and He'll *never* let you down. That's
better than any human father. He's always there."
(Divorced woman, mother of two children in her mid-
forties)

It may be that the needs and desires of some of these
evangelical women are not so different from many of their more
feminist or mainstream counterparts, but rather that their means
for achieving a satisfying, or at least reasonable, life differ. The

63

balance rests in favor of accommodation rather than resistance. And secular means having failed them, they turned to religious resolutions.

Moreover, while many of them argue that men and women are different by nature and that their roles should reflect those differences, they recognize that this is not always the case in practice. In a number of instances, it became evident that both men and women of this community clearly saw the discrepancies between philosophy and practice, hope and happenstance. For example, the issue of submission and independence was discussed with a couple in their mid-thirties, Carl and Marcie, both graduates of an Ivy League University. They both nodded knowingly (recognizing my interest and difficulty in understanding the concept and practice of "submission"); they agreed that the wife should submit to the husband. Carl went on to explain (he did most of the talking at this point):

Carl: There must be someone in authority—it just doesn't work if there are two leaders or no leaders. I know it sounds hard, but the man is the God-given leader and the wife must submit to him and he must love her. That's very important—he must *love* his wife. It should be that if both have jobs in different places, both should be dying to go where the other's job is—that's love and commitment. . . . When we were married, we both threw it all in. We joined in Covenant so we knew what that meant in terms of roles.

Rose: Do you consider yourself [directed to the husband] the leader in all cases in your family?

Carl: [Laughs] Well, yes. But not always. My wife is actually better at accounting than I am, but we know that as the man, I should be running the finances. So I do it even though she's better at it than me. I'm not a natural leader; I've had to work at it. I'd just as soon sit back. Now Marcie is a leader. I've had to learn to take on responsibility—it hasn't been easy.

Rose: Do you think this has been true in a lot of the marriages in the fellowship?

Carl: Yeah, I'd say about half of the marriages here show strong competent, active women and easy-going husbands.

Rose: You said that God directs your decisions; that you ask Him for advice and then follow His instructions. [Both nod in agreement.] What happens if you, Carl and Marcie, each hear different things from God. How do you reconcile this, if you each really believe that you're hearing the Will of God? [They both look at each other and smile.]

Carl: The wife should submit, even if it ends up that the husband is wrong. It [contradictory interpretations of what God is telling each of them] rarely happens in our marriage though. Although a couple of times, I have been wrong. One time in particular we both thought we had heard the Will of God. Marcie submitted, as it was right to do and God blessed her, and therefore us. Boy, I almost ruined everything—my job, the family. . . . But because Marcie had done the right thing [in submitting], God rectified the situation. [Marcie nods in agreement]

After Marcie and Carl were married, Marcie taught school. When their first son was born, Marcie chose to stay at home.

It was hard when my fifth year came up and I let my New York certification go. I knew I had chosen to stay home with the kids and my family. But I needed an outlet for my creativity and my teaching ability. I didn't realize then that I could teach in many ways, like someone calling up for a recipe, or saying that their child was doing such and such and what did that mean? Now I have a little catering business and the young women in the fellowship come over as we're preparing the food and we talk. They're learning how to be young women in Christ and that's been really neat. You can teach in a lot of different ways.

Marcie then went on to explain how good her family life had been, although it had been difficult for her not to continue in her professional role as an elementary school teacher:

> The first year my son was born was really hard. I wasn't
> sure we were going to make it. But Carl was really good—a
> very loving husband. I am an enviable woman. He is my
> spiritual father in the Lord; he brought me to Christ and he
> is my cover and the head of our household. I sit at his feet
> in amazement, much as the church sits at the feet of Christ,
> the bridegroom.

By way of comparison, Marcie then talks about a college friend
of hers who came back recently for a wedding:

> She is thirty-two and told me that she had built her career
> as a business woman, and now there aren't any men
> around. I'm so thankful that didn't happen to me. It's really
> sad.

The struggle for identity, therefore, is a concern. The coping
mechanisms of many of these women tend towards eliminating
rather than working through their frustrations; they accept the
traditional notion that the wife's identity is subsumed under that
of the husband's. Consider Marcie, who views the struggle for
identity as an independent woman to be a curse: "I'm so glad I
didn't have to fight for an identity—to be *someone*."

But for other women in the fellowship, it is an issue of
growing concern. For instance, Sally (a wife in her early thirties
and mother of two small children) and her husband are
considering moving again. Although hard-working, her husband's
employment situation had been rather tenuous for several years
and he has been periodically unemployed. Sally stays home with
their two children. As they were considering a move to another
state which Sally was not thrilled about, I asked her how the job
hunt was coming—a process in which the whole community was
involved.

> Oh, there's one lead, but I don't know. I'm getting tired of
> always thinking about Paul and what he's going to do. It's
> not just him in this relationship. I'd like to do some things
> too.

Sally is not the only one who harbors some resentment over the prescribed roles that in theory she subscribes to. But what do she and others want to do about it? A seminar on women's roles, run by the wife of one of the elder's, explored the following kinds of questions:

What is my position or role within the church? The men have their ministry, but what do we have? We take care of our husbands and support them, but what else is there?

According to Sally, it was a beginning. She certainly is not looking for a revolution, but she did quietly hint in front of her husband that, "There may soon be some changes." Her husband then replied that, "The time may have come when some things can change." Sally quickly added, "But, the women are basically satisfied."

Our discussion raised questions about the "incontrovertible" nature of men's and women's roles, and why there may be role shifts or redefinitions of gender roles. According to Sally, since women, historically, had been the ones in the church with the men staying at home on Sundays, the fellowship needed to bring the men into the church "for they are the natural heads." Once, however, men are established within the church, women can become more active. Her husband supported her argument, at least in part: "That's right. Then we can consider giving the women more influence. But I don't know about governmental authority"—and here he stopped.

This statement implies that Covenant women see themselves as knowingly and willingly stepping down and relinquishing authority and power in order to attract their men into the fellowship. They see themselves as legitimating men as the "rightful and natural" (that is, God-willed) leaders of the church, government, and family. By defining themselves as soft, they believe they have allowed their men to appear as strong and in control. In the process, many men, in fact, have come to feel more competent, capable, and responsible—but only at the expense of the women. The women had to be kept in their place. No longer was it even possible for them to offer spiritual guidance to other women without the intervention of men who had to "cover" them. The second implication of Sally's statement is that once men are

67

strong enough not to be threatened by the women, then they "can consider giving the women more influence." Influence can now be doled out, but it continues to be controlled by the patriarchy.

Demographic factors

With approximately 250 full (committed) members, the Covenant fellowship consists primarily of young families with small children and single people, although there are a few people over the age of forty. The founding members of the late 1960s were mostly in their late teens and early twenties, and the relative youth of the leadership reflects the youthfulness of the group: the elders are all in their mid-thirties, the oldest elder being thirty-six. The mean age of the fellowship is twenty-eight. An emphasis on family life and the youth of the membership has led to a proliferation of young children; approximately half of the fellowship is under the age of fifteen.

While a wide range of socio-economic classes are represented, the elders and members describe themselves as primarily middle- and lower-middle class. Most come from white, middle-class families; some were raised in mainstream Protestant or Catholic homes; and others report no religious upbringing. College professors, farmers, skilled laborers, businessmen, and social workers comprise the fellowship. The average income ranges between $15,000–30,000. Minority members are welcomed but rare; compared to the general area population, however, they are proportionately represented.

The fellowship is set in a rural township outside of a university town of 50,000 people. All of these factors—theological, organizational, and demographic—interact in ways that uniquely influence the school they sponsor and the children they socialize.

4

School Life: Covenant School

We can no longer send her to the wolves. (Head elder)

Origins and organization

Sarah, the head elder's daughter, was five. She had just started kindergarten and her parents were not pleased. "We must do something. It's not right to deprive her of the word of God. We've got to think of an alternative." They decided to withdraw her from kindergarten and find a tutor. But after the months passed, they questioned whether the isolation from other children was a good idea. With others in the fellowship, they began to pray about what they should do.

There were not many children yet, but they were anticipated, for it was a young group and many had just married and were starting families. With the prospect of increasing numbers of children, they prayed about starting a school. Like the establishment of many Christian schools, the initial motivation came from the pastor at a time when his children were approaching school age. "For three months we fasted and prayed for the Holy Spirit to give us an answer by sending us a man to start the school."

"Then I came," explained a lively woman in her mid-thirties. Hilda had been studying education and teaching in the United States on a Fulbright Fellowship when she came to visit Covenant school. "I thought it was part of the Jesus Movement—with rock music and drugs." But Hilda stayed, and the Covenant fellowship welcomed her as the first principal of their school.

Well, I wasn't a man; and I had planned to go back to my country [Sweden] but the Holy Spirit seemed to be telling all of us that I should start the school. That first year [1974], I had six students ranging from kindergarten to 6th grade: the elder's daughter, two Harlem street kids, one student who had been labeled mentally retarded, one who was brilliant, and one student who had been kicked out of public school. The school literally originated from nothing. It had no expressed statement of faith, no principles or philosophy of education as guidelines, no curriculum or programs, no books or equipment, no classroom and no money. It was built out of faith.

That year, 1974, as principal and sole teacher, she taught the six students in a one-room schoolhouse setting, using the facilities of the church that formerly had housed the newspaper. From 1974 to 1981, the school expanded to approximately 110 students, ranging from preschool to 9th grade, with eleven teachers and one secretary. In the last three years, it has contracted slightly to ninety-nine students, ranging from kindergarten to 8th grade. Deciding that it was preferable for children to stay at home under the guidance of their parents until the age of six, they discontinued their successful preschool program. (They realize and accept that this decision may engage them in a legal debate with the State Board of Education whose guidelines state that children should begin school at the age of five.) As a complement to this decision and as a response to a recognized need among parents, parenting education workshops were organized for parents and newlyweds. At the upper end, they decided to have students make the transition to public school after 8th grade. They thought that students were sufficiently spiritually prepared to make the transition and that the public school would provide a good testing ground for the 9th graders.[1] As of 1986, some parents in the fellowship are becoming more interested in teaching their children at home. While this is a minority, it is causing some friction between the fellowship's desire to support parents in their role as the primary educators for their children and to support the school which they believe offers a superior education. The friction challenges their sense of consensus regarding the nature and roles of parenting and Christian education.

As of 1983, seventy-two students coming from forty-eight families attended Covenant school. As the fellowship members have grown older and increased in number and as the society has turned away from the turmoil and experimentation of the 1960s, the student population at Covenant has become more traditionally middle class.

Covenant students from the 5th grade on have attended, on average, 3.15 years in public school. Only 10% of them have attended only Covenant school, and another 10% only Christian schools. The majority (60%) have spent most of their schooling in Christian schools (either solely in Christian schools or less than three years in public school). There is no distinctive time that marks the transition from public to Christian school; rather, students entered Christian school at all grades. It was too early to tell how many students would go on to higher education, although the administration estimated 90% of them would eventually attend a variety of secular and Christian colleges.

Teachers at Covenant come from a diversity of religious backgrounds, from Catholicism to mainline Protestantism to no religious upbringing. All of the charismatic teachers received B.A. degrees from secular colleges; 80% have M.A. degrees, mostly from secular colleges. Eighty percent taught for at least two years in public schools. The current principal taught in public schools for twelve years. All of the teachers are members of the Covenent fellowship.

Single female teachers were paid less at Covenant than men or married male teachers. The explanation given was that women did not need to support families; they were considered supplemental earners. The average starting salary was in 1983 $9,500. The school budget per student was $2,050. There were six classrooms and a student-teacher ratio of 9:1.

As an outgrowth of the school, two satellite schools were established. Both lie within a twenty-mile radius. All of the sponsoring fellowships are similar; Covenant trains the principals and teachers, many of whom previously taught at Covenant. Nonetheless, differences do exist and are attributed to differences in their constituencies.

Covenant emphasizes the arts more; dance and music are very important to us. We've got a lot of artists and professionals in the community. [Covenant 2] is mainly a farming fellowship, and [Covenant 3] consists primarily of farmers and small businessmen—they tend to emphasize different things. They're probably more traditional and back-to-the basics than us. *That's good—how you worship and how you train your children is an expression of who you are.* There are absolutes and guidelines, but different styles. (First principal)

At Covenant, fairy tales are used and elves and other fantasy creatures adorn the walls. But teachers at Covenant 2 explicitly state that no mention of witches, elves, the tooth fairy, Santa Claus, or the Easter Bunny will be made—they consider such references sacreligious.

The original principal directed the school "under the cover of the head elder" for six years. When she left to start schools in new communities, a Council on Education was formed. The Council consists of three elders, the principal, and three parents. In past years, the school was partially supported by the fellowship and partially by tuition. As of 1982, the fellowship has assumed full responsibility. Members tithe 10% of their income for the support of the "fellowship," and an additional 4% for the support of the school; parents contribute 2% more for each child in school, up to three children. This is a substantial sacrifice for many people, but the fellowship decided that educating the young—whether they are their own children or not—is of primary importance. The school is a community effort.

Physical environment

Through the doors to the barn parades a constant stream of children, parents, teachers, elders, and other members of the fellowship. The barn is a very familiar place for all of them—it is where they attend services; hold weddings, baptisms and funerals; go to school; teach; sing; preach; dance. Aerobics classes, theatrical productions, counseling sessions, and family workshops are held there. Parents pick up produce supplied by one of the local farmers in the art room; both here and in the multi-purpose room, as well as in the 7th–8th grade classroom (where people gather after services), parents take notice of the work of the students and the murals which depict the current Bible lesson for the school.

The school reminds one of the cozy one-room schoolhouses of the past. The classes, however, are spread throughout the barn and addition. Stoked by students, a wood-burning stove heats the 7th–8th grade classroom. The floors are covered with brightly colored carpet squares that conjure up images of Jacob's coat of many colors. Students' art work and writings and colorful murals that illustrate Bible stories adorn the walls.

On the main floor of the addition, a large open area separates classrooms and serves as the auditorium, cafeteria, and play area when the weather is bad. During school worship, the younger children sit on the carpeted floor; likewise, lunch is eaten on the floor. One couch and two chairs sit alongside one wall; otherwise, there is no furniture. In addition to the kindergarten, the 3rd–4th and 5th–6th grade classrooms, the principal's and secretary's offices, and the teachers' room feed into this area.

The space serves as a communal gathering area—all have ready access to it. Students of all ages eat together; brothers and sisters can mingle easily and tell each other about what they did that morning in class. Without really supervising, one is aware of what is going on from the teachers' room; likewise, the secretary's office has a large window through which she can survey the multi-purpose room.

Downstairs are the 1st and 2nd grade rooms, and an additional smaller classroom that is used when the 2nd and 3rd graders are separated for reading. Since partitions divide the rooms, people are conscious of not being too noisy. When one of the teachers leaves the room, students are left with a feeling of being on their own but if they get too loud, the next door teacher can monitor them. In order to leave the 2nd grade room, one must exit through one of the other two rooms. Both because of the proximity of the rooms, the lack of sound-proofing, and the frequent traffic in and out of rooms, students are taught—out of consideration for their fellow students and teachers—to be quiet and to attend to what is going on in their own classroom. This they do remarkably well—both when their classroom teachers are present and absent.

The 7th–8th grade classroom is in the old portion of the barn, somewhat separated from the rest of the school. It is an open area, partitioned off by beams and rows of the old traditional desks. A baptismal sits off to one corner, and the wood-burning stove and church library preside over the back of the room. The art room is next door. The science room, replete with a refrigerator, stove (it used to be the church kitchen), and science equipment donated by local colleges is located in a room off to the other side.

Physical education classes are held at a nearby reformatory school which gives Covenant access to their facilities. Students are bused there twice a week. Out behind the barn are fields and a playground.

Two bathrooms, one for men and one for women, are shared by the students, teachers, elders, and parents. The atmosphere is quite different from the average public school bathroom where students often go to retreat, take a smoke, or write graffiti on the walls. Not only are the bathrooms used by everyone, members of the fellowship (including parents and teachers) clean and maintain them as well as the rest of the school and church.

Desks are positioned in rows that face the teacher's desk and blackboard. Round tables facilitate group work. All students have their own lockers in the back of the room; they are free to get up and get what they need during the class.

Educational philosophy

In an attempt to save Sarah and others from "the wolves," Covenant founded a school based on Christian principles. Initially, no formal plan for the school existed. Rather over the years and through "the direction of the Holy Spirit," a philosophy was hammered out. "The growth of the school was organic, always changing in accordance with the working of the Holy Spirit."

In the frequent references to "being open to the workings of the Holy Spirit" and the resistance to a standardized form of instruction, the school reflects the values and norms of the adult fellowship. The elders and teachers at Covenant School see their school as falling somewhere between legalistic, religious education and permissive, humanistic education. Drawing from a Montessori model of education which emphasizes creativity and the development of individual potential, they seek to place everything in God's perspective. They believe that children should be exposed to worldly things and secular materials in order to judge what is godly and ungodly. As the principal explained:

> As educators who desire to see the King glorified among us, we join Jesus in His Highpriestly prayer: "I do not ask Thee to take them out of the world, but to keep them from the evil one. They are not of this world, even as I am not of this world [John 17:15–16]."

Covenant educators want to teach their children discernment. While they want to save them from the "wolves," they do not want to isolate them. Much as adult members of the fellowship are given the freedom to decide what books to read, movies to see, music to listen to, and drinks to consume with moderation as their guide, so do they give their children the freedom to explore and make judgments. They hope that their children will reform—indeed transform—society, not withdraw from it. They believe this requires an understanding of the world, its practices, and its people.

The following interaction serves as illustration. One day during morning worship, a fourth grade boy asked everyone to pray for his cousin who had died in an automobile accident. He had been drinking and had run off the road. Another boy in the class challenged him,

Student B:	"I thought you said he was a Christian."
Student A:	"I did."
Teacher:	(intervening) "Just because he drinks, does it mean he wasn't a Christian? Can Christians make mistakes? [Pause] Can Christians be Christians and still drink?"
Other Students:	(in chorus): "Yeah."

> *Another Student:* "It's O.K. to drink beer. My Dad does."
> *Teacher:* "We believe it's O.K. to drink in moderation—so long as one is in control of it."

While members of Covenant are free to attend movies and other secular events and read books at their own discretion, they too discuss the limits of their self-control and their effect on others. During a teachers' meeting, one teacher selected Scriptures that addressed the issue of perfection. She talked about "how easy it is, given the freedoms we have in our fellowship, to fall away from the Lord." Others nodded in assent. "We have to keep questioning and putting things in God's perspective."

How do the Covenant people teach their children? What values do they want to transmit to their children? How do they define their goals and responsibilities as educators? The primary emphasis on love and building positive relationships in the fellowship carries over into the educational philosophy of the school. The following responses by teachers are typical:

> My goals as a teacher? 1) to have them love the Lord with all their heart and soul, 2) to have them love their neighbor as their brother. These are the fundamentals. Oh, also forbearance. Then I guess there would be curriculum goals: to be able to communicate effectively—mostly in speech since that's how we most influence people. In order to do this, you must first know what you think—to be able to evaluate and select from your environment and then to be able to clearly communicate. Other goals: to teach them to be kind, loving, to spell correctly, to speak accurately, to have a broad vocabulary. (English teacher)

> Love has high priority. To love one another is a goal—as teachers we should be givers of love. Through relationships with other children, the child will have the opportunity to work out kingdom principles on his own level: sharing, communicating effectively with others, being cooperative and sensitive, preferring others to himself, learning responsibility, respect, and forgiveness. . . . It's important

to help the children build a positive self-image and to exercise self-control. (Principal)

Covenant School, with primarily a middle-class constituency, wants students to internalize values. The school handbook states this explicitly:

> The goal for discipline is that the students will learn to operate from the spiritual rules within rather than outward laws. Hence, the attitude of heart is seen as more important than the actual wrongdoing. Because of this, the school operates with few external rules.

The degree of supervision and routinization is low, the degree of complexity high. Both students and teachers are encouraged to express themselves and explore their values and beliefs.

Trying to resist the institutionalization, and therefore the routinization of Christian life, teachers, elders, and parents grapple with how to transmit their faith and values to their children in a dynamic way:

> The history of the church is marked by a repeated moving of God's Spirit, raising up men and women as reflections of His Kingdom here on earth. During the life of the next generation, however, the initial exuberant expression of Christ has tended to dissipate and become reduced to institutionalized patterns of behavior. The vitality of life experience in the Lord was missed in the translation from father to son. One of the most challenging and difficult questions that faces anyone whose responsibility is to train children in God's ways is *how* to transmit spiritual life from one generation to the next without losing the essence, which is a dynamic faith and a Christ-like character. (Covenant handbook)

The most characteristic feature of Covenant's organizational style is the readiness to change. This past year, teachers who had been teaching one subject or grade level were asked to teach another. Although an undermanned work setting such as this often requires such flexibility, the changes went beyond the demands of the situation. Much of the change was initiated to challenge teachers, calling them to grow even more. Thus, one teacher may be teaching art, physical education, 5th grade mathematics, 8th grade science, and 7th grade English.

Curriculum

In stressing the uniqueness of the individual and the power of the collective, the Covenant people teach that there are a variety of viewpoints and people to learn from—one should listen, discern, and teach in return. For example, Covenant uses the Follett Social Studies series that is used by many public schools. They have chosen the series because, as stated in the Teachers' Edition (1977),

> [it] gives students ample opportunities to explore values—their own values, those of other individuals and groups, and those of the society in general. The methods employed allow meaningful exploration that will provide greater understanding. Particular emphasis is devoted to the democratic values that are an important part of our American heritage. The authors believe strongly in a free society based on individual responsibility and mutual cooperation, and the content reflects this belief. (Covenant handbook)

This choice reflects, in part, a greater willingness on the part of these charismatics to expose their children to more diversity and exploration of values than many Christian schools. But the series still stresses traditional American values.

The emphasis on foreign languages at Covenant school is strong, although the program depends on the year and the personal resources available. They once had Spanish, French, and German programs, but in 1982–1983 they taught no foreign languages. This year, they are offering French again. Foreign visitors and missionaries visit the school and tell of their country, teaching them songs or Bible verses in their language. The faculty at Covenant were the most articulate of any I talked with as to why foreign languages were an important part of their curriculum —part of the reason stems from their charismatic orientation:

> Learning a foreign language for the purpose of communicating clearly and effectively with one another whose very habits, thoughts, and actions have a different orientation, is exemplified in God's gift of "tongues" which he endows to all men who wish to communicate clearly with Him. "Tongues" is the heavenly language that allows us to speak to our Father in the quickest and most effective way without the entrapments of our native language. Goals: To have rewarding exchanges with those who are not like us [without compromising scriptural precepts] in order to foster unity rather than division.

These subjects are taught according to a traditional public school schedule, with additional time set aside for worship. The following is a basic schedule of the time alloted to each subject area according to grade level.

Table 1 Time allocated by subject area (hours per week)

Subject	Grade 1–3	Grade 4–6	Grade 7–8
Spiritual Training	2.5	3.75	3.75
Integrated Educational Activities	2.5	2.5	0
English Language Arts	4.5	3.75	3.75
Mathematics	4	3.75	3.75
Science	1.5	2.25	3
Health	.75	.75	.75
Social Studies	1.5	2.25	2.25
Spanish	1	2.25	2.25
Art	2	1.50	1.50
Music	1.5	1.50	1.50
Physical Education	2	2	2
Study Hall/Other Activities	2.5	.75	1.75
Lunch	3.75	3.75	3.75
Total	30 hours	30 hours	30 hours

During 1981–1982 (the year I began research in the school), Integrated Educational Activities were slotted for every Wednesday afternoon. This involved interdisciplinary studies and field trips involving all elementary school students and teachers in an attempt to achieve a more holistic approach to education:

> Jesus is an example to us of a holistic educator. He did not
> read the disciples a list of rules to follow in order to be
> godly men; He taught them by living and sharing his life
> with them. Christ's school was life itself. . . . In today's
> society, education has become fragmented and
> compartmentalized.

> The goals of Integrated Educational Activities is to reveal
> God's Kingdom to the child in a more realistic way by
> bringing unity to the various segments of academic subjects.
> [Another primary] goal is to provide activities [for] social
> interaction between students. In this environment, peer
> relationships may be nurtured, hearts may be knit together,
> and the formational bonds of covenant love laid. (Covenant
> handbook)

Teachers agreed with the philosophy of the program and applauded the attempt, but found it extremely time consuming and logistically difficult. Discontinued after two years, many hope they will be able to reinstitute it in the future. The schedule, then, changes to some extent from year to year depending on the talents of the teachers and the needs of the students.

Secular texts are used and Christian principles integrated. The following description of a 3rd grade English class serves as illustration. The students were reading a story about men who were drilling for oil when a flood came and devastated much of the area. The men became discouraged. The teacher begins the class discussion:

Teacher:	What would you do if you were those men, or involved in such a project? [No answer] What would your Dad do?
Student A:	If drilling for oil, go to another well.
Teacher:	Well, that's one thing that you might

	eventually do. But this is only an example—what if it were any project?
Student B:	Pray first.
Teacher:	I think that's what your Dad would do—pray first.
Student C:	See if what they wanted was there.
Student D:	Ask the Lord if drilling there was the right thing to do.
Teacher:	Yeah, that's how I think we should function. Sometimes people don't understand. What did people think of Noah? People thought he was crazy. They laughed at him. Do you think Noah was discouraged?—Same sort of thing. If these men knew the Lord, they would get down and call upon the Lord, and ask for God's direction and strength. Sometimes God says to have endurance. Sometimes we don't think it's going to work.
Student C:	These men won't pray.
Teacher:	I think you're right. But for *us*, it's the natural way. The men we know and your dads would pray.

A different English teacher in the 5th–6th grade class, discussed the difference between Truth and truth in relation to the students' reading of *Tom Sawyer*:

Teacher:	Rich, what is the difference between Truth with a capital "T" and truth with a little "t"?
Rich:	I don't know.
Teacher:	What else do you capitalize? How do you close a letter?
Rich:	In Christ.
Teacher:	Right. What else?
Student B:	One is the Lord.
Teacher:	Right. One is the Lord and the other is just a little human being. Truth equals God's Truth, and truth equals human truth. What is something true about Tom Sawyer?
Student C:	He doesn't like to work.

Teacher:	Is that true of young boys—[smiles]—that they don't like to work?
Student D:	[An emphatic] Yes.
Teacher:	I have a suspicion that there is not much of God's Truth in *Tom Sawyer*. That's something you as Christians have to discern if there's God's Truth in stories, or movies, or poetry. Check it—if it doesn't conflict with the Word, then it's ok; if it does conflict, then it isn't Truth. Have you seen *Tootsie*? It goes against God's Word—it's funny, and good, but you have to measure it against the Word of God. You can read lots of different things, but you have to be discerning. Ask your parents if you have questions about it.

The majority of schooltime, however, is spent on straight-forward presentation of academic material, be it talking about series and parallel circuits in a class on electricity or algebraic formulas in math class. Science and social studies classes address current social problems:

> Confronted by an energy crisis, threatened by pollution,
> confounded by a food shortage, and burdened with zooming
> world populations, our society is in need not only of
> scientists who will pioneer discovery to solve these issues,
> but also an informed population who will understand them.
> (Science teacher)

Health and sex education are taught: "It's not facts that are the problem, it's what we do with them. We stress the importance of friendship both within and outside of marriage. We don't teach that sex is a sin, but rather a gift to be saved until marriage." (First principal)

As part of classwork, students and teachers will play games such as the "Ungame" which is a Christian rendition of Values Clarification. People can pick cards from one of three piles: Light Hearted, Christian Beliefs, or Deep Understanding; they pose questions such as:

What is your purpose in life?
Describe the ideal life.
What does freedom mean to you?
When do you feel closest to God?

One can be sent to Worry Wharf or Happy House or land on a spot where you pick a card that presents tiny sermonettes:

If there is unnecessary laughing, some people may be afraid to share their feelings. Be aware of the mood that you create. Bless the person on your left.

Kindergarten through 2nd grades have their own classroom teacher. Students in the upper grades have their own classrooms, but teachers rotate according to subject. In the combined classes (3–4, 5–6, 7–8), students are often broken up into separate working groups. While the teacher is instructing one group in math, the other group is reading, working on exercises, or taking a test. Students learn to tune out fairly quickly, and attend to their own work. However, if they finish their own work early, they are likely to listen in on the other class.

The school day always begins with class worship; on Fridays, the whole school comes together for joint worship. Typically, the first forty-five minutes are spent singing (accompanied by guitars in the upper grades), reading the Bible, talking about concerns, and praying. Readings from different editions of the Bible are compared. Rather than reciting Scriptures, students are asked to interpret and apply them to their own lives.

During a Bible reading in the 5th–6th grade, the teacher interrupted the student who was reading to ask what "cutting the root of the tree of evil" meant:

Student A:	That people must repent, turning your ways around.
Teacher:	If you don't?
Student B:	[Pointing to the ground] Go down there.
Teacher:	Where? [grins]
Student B:	To Hades.
Student C:	[Seriously] I thought that was a country [they

	usually refer to Hades as Hell].
Teacher:	[Laughs warmly] That's Haiti.
Student D:	It means that we should bear fruit, you know the good fruit.
Teacher:	No, I don't know. What is fruit?

Teachers and students pray spontaneously, "when it feels right." Certainly expectations direct them: they should pray; moreover, they should pray *for others*. But the process of prayer is subtle. Almost by tacit agreement and without visual clues, even the youngest students seem to know when it's time for them to pray (they do not "need" to pray out loud every time), taking turns, and letting others finish before they begin. Students likewise initiate songs and dances, thus helping to direct the course of worship. The emphasis is on *individual expression*.

The curriculum promotes individual exploration also in forming and solving problems. An example from the 2nd grade further illustrates. The students read the following poem,

> I love my thumbprint
> Nobody has my thumbprint . . .
> But myself . . .
> Mine will always be the same
> So will I be the same forever and ever.

Before making prints of their thumbs, the teacher asked whether or not they thought they would stay the same forever:

Student A:	agrees: Yeah, you're born to stay the same.
Student B:	disagrees: When you go to heaven you change.
Student C:	disagrees: If you hurt your thumb, it changes.
Teacher:	Is one right or wrong?
Student A:	No, we're all right. We're the same here, but different in heaven.
Teacher:	I'm proud of you. It's good to think for yourself and then have reasons to back up what you think. You help me to think of other reasons.

Students are encouraged to question, and when teachers deem it appropriate they will take time to address the issues that students are concerned with rather than sticking to the material. Furthermore, students are free to say what they are thinking. For example, one question in the Ungame was, "What song would you like sung at your funeral?" One student promptly gave the name of a popular song, "I'll get there one way or another." Everyone laughed, and others went on to suggest more "traditional" songs.

In the 5th–6th grade class, a student interrupts the flow of the conversation and asks:

Student:	If Joseph and Mary got angry with Jesus because he stayed in the temple, would that be sin?
Teacher:	[A little taken aback because of the discontinuity] Well, did they get angry?
Student:	No.
Teacher:	Then it's not an issue.
Student:	[Pursuing the issue] It's not a sin to be angry at what someone does, but at the person?
Teacher:	[Takes time to discuss anger briefly since it is apparently a real concern for this student, but then gently reminds the student that he should pay more attention to what is going on in the class.] It's important to discuss why you're angry so a wall of hatred won't be built and so the enemy can't use it against you. You can be angry but not in sin. Jesus got angry at the moneychangers. Sometimes we need to release our feelings—our angers and our anxieties. But we can also do it in sin. Then we have to ask for forgiveness. But your question is not valid. You have to ask God for discernment in reading.

Teachers expect their students to attend to what is going on in the class as a whole and to work together as a collective. In the 7th–8th grade class, the following interaction took place when a student who was not paying attention asked a question that had just been answered:

> *Teacher*:   Were you listening? Can you read? [Teacher
> points to the board and other kids laugh.] John,
> I'm asking because I know you need your
> memory prodded. That's the hardest thing for
> you. You have a fine mind. You need to
> discipline yourself to use it. Do you have the
> desire?

Later on in the class, when John made a good point, the teacher
enthusiastically responded,

> See how much you can do if you just try! [Kindly] It's very
> important to lay a good foundation. Have you ever tried to
> build a house on a rocky or soft foundation?—it will
> crumble [the Biblical application was particularly
> appropriate for this boy, whose father is a builder].
> Whether someone forces you or not, you have to want to
> desire to do it. It's got to be something within.

Another teacher took aside some students and asked them to
encourage their classmate:

> As you know, Steve hasn't been doing too well on tests. We
> want to encourage him to do better, and to get more work
> done at home. You can help him by asking if he's done his
> work yet, or seeing if there's something you can help him
> better understand. If he knows you're concerned in a real
> way, he might become more serious about his work. We all
> need to take responsibility.

Teachers consider it their Christian responsibility to delve
deeply into the feelings and inner thoughts of students. Attitude,
not behavior, is the crucial concern; the motivations and
intentions of the students are critical.

While adults are concerned with the innermost feelings and
thoughts of the children, they give their students a fair amount of
control over their external environment. Kindergarteners, who
spend half-a-day at school, often walk unsupervised from one
room to another even if it is in a different part of the building.
Classes are often left unattended. Rather than creating a

structure in which students have no freedom to stray, teachers at Covenant school give them much opportunity to explore—both their surroundings and their limits.

The freedom of movement exhibited in church generalizes to the school environment. At Covenant during the worship time, people stand and sit as "the Spirit moves them." Some close their eyes, raise their hands, clap, dance, pray out loud or silently, and move in and out of the service. Certain expressions are considered appropriate depending on the situation, the atmosphere, and the type of song that is being sung; thus, the cues are more complex and subtle than in many conventional services. In school, Covenant children likewise are free to dance or sit, clap, etc. during worship times. They volunteer suggestions for songs and prayers. During class they are expected to sit and do their own work, but there is much greater leeway for getting up to go to one's locker in the back of the room, or to the bathroom. Unless students are disruptive or continually avoiding work, it is assumed that they have a legitimate reason for needing to get up. The choice is left to the student until he or she abuses it. Students often work together in group projects or quietly help other students with their work. Often during worship times, class discussions, lunch, and activity times, students will gather together on the floor. When moving from one classroom to the next, students quietly move along on their own without adult supervision. Seeing students file along in a single line is a rare occurrence; in fact, this is one of the concerns that Covenant teachers harbor. "Could our students form a single line if we asked them to right now? Maybe we need to teach them to be more orderly" (unsolicited comment from a Covenant teacher).

The degree of formalization is low. At Covenant no formal dress code exists. Students' clothing, like adults', is informal. In the evening worship service at Covenant, people wear anything from jeans to suits. Ten years ago, the majority of the membership wore "straggly jeans"; five years ago they decided it would be more pleasing to God and make a better impression on others if they wore "good jeans"; today, some men and women still comfortably wear jeans or informal slacks, but the elders tend to dress in suits or sport coats and the women in stylish dresses. Make-up and jewelry are common; "women should look feminine." But attire is not a primary issue. Likewise, children in

87

the school should be cleanly and neatly dressed, but both boys and girls may wear jeans or pants, sneakers, etc. The only restriction, to my knowledge, is that slippers are not allowed in school.

> One parent complained about us deciding that her child should not wear slippers in school. She thought if it was supposed to be a familial environment then slippers should be allowed. But that was going too far into informality.

Boys' and girls' attire resembles that of public school students in terms of fashion. Girls wear both pants and shorts and skirts and dresses.

In fact, while many adult conversations focus on the difference between female and male roles, needs, responsibilities, and expectations, in practice little distinction is made at the school. Still, they are often referred to as important:

> We are preparing them for manhood and womanhood in the Kingdom of God. (Teacher)

> I want each one to be what God made him to be. [Pause] I want them to be good husbands and wives, that's what! (Member of school board, parent, volunteer)

Although the school is given the responsibility of inculcating the fellowship's, and therefore the parents' values, it is rarely explicit about appropriate gender roles for students. Boys and girls are not segregated by sex except in sports, and often girls are (and are perceived as being) more assertive and "quicker" intellectually than a number of the boys in the class. When I asked the principal about this, he thought for a long time. While he was usually quick, though careful with words, here he had to search for an example of how Covenant's philosophy of female and male roles was expressed through action in the school. He couldn't think of an example, but in response said:

> You know, you're right. There doesn't seem to be much difference in how we treat boys and girls. We're going to

have to think more about this. In the fall, maybe we'll
institute a six-week course on sex roles.

(You never know what the unintended consequences of your
research may be—this was certainly not my intent.)

Social relations

In studying educational systems, it is important to ask not only
what is being taught and how, but to whom and by whom—and
in what kind of social environment. Large-scale studies of
schooling focus on objective variables such as school size,
student–teacher ratio, attendance, amount of homework, and
budget. While these are important variables to consider, they
miss the meaning and ethos of the environment in which
students, teachers, and parents participate.

Institutions consist of people interacting with one another,
creating, observing, and breaking agreed-upon norms of social
interaction. Therefore, one of the best means of understanding
an organization is to examine the ways in which people relate to
and communicate with one another. In addition to observations,
interviews and informal conversations, surveys asked students,
teachers and parents to describe their relationships with one
another and to check off which adjectives most characterized and
least characterized their relationships with one another.

In general, people at Covenant describe their relationships as
supportive, friendly, meaningful, open, and helpful. But there
were variations in how students, parents, and teachers ranked
their relationships with one another. And there is competition as
well as cooperation, conflict as well as consensus.

A high degree of value consensus brings people together at
Covenant. People stand together against a common enemy—
Satan. They constantly remind one another that one of Satan's
most devious tools is accusation. "He will magnify the defects of
other Christians before your eyes, so that he can tear us apart."
The Covenant people work hard at "building one another up" in
positive but confrontational ways. Conflict is not avoided but

attacked head on. "One has to discern when conflict is disruptive—when it is the work of Satan, and when it is positive, promoting growth and strength" (Elder). The Covenant people would agree with Charles Cooley's assessment that

> conflict of some sort is the life of society, and progress emerges from a struggle in which an individual, class, or institution seeks to realize its own idea of good.[2]

Conflict is recognized at the individual, institutional, societal, and spiritual level. Rather than viewing it as divisive, the Covenant people see certain kinds of conflict as integrative. Richard Simpson's distinction between non-communal and communal conflict helps clarify their conception of positive, communal conflict:

> Non-communal conflict results when there is no community of ends between the parties to the conflict, or when these parties believe that no common ends can be discovered so that a compromise may be reached. *Non-communal conflict is seen as disruptive and dissociating. Communal conflict, i.e., that based on a common acceptance of basic ends, is on the contrary, integrative.* When men settle their differences on the basis of unity, community conflict will ensue; when they settle their unity upon these differences, non-communal conflict will ensue.[3]

Not only community members, but parents and children and teachers and children join together to fight a common enemy. They are involved in a daily mission together; each person, no matter how young, has an important part to play.

By blaming certain kinds of conflict on third-party demonic forces, the parties immediately involved in the conflict are relieved of guilt and responsibility. Through discussion and prayer, people can air the problem and present their cases to the Ultimate Judge. Because submission, humility, forgiveness, and openness to the Holy Spirit are primary values, both parties can save face.

The sharing of concerns before prayer is the time when issues are raised. If there is consensus, or "a oneness of heart," then people will pray with collective force. If not, then people will pray to God to grant them discernment, to open them to His will, and to unite their hearts. They will not publically present competing petitions to God. The power of prayer is that it keeps the lines of communication open; people must respect one another's desire or need to pray. According to a number of people at Covenant,

> Prayer is the most powerful tool we possess as Christians: to petition God for our needs, seek His will, intercede for those around us, and ward off enemy attacks.

The school day opens with prayer, and teachers pray with students after disciplining them. If teachers see that there is conflict between two students, they will often intervene, probing into what the "real" issues are. For example, teachers will bring the two children together and ask what transpired between them; what it feels like to be called names; what the one student may have done to provoke the other; and why they need to care for one another. If necessary, class time will be used to discuss the problem with these students, while giving others in the class work to do. The session is either ended with prayer or the suggestion that each person go off, look deep into their hearts, talk with God, and then come back together again to discuss it further.

Relationships at Covenant are intimate and intense. They are characterized by much interaction, confrontation, and open communication. People are expected to participate in the group, both sharing their own concerns and responding to those of others. As many social scientists have noted, "the greater the intensity of the relationship, the greater the likelihood of conflict."[4] Both the intensity and the conflict can be witnessed at Covenant.

Teacher–student relations

Covenant school stresses the importance of the teacher–student relationship. According to the school literature and interviews, the first prerequisite is for the teacher to give unconditional love to students. "The Lord's commandment to love one another transcends all other considerations" (Covenant handbook).

Teachers are intimately involved with their students. They know their parents and siblings and are aware of their private lives. Both within and outside of the classroom there is a lot of joking, touching, confronting, and general interaction with individual students and groups of students. Teachers work hard at bringing diversity to their classrooms and involving students in creative projects. This enhances the amount of joint activity between teachers and students. While the traditional lecture format is the most common form of instruction, teachers encourage class discussions and participation of students in designing special activities: plays; foreign meals accompanied by the music, costumes, and pictures of the country; and mock radio shows. Although this is more common in the lower grades, the junior high school students are involved in preparing music (most play guitars) for the school and church services.

But confronting or "calling one another up" is also an important form of social interaction at Covenant. Teachers recognized this: "If these kids were in public shcool, they would be considered angels. Because we want to develop character and spiritual growth, we keep confronting them—they can always be better. In that sense, we never let up." They echo here Émile Durkheim's famous analysis of the society of saints:

> Imagine a society of saints, a perfect cloister of exemplary
> individuals. Crimes, properly so called, will be unknown;
> but faults which appear venial to the layman will create
> there the same scandal that the ordinary offense does in
> ordinary consciousnesses.[5]

And the pressure is on teachers too, for they are to serve as "living examples of Christ." One of the most characteristic adjectives used by both students and teachers to define their relationships was "challenging." Not only must they teach their own subject areas, but also morality, spirituality, and godliness. All are aware that they expect a lot from themselves and from others.

In fact, prayer times are often used to confess shortcomings and difficulties; to ask for forgiveness (from one another and

God) and for guidance to become more perfect.

> Lord, help me to be a good teacher today. Let me be
> patient with the children. Help me to teach them what they
> need to know and to encourage them in your love.
> Yesterday, I was short with some of the students. Let them
> forgive me. Help the children to work hard today, to learn
> what they need to learn, and to be kind to one another. (1st
> grade teacher praying with her class)

During these prayer times, students and children alike share personal problems and concerns.

The atmosphere that prevails at Covenant is one of trust. The school encourages autonomy and initiative that is sensitive and responsive to others. A high priority is placed on submission to authority as an act of individual choice. Constraint is used, but only after students have tested the limits. The faculty expect their students to behave and to treat one another kindly; when they fail to do this, teachers express their disappointment. The 1st grade teacher explained:

> They know what I expect, and they know right from wrong.
> I tell them you are mine. I am your teacher and you are my
> students. We have a special relationship. They don't need
> spanking because I've got their hearts. They know if they
> disappoint me.

Spanking is used as a disciplinary measure at Covenant. In the lower grades, an average of two to three students are spanked each week. But in general, withdrawal of approval rather than the assertion of rules characterizes the approach to discipline. The establishing of rapport in relationships rather than rules and the exercise of traditional authority over legal rational authority predominate.

Teachers see children not only within the context of school, but at church services and functions and in the students' own homes. Teachers will also have students over to their homes; sometimes they come because their own children are having a party or because there is a "Body Life meeting" (a home worship service). The 2nd grade teacher, for example, would invite the "student of the week" over to talk, play games, and have a snack after school.

When students were asked what they most liked about the school (or what they will miss most when they leave for public high school), they are unanimous in stating that it is their relationships with teachers who really care about them.

In general, both students and teachers described their relationships with one another as godly, helpful, happy, supportive, meaningful, and good. Teachers, however, rated their relationships with students as more secure, warm, challenging, familial, orderly, and colorful than students rated their relationships with teachers. Part of this may reflect the effort that many teachers everywhere put into their teaching—and the expectations and desires they have for the process. Indeed, one of the sharpest ironies of schooling is that it is generally a more creative and challenging process for the teacher than for the student. There was also some disagreement ($p = .07$) over how "easy" each thought their relationships with the other to be; teachers thought that their relationships were easier than did students. While neither students nor teachers thought that their relationships were boring or hostile, teachers thought they were significantly less boring and hostile than their students. But both agreed that their relationships were not cold, bad, worldly, hostile, or hard.

Parent–teacher relations

At Covenant, parents agree to submit their individual and family lives to the leadership of the fellowship. If a problem arises in school between parents and the teacher that cannot be resolved, an elder will intervene. This, however, is very rare and is done subtly. If the parents are thought to be at fault, an elder will confront them, sympathizing with "how difficult it is to see your children objectively—especially since they are a reflection of you. It may be that you cannot see the problem that your child is having because you have the same problem." The elder and the parents and the teachers will then work together on trying to resolve the problem. To clarify the process, a convenant document specified the lines of authority:

Figure 1 Authority Structure at Covenant

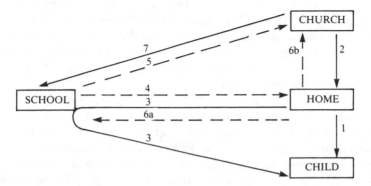

solid line = carries authority
broken line = can make suggestions (not authority)

1) The mandate to train the child into holiness and Christ-like character is given to the parents. The authority and responsibility for education lie with the parents.

2) In Christian community, parents have opened and submitted themselves to the authority of the church to speak into their lives. The leaders train the parents who in turn train the children.

3) The home delegates authority and responsibility to the school for education. The school becomes the extended hand of the home and thus serves it.

4) The school as a supporter in the education of the child can approach the home with corrective or directive suggestions, but it carries no authority.

5) In cases where the school feels it necessary to see a change come about in an area of a child's life, it approaches the home first. If there is no change, the school goes to the church leaders with its opinions and suggestions; the church goes into the homes with the authority to correct.

6) If the home has adverse feelings about an overall direction in the school: a) it approaches the school with suggestions; then, if agreement is not reached, b) it goes to the leaders who have the authority to change the direction.

7) The church makes the decision to have a school and therefore rules the school governmentally.

In all this, we believe in a God to whom we all are submitted and desire to be led by the Holy Spirit to hear His answer.

Many parents are personal friends of the teachers and together they are involved in many of the same social activities. Most parents see teachers at least once a week at church services (only 5% of the students' parents are not members of the fellowship), and on average two to three times a week. Such frequent encounters give them the opportunity to talk about school and the children in an informal way.

Also, 40% of the parents volunteer on a regular (at least once a week) basis. Although most volunteers are mothers, a number of fathers do help out with field trips, special shop classes, lab experiments, and art classes. Parents tend to volunteer in the same classroom as their children. Often they will follow their children from one grade to the next. For example, a mother will volunteer the first year in kindergarten and the next year in 1st grade. The primary objective and interest is to spend more time with their children; to come to understand their children better by seeing them interact and perform in environments other than the family; and to acquire a better sense of what is going on in the classroom, hoping to increase parental awareness, involvement, and empowerment.

Relationships between parents and teachers tend not to be based upon problems that students are encountering but upon common interests; such overlapping networks and interests mean that communication between parents and teachers is not determined solely by how the child is doing in school.

Nonetheless, overlapping alliances and roles can become problematic; networks can be entangling. Since parents are considered to have ultimate authority and responsibility for the training of their children, teachers are supposed to defer to parents. As professionals, however, who see children in contexts outside of the home, teachers may see things that parents do not see in their children. Considering it their "calling" to point out certain things (lying, cheating, a bad attitude, laziness), they may run into conflict with parents. At many levels, the community encourages working out these types of conflict which "can prove to be painful but growth-producing."

In any organization, communication is critical for exchanging information and negotiating and resolving conflict. At Covenant, prayer is often used as a means to build solidarity and resolve conflict. Prayer is used regularly to open and set the atmosphere of all meetings; after disciplining a child; to communicate needs and concerns; to acknowledge consensus; and to celebrate. When I asked one teacher whether she prayed with parents when they were discussing problems that a child was having in school, she answered,

It's tricky. Since the man is the head of the household, I should not initiate prayers—it's really up to the husband. Yet as a teacher, I have authority because God has entrusted these children to me; He has anointed my position. But I am still the servant of the parents who have the ultimate authority; besides as a woman, I have to be careful not to overstep my boundaries. It's sometimes uncomfortable because you feel you need to pray but nobody is sure who should initiate it.

A high degree of consensus, however, is evident in how teachers and parents evaluate their relationships with one another. In general, they describe their relationships as supportive, friendly, meaningful, open, helpful, godly, challenging, and familial. In only four out of fifty-nine adjectives, did parents and teachers significantly differ in their ratings: teachers rated their relationships with parents as more familial and less carefree than did the parents; and parents rated their relationships with teachers as more cheerful. While both thought that "cold" was the least characteristic adjective, parents were more emphatic.

Furthermore, both teachers and parents report that there is a high degree of consensus between them. When it comes to ranking the values that they cherish most strongly, there is likewise a high degree of consistency. In ranking Milton Rokeach's terminal values, everyone chose salvation as the most important value; and there was general consensus that family security, friendship, and wisdom followed as the next most important values.

Conclusion

Covenant school reflects the organizational style and purpose of the fellowship that sponsors it. In fact, the community's goals and methods are accentuated in the operation of Covenant school which serves as one of their experiments in cultural production. Through the school, the Covenant people are communicating their view of the world as a place in which individuals are actors who, in cooperation with one another, can effect the world. Moreover, they are preparing their college-bound children for professional jobs through which they will be able to exercise their Christian influence. Rather than conforming to the demands of a specific job that one should do well, the Covenant people anticipate their children entering into—even creating—roles that will enable them to act on the world. Thus, their schooling stresses the acquisition of analytical skills, flexibility, self-direction, and the persuasive use of language. Group work, discussions that explore a spectrum of values and beliefs, and various strategies for formulating and resolving problems characterize school life.

To Live in Fellowship:
Lakehaven Community

To me America is God. God has brought America together
and now we're slowly losing it. (Principal and deacon)

When I asked him what the "it" is that America is losing, the
principal responded: "Take welfare for instance. It's got its place
but it's sorely abused. We need to be able to function without it.
[Pause] It's a sad thing. . . . The church is declining—just look at
our nation. It all started to decline in the 1960s when God was
thrown out" [here he is referring to the 1963 Supreme Court
decision prohibiting school prayer].

While the Covenant members see themselves as pioneers,
forging ahead to create a new, better world out of the old, the
Lakehaven Baptists see themselves as guardians of the past,
preservers of traditional values and lifestyles. By attempting to
"return to the values that once made America great" (a
statement publicized by Jerry Falwell but commonly expressed by
many fundamentalists), they want to restore America to a
Christian nation, as God's country.

While they decry the evils of the secular world and resist
commercialized mass culture, these Baptists strongly support the
leaders of our nation, the doctrines of democracy, and the free-
enterprise system. Patriotism is an integral part of their
Christianity. As tangible reminders, American flags appear in the
sanctuary, in the auditorium/cafeteria, and even on men's ties.
Patriotic hymns and pledges of allegiance to both American and
Christian flags have a voice in many church and school
gatherings. Political leaders are regularly prayed for by name.

(The charismatics also pray for "the leaders of our nation, may they be godly men," but they rarely refer to them by name and no American flag is to be found in the church or school.)

The Lakehaven Baptists consider threats of the energy crisis, overpopulation, food shortages, and limited natural resources to constitute pseudo-problems. They believe these are tactics used by secular humanists to legitimate abortion, sterilization, euthanasia, and communism. They do not care to question much further, to research the matter, and weigh the evidence. It is written by godly men, and so it is. The world is defined in terms of good and evil dichotomies; in theory, little gray matter exists to muddle the mind.

The orientation towards a meaning system that explains simply the complexities of life affects the nature of their discourse. While the Baptists are wonderful at keeping a friendly, light conversation going, they avoid extended discussions of either politics or religion. Generally they assume agreement on the things that matter to them, in part because they come from similar backgrounds and in part because they embrace a common faith. They do not want to engage one another to the point of confrontation nor do they want to test the degree of consensus. Rather they respect the individual's right to privacy and shy away from analysis. Aside from sermons where the nature of the world and God receive extended attention, political discussions tend to be short. People skillfully change the subject to small talk or make a pun in order to avoid too much serious talk about "heavy" subjects. For example, when we were discussing the decline of American society, the principal soon (within three minutes) ended the conversation by relaying a joke that he had heard Jesse Helms recently tell. "How do you know when a Russian's lying?" [laughs] "When he starts moving his lips."

Thus, while the Lakehaven Baptists share many of the same fundamental beliefs as the charismatics, they do not examine them in the same way. In a very real sense, the Baptists' statement of faith is codified and settled in the pastor's desk drawer. What they believe seems to be taken for granted; the traditions are well-known and do not need to be questioned.

Trying to live up to the Christian ideal, however, is not easy. Dissonance between beliefs and behavior can create enough discord that people need to be reminded not only of the guidelines for living a Christian life, but also of the fact that they are doing better than many. Guilt and shame are fed with the hand of love and consolation offered to the discomforted. For example, a Sunday morning prayer draws attention to those who are not in attendance and offers indirect reinforcement to those who are:

> This is a prayer for those not with us—some because of
> sickness, some because of travel, some because of hardness
> of the heart. This disturbs us and concerns us that they
> reject Your house. Help them to confess their sins and turn
> back. And help us to welcome them back with love.

Distinguishing between those who are saved and unsaved serves the same purpose. The process not only consolidates one's identity with the righteous, but it also allows the authorities to warn, indirectly, of the evils that could befall one if he or she were not saved and faithful.

The Christianity of the Baptists serves to chastise, comfort, and control, reminding people that they are saved from eternal damnation *and* have the responsibility to be *good* Christians. Guilt acts as an effective means of social control, particularly in the process of socialization.

"To fear God is to know God." The fear these Baptists emphasize is the fear of displeasing God, as a child would fear the displeasure and withdrawal of his parents' love. The fear that induces respect, rather than the fear of the wrath of God, predominates. Sermons focus on God's love for them as His children and His desire for them to be obedient and faithful. (This contrasts with the charismatics' emphasis on the reciprocal love between Christ and man and between one another in the community.) The Baptists refer most often to God as a loving Father; He is a parental figure. The charismatics speak most often of Christ as a friend, and then as the bridegroom. These are good denoters of how people perceive their relationship to Christ; what their rights and responsibilities are; and how power is perceived.

The Baptists' belief in original sin and the voluntary nature of man's transgression frames their mistrust of both themselves and others. They believe that peoples' wills need to be broken or at least strictly constrained. Furthermore, the individual will need to be kept in check across the life course; adults as well as children need to understand liberty as "freedom under authority." In order to protect individual liberty, specifically privatism, the individual must sacrifice personal freedom and conform to collectively constructed limits that serve to protect everyone. For example, the Baptist fellowship disapproves of any alcohol consumption or attendance at movies or dances. It is not that they consider all alcohol poisonous or all movies depraved, rather they harbor doubts about the limits of their own self-control. "You can't always trust yourself." Furthermore, "even if you could, you should not indulge because your actions may cause your brother to stumble" (Monitor).

In talking with Baptists about entertainment, however, I found that many were familiar with the names of popular films. When asked whether they had considered seeing the film about the Olympic runner, who as a Christian refused to run on Sundays, they volunteered the name—"Oh, *Chariots of Fire*—no that probably wasn't so bad. But you shouldn't go to the theater, because others might see you and say, 'Oh, there's Mrs. ____ and she's the principal's wife.' You might make others stumble." When I asked about television, they considered it to be a problem. Because you can "watch it behind closed doors, so to speak, you aren't making anyone else stumble, but you could lull yourself into watching something you shouldn't see. When you're relaxing after a hard day, sometimes it's just hard to get up and turn off the T.V., even though you know you should" (Monitor). Nonetheless, Baptists do watch television; in private, one is granted greater freedom. However, in public—because one might fall—all should abstain.

They object to television for the same reasons they object to rock music: programs are filled with the corrupting influences of sex, violence, and disrespect for authority. "For example," offered the pastor

> women will sit around and watch soap operas in the
> afternoon, and watch everyone running around and sleeping
> with everyone else. It shows deceit. There just isn't any
> respect for commitment anymore. Or take, for example, the
> *Dukes of Hazzard*—here in this tiny town we have two

juiced-up orange cars with the number 1 painted in white on their sides. These kids act just like the Dukes who speed around in their cars. They can steal and shoot and still be the good guys because the guy who's really corrupt is the sheriff. It just doesn't teach young people to be respectful of authority.

Social organization

Anyone brought up in a mainstream Protestant tradition would be familiar with the eleven o'clock Sunday morning service of the Baptists. Bulletins handed out by ushers provide an overview of the service and cue people to its order—when and what hymns to sing; when, what, and how to pray; and when to sit and stand. People sit in pews facing the altar where the minister and his associate reside. To the left are the organ and choir stall filled with twelve men and women ranging in age from seventeen to seventy; all are dressed in white robes. Flowers bedeck the altar. The service is neatly orchestrated to fit within the hour. Participation is communal and directed by the clergy, except for announcements when individuals can speak out on their own accord.

One distinctive feature of the service, which was otherwise quite similar to the average major Protestant worship service, was recognizing visitors by having them stand and introduce themselves. Ushers then brought them a gift: a pen printed with the church's name and address, and a spiritual tract.

Sunday evening services, filled more with music and Scriptures than sermon; Bible studies; intercessory prayer groups; youth groups and athletic events; and special missions days fill the week for many of the congregation.

In contrast to the more sect-like nature of Covenant, the Baptists are more church-like in their organization. Characteristic of the "church," the Baptists are more conservative but also more compromising in accepting greater variation in commitment by their members. Its membership tends to be inherited, its leaders ordained and imported, and its services more restrained and ritualistic.[1] The question of the degree of acceptance of the secular world, however, is complex. While the Baptists tend to be more separatist in doctrine than the charismatics, they are more involved in the surrounding secular community. While the charismatics tend to be more tolerant in their theology, they are more exclusive in their community. The Baptist church represents less an exclusive, moral community or strictly speaking, *fellowship*, and more a socio-religious gathering or *congregation*.

Leadership

Reverend Mann is the pastor at Lakehaven. In cooperation with the deacons and Board of Trustees, he runs the church and ultimately oversees the school which is headed by Principal Luthy.

Reverend Mann is a very congenial, warm person. He is the kind of person whom you feel you can talk to and depend upon. Direct and down-to-earth in his speech, he describes himself in this way:

> I'm no scholar. I don't think I'd like to research or to have to read a whole lot of books. No, I'd rather be cooking hash browns. [laughs] After I graduated from public high school, I got a job in a photography lab in New York City and made relatively good money. I worked there for a year. My father was a pastor. My mother asked me if I had thought of Bible college. I said, "No." I was the type who'd get the report done the night before by looking at the cartoons and making up the rest of the story. I just wanted to put all my books away. I would hate it if I had to study every week. Well, I ended up at Bible college and I hated it. I wanted to come home after the first month. But I graduated in three years.

An unpretentious person, Pastor Mann relates well to people without compromising his beliefs. "Sometimes I'm surprised," he said. "You know, if I were living in sin with a girl, I wouldn't come in and talk about it with a minister." The tone is neither condescending nor cynical; it is honest and direct.

Much of this has to do with his remembering well his teenage experiences and the suffering that he had endured. He talked about being in the 8th grade and hating school. He ran away from home and hitchhiked to New York City. He slept on the streets for two weeks before hitchhiking to his brother's home where he stayed for a few more days before being convinced to go home and back to school:

> It's as though I had never been gone. The teachers seemed
> to ignore the fact that I had been gone. They didn't worry
> that I had missed work, and didn't make any attempt to
> help me make up the work.

Things got better after high school (which, like junior high school, he found trying, humiliating, and uninspiring). After Bible college, he married but then lost his wife and two daughters in an automobile accident. He later remarried; his second wife had been teaching in a Christian school. Their first son died six days after birth:

> This brought the two of us together. You know, before
> Nathan, we would sometimes be sitting and watching T.V.
> or reading, and something would remind me of my first wife
> and daughters and tears would come to my eyes. Judy had a
> hard time understanding that and would feel
> uncomfortable, but I think after Nathan she knew what it
> meant to lose a child. It really bonded us together.

Without dwelling on his past, Pastor Mann uses his own experiences to bring him to understand better the sufferings of other people. But while he expresses more compassion than he does condemnation, he strictly upholds definite standards and judgments.

When one of the girls in his congregation and school became pregnant near the end of her senior year of high school, there was no hesitation in expelling her. "The rules do not permit a pregnant girl to continue in school. She is responsible for the consequences of her sin." But Pastor Mann also believes that many people, including the girl's family and the father of the child, should be more supportive to her and accepting of her condition. Consolation and support are mixed with a strict reading of the law that holds the girl responsible for her sin but also forgives her of that sin. The divergent interpretations of this last clause has created conflict within the church.

For example, when the father of this girl asked if there was anything they could do to reconcile the situation, the pastor counseled them to ask for the forgiveness of the church (the congregation). This they did. The father confessed that he had advised his daughter to deceive the school by hiding her pregnancy so that she could graduate; and the daughter asked for forgiveness for her sins of fornication and deception. At the end of the confession, the pastor asked those who forgave them to stand:

> All but one couple stood. I am sorry for that couple who
> could not find forgiveness in their hearts. But the church
> forgave them and decided that the girl would receive her
> diploma since she had completed all her work. But when
> the father asked if she could now go on the class trip and be
> in the graduation, he didn't understand that she must pay
> for the consequences of her sin and that to allow her to
> would go against the rules. "But," the father said, "I
> thought you said we were forgiven?" "That's right," I said,
> "but that doesn't undo what you have done." After that,
> the whole family packed up and left the church.

At Lakehaven, one offers comfort and support within the context of proscribed rules. External conformity to rules takes precedence: "Otherwise there would be no order." While Pastor Mann holds very definite beliefs, he is not as rigid doctrinally as some of those involved in the school leadership. Full of puns and stories, he is able to talk with people without being overly judgmental or righteous. He emphasizes God's law but also his love and compassion. He also tends to resist the "highfalutin":

> On Wednesday nights, we break into prayer
> groups—intergenerational groups. It's surprising how
> similar little children's and eighty year olds' prayers are. It's
> the ones in between with the formal, long, elaborate
> prayers. People judge—they think they need to be long and

formal. . . . What we need is to be considerate of one another.

I talk with people about being saved, to let them know that they can have eternal security and won't have to live after death in the fires of evil.

Although Pastor Mann speaks of the fires of Hell, he does not conjure up images of evil and fear as much as he does understanding and comfort.

His right-hand man and the principal of the school, Mr. Luthy, likewise would not consider himself a scholar. After graduating from high school, he was a truck driver for a number of years. Then his wife and he joined a Christian singing group that toured around the United States and Canada witnessing to churches and schools. Mr. Luthy grew up in the area; his wife and he met in church. She now assists him in the classroom as a monitor.

The anti-intellectualism that runs through sermons, school lectures, and personal conversations represents a distrust of "experts" and an overly rationalized society. According to people at Lakehaven, what we need more of is plain, good-old-fashioned reasonableness: that is, a healthy mixture of faith, good sense, and thoughtfulness. Given that things are precarious, we should honor the well-tried institutions of family, church, and community. Only through the long-standing traditions of these institutions and solid friendships, can we create a sense of order and coherence that can be depended upon.

Demographic characteristics

Nestled into a sleepy village of 800 people, the Baptist church presides over Main Street. American flags attached to telephone poles line the street. Politically and socially conservative, the local community is traditional, relatively stable, and poor. The area, and especially farmers, have been particularly hard-hit during the recession of the 1980s.

Most of the Lakehaven members grew up in the vicinity and experienced the security and watchfulness of a small-town environment. They tend to come from rural, white, working- and lower middle-class, fundamentalist families. The congregation is older than Covenant's, with the majority of people being near or in retirement age (approximately 40%), with another large cluster of young people starting their own families. The middle-aged (ages forty to sixty) are largely unrepresented. Approximately twice as many women as men attend church services, partly because of the greater number of older, widowed women, but also because of greater involvement among younger women than men.

The latter is an issue for both the church leadership and the lay women. Although women are considered to be more spiritual by nature than men, both the pastor and many of the women wish that men would take their religion more seriously. Women of all ages said that what women in the community looked for in a husband was a Christian man. They also agreed that Christian men were hard to come by.

According to the pastor, men would sometimes pretend they were interested in spiritual things while they were courting a woman, but once they "caught her," that would be the end of their church-going. After marriage, husbands would ride around with their "buddies" while their wives went to church:

> I can see it on their faces. On Sunday mornings I'd say,
> "Good morning, where's John this morning?" and I could
> just see her face cringe. I knew she wanted to be able to
> say, "Oh, he's sick or he had to go work," but she couldn't
> when he was out waxing his car or playing ball. I decided to
> stop asking for the most part. I don't want to make them
> feel too badly.

Likewise, the women wanted their daughters to marry good Christian men. For both the mothers and their daughters, this seemed to go hand in hand with someone who would be hardworking, even-tempered, and non-drinking. One senior high school girl responded that she would like to get married a few years after high school to a "Christian man, mild-tempered; someone about six feet tall would be nice."

In contrast to the recent past, the young people of Lakehaven are now tending to "delay" marriage until ages twenty-three or twenty-four. Traditionally, they married in their late teens. As with those interviewed in Lilian Rubin's *Worlds of Pain*,[2] marriage was a way of getting away from home, of asserting your own independence, of escaping bad family situations. "Many of them have dreams of the man on the white horse sweeping them away—well, reality can hit pretty hard. The romance doesn't last for long" (Pastor Mann).

Much to the pleasure and surprise of many of the adults, more and more of their young people are postponing marriage and going on to college. Most of the recent graduates of the Academy represent the first generation of college-bound children for their families, and they are proud that they are able to attend and achieve at community and Christian colleges. But parents' and teachers' encouragement is mixed with pessimism about their children's futures. The message is a mixed one. They tell their children that "they must learn to be punctual and obedient, to follow rules and respect authority, and *if there is a way*, to go to college" because they know that they do not have much chance even for a skilled laborer's job without a college degree (Academy mother and monitor). "They must learn how to listen to the whistle blow" (Pastor). Parents also encourage their children to get more schooling and secure a job before they get married so that they will be more economically self-sufficient. Otherwise, it "can put a real strain on the family and times are tough enough" (Pastor Mann). As one mother of a daughter who will be attending Christian college put it, "George says [to their daughter], 'you are going to get yourself a college degree before you get married and start having children.' Somehow we'll find a way of putting her through college. It's just important that she be on her feet before she starts a family."

Many of those who marry young, especially when they were "caught" by pregnancy, do live with their families. Moreover, almost everyone works. Of all the married couples, only one woman in the congregation is not working. The rest of the women have jobs and grandmothers are the ones who most frequently look after the children. There is no "formal daycare" in Lakehaven, although a few mothers do take in other people's children in the form of family daycare.

The women and men of Lakehaven are, for the most part, trying to make do. Economics is the overriding issue. Gender, per se, is a moot point. While the Covenant people are conscious of creating a strong sense of female and male culture in order to complement the strong conjugal bond, men and women in the Lakehaven community struggle to come together in spite of their long-established differences. The Baptists do not glorify a notion of female and male character; rather, they accept it as one of the realities of life.

My questions about expectations for men and women, husbands and wives were interpreted more generally. While people at Lakehaven know that they do not like textbooks that attempt to invert traditional sex-role norms, such as a father washing dishes with his daughter or a mother washing the car with her son, they talk very little about female and male roles or relationships. Although gender differences are recognized and resentment is expressed, especially by women who feel strapped by children as well as a job outside of the home, this rarely is the topic of conversation. A different ethos for female and male culture, a lack of understanding and communication between the sexes, and a strong sense of suspicion between the sexes are taken for granted. Frustrations tend not to be shared or alternatives explored among the adults. But there is some sign among the young men at the Academy that they want to be closer to their girlfriends and future wives. Two of the senior high school boys, in responding to a question about what they would look for in a spouse, responded: "Someone whom I can talk with—someone who's easy to get along with. I want a friend." At the same time, a majority of the Academy students believed that wives should submit to the authority of their husbands.

The majority of the congregation is composed of skilled and unskilled laborers, factory workers, farmers, truck drivers, and secretaries. A few members teach at the local public school where they are still able to celebrate Christian holidays with crèches in the classroom at Christmas time. According to the elders and members, the majority of members belong to the working and lower-middle classes. Some of the farmers, however, belong to the middle and a very few to the upper-middle class.

The members of Lakehaven come mostly from fundamentalist

families. By and large, their religious identification is shared with previous generations and is continuous with their past. Their local community, imbued with their theology, serves to uphold tradition and protect the rights of individuals through social sanctions rather than litigious means. Covered-dish suppers continue to bring people together to chat about the happenings of the week.

Within the biblical, republican tradition, members of Lakehaven equate Christianity and patriotism. For the Lakehaven Baptists, their sense of meaning and belongingness stems largely from the groups they identify with—their family, their church, their local community, and their country. They do not expect to distinguish themselves as individuals; rather, they strive to be solid family and community members and to hold down a good job. Patriotism is important because it allows them to feel proud and to pay homage not only to their country but also to themselves as law-abiding and godly Americans. They are angered by those who challenge the traditional, patriarchal family and the virtues of the rural past and small-town America because attacks on those traditions threaten their very identity.

The Lakehaven Baptists do not have great expectations for the future; in fact they think that Armageddon is on its way. The morning after some earthquake tremors were felt, people spoke about the possibility of it being "Judgment Day," although they were neither dismayed nor surprised when this did not occur. Rather than preparing for the future, they are attempting to preserve the past and to be faithful stewards of what they receive. And this they communicate to their children.

The Lakehaven Baptists know that life is a struggle, that in the words of John Masefield:

> To get the whole world out of bed,
> and washed, and dresseed, and warmed, and fed,
> to work, and back to bed again,
> Believe me, Saul, costs worlds of pain.

They would not deceive their children by pretending otherwise, by telling them that they can "grow up to be anything they want to be" or that "the world is their oyster." That, they know, is foolishness. Instead, they try to prepare them for life as best they can by bringing them up strictly in the ways of the Lord.

6

School Life: The Academy

Origins and organization

> All our children were enrolled in Christian school before we moved. When we came here, we looked around for a Christian school but there wasn't any in the area. We didn't want to send them to public school. So we talked to the pastor and some other parents who were interested in the idea. That was in the spring of 1974. By the fall, the Academy was taking in students. (Founding parent and volunteer mother)

Unlike most who build their schools one or two grades per year, the Baptist school opened with all twelve grades—a situation that the A.C.E. curriculum makes possible. Schools buy the curriculum, paying $5,000 for a three-year contract in which they agree to use only A.C.E. materials, curriculum, equipment (all of which costs extra), and procedures. In one-week training sessions that principals and pastors are required to attend at A.C.E. headquarters in Lewisville, Texas, they work through PACEs and take tests identical to those their students will take. The only difference is in content—they are tested on A.C.E. procedures, how to set up a school, etc. Back home, teachers and monitors will be tested on the classroom procedures that they in turn will enforce.

Since the emphasis is on learning, not on teaching, teachers need not be highly qualified nor highly paid. Two of the three supervisors have B.A. degrees from fundamentalist Christian colleges and one a degree from a state university; all come from fundamentalist backgrounds and attend Lakehaven Baptist Church. None had former teaching experience in public schools, except one who had student-taught in public school. All of the monitors have their high school diplomas and one has a B.A. degree from a Christian college. The principal and supervisor of the 6th–9th grades used to be a truck driver and a Christian singer on tour.

The average starting salary (1983 figures) for supervisors is $9,000; monitors, who work full-time but are less qualified, begin at $2,100. The Academy likes to hire couples, and two of the three classrooms are run by a husband–wife team. In each case, the husband is the supervisor and the wife the monitor. All of the monitors are women.

According to A.C.E., the combination of a pre-packaged system of individualized instruction, clearly delineated rules and regulations, and specifically designed furniture, allows the supervisor to direct a large number of students who are working at different academic levels. The student–supervisor ratio at the Academy is 25:1, and students are grouped kindergarten–5, 6–9, and 10–12 grades. A primary objective is to enable schools to start up quickly and inexpensively.

Within two to three years, approximately 100 students were attending the school. As of 1983, there were approximately seventy-six students representing forty-five families. Students are drawn predominantly from the congregations of three Baptist churches: one-third of them come from the sponsoring church, and about two-thirds from two churches in neighboring towns. Approximately 15% are unchurched. Baptist students in the 5th–12th grades spent, on average, 3.19 years in public school. While many of them had attended only the Academy (32%), a number (27%) had attended public school for three or more years. Many of their parents were farmers, skilled laborers, truckers, secretaries, and housewives.

The budget per student is $618.42. Since students pay for their own PACEs (approximately $65 annually), the school does not assume the cost of textbooks. The tuition is $1,800 for four or more children per family, $1,600 for three, $1,400 for two, and $900 for one.

Members of the Baptist church offer varying reports about the degree of consensus and commitment to starting a school. Since church and school records were not available (for reasons of protecting individual privacy), I must rely on individuals' retrospective accounts of the developments of the school. It appears that the idea of the school was quite controversial. According to the current pastor, the congregation numbered 300 in 1973; it declined to 150 when they decided to start a school. Thus, when another person reports that 95% of the congregation was in favor of the decision to start a school, it appears that she is talking about 95% of those who decided to stay after half of the congregation left to join other churches.

Indicative of the tension within the congregation, there have been four pastors and three principals within the past ten years of the school's existence; this is unusual for independent Baptist churches whose ministers tend to have a longer tenure. A number of the dissenters were older people whose children were grown and were not willing to support the school financially. Others felt that the public school, in conjunction with Sunday school and church, was sufficient. In fact, the public school is a rural school and a number of its teachers are members of the Baptist congregation. Furthermore, regular announcements about community religious activities were already being made over the intercom in the public school and teachers were being allowed to display religious symbols (e.g., Christmas crèches) in their classrooms.

Unlike Covenant where all members send their children to the church school, some members of the Baptist congregation continue to send their children to public school or even teach them at home. In some cases, one child in the family will attend public school and the other attends Christian school. Parents discuss how the different types of instruction better meet the needs of their individual children. Thus, one child who was withdrawn, slower in learning, and "neglected" by the public school was enrolled in the Christian school, while her brother continued in public school.

This lack of unanimity has continued to create conflict. In 1982, people were not sure whether the current principal (who was brought in the year before) or the school itself would last. Some members of the congregation felt they were being discriminated against and judged as less committed Christians because they did not send their children to the Baptist school.

The pastor and principal held meetings to reassure people that this was not the case—although, in fact, there appears to be a good deal of truth to it. A volunteer mother, and one of the founders of the school explained:

> People have got to realize that the school is not separate
> from the church but a ministry—it's like missions work.
> Tuition is $1,000 a year—but people can find ways to pay it
> if their priorities are right. I'd do anything—wash
> dishes—to keep my kids in [Christian] school—I'm that
> convicted. But it depends on your objectives—a lot of
> people don't have their kids in [Christian] school that are
> members of the church. But I'm not judging them. They've
> got their convictions. That was one of the problems of the
> church—they felt paranoid that others were judging them.
> What I think is bad is to put your kids in and then take
> them out. That's bad testimony. Can't understand it. One
> family is farmers. They took two of their kids out and put
> them in BOCES [a public vocational training program]. My
> husband was a farmer too—he says all that family needs to
> do is sell one cow—it's a matter of priorities.

In another attempt to resolve conflict, the church constitution was changed to grant church members greater representation in school decisions and the church board greater authority over school finances. Previously, the school board autonomously made all decisions regarding the school, although the church treasury paid for it. Now the school board, consisting of seven members including the principal, pastor, and parents and fellowship members, make decisions regarding the finances of the school. The church supplies the buildings and heating; the rest is supported by tuition. The other churches that send students to the Academy may send one representative but he or she has no voting power.

Due to the high degree of formalization and centralization, the reliance on tradition, and the emphasis placed on conformity, there is little overt discussion about authority at the Baptist school and church. When conflict erupts, however, it tends to be volatile and threatening to the authority structure.

At the Academy, authority is highly centralized. The principal is clearly the one who runs the school. When he deems it necessary, he informs the pastor, other teachers, and parents of policy decisions; problems with certain students; meetings; etc. Although the pastor meets with the principal and staff every morning for prayer and his office is located next to the principal's and in the midst of the school, he often is not aware of school events or policies. He is an interested and benign participant, rather than an active, authority figure.

For example, the principal, without consulting anyone, agreed on the spot to my doing a study of his school.[1] The first day I arrived at the school to begin my research, neither the pastor nor the teachers knew in advance that I was coming or what I would be doing. Moreover, few of them asked once I explained my interest in Christian education. This experience was quite striking in contrast to another area Baptist school that refused to give me entry after a summer of negotiations, and to Covenant which after three months of negotiations had me come before the school board for two hours of questioning before they decided to approve my study. The only time the principal of the Academy consulted the pastor, who in turn consulted the Church Board, was when I requested to look through the church and school records. The request was denied.

The Academy uses Accelerated Christian Education (A.C.E.), a system of individualized instruction that is distributed nationally and internationally by a for-profit corporation whose head-quarters is in Lewisville, Texas. Naturally the type of system chosen influences how people relate to and think about it, and characteristic features of the fellowship influence what type of system they decide upon in the first place. The interesting paradox is that the Baptists who stress tradition and conformity, have adopted a system that is much more innovative and different from their own or the general public's educational experience. A.C.E. has taken the scientific management of schools to the extreme. Their model more closely approximates that of the factory or office: there are "supervisors" and "monitors" rather than "teachers"; student "offices" rather than desks; and "testing stations" that create "quality control." Students are "promoted" from one level to the next.

Physical environment

The Academy is housed in the Baptist church, a structure that has long presided over Main Street. The three classrooms (grades kindergarten–5, 6–9, and 10–12) are separated from one another. Little interaction between groups occurs; in fact, it is a special privilege for students to run errands between the classes or for junior or senior high school students to help out in the lower classes.

Classrooms are neatly arranged. Student offices, seven or eight to a line, are built together as a long wooden desk, divided by blinders for each student. The cubicles are designed to promote independent work and to limit student interaction. Although they are in close contact, students do not have ready access to eye contact with anyone—including the teacher. Instead, they are to direct their attention straight ahead, sitting straight in their chairs with feet firmly planted on the floor; without turning around they can raise one of three flags in order to get the supervisor's or monitor's attention. Two rows of cubicles, placed back to back, line the middle (just off-center) of the room; additional rows face the walls. Each room contains twenty to forty student offices. Typically each student office contains a Bible; Kleenex; the PACEs the student is working on; pens, pencils, and paper. Upper-level students also have dictionaries. Everything is in plain view; there are no drawers in which to hide artifacts from the teacher's purview.

Unlike the traditional classroom where the teacher's desk defines the front of the classroom and is the center of attention, here the scoring table serves as the focal point. A long table, designed for students to stand at and correct their work, occupies the center of the room. The various subjects and levels are represented by booklets that sit upright in the middle of the table. Under the A.C.E. program, the ability of students to *learn* rather than the ability of the teacher to *instruct* is central. In fact, the teacher's desk is placed off to one side of the room and receives little attention; instead, the supervisor is busy navigating the room and responding to flags that students raise. Furthermore, teachers' desks have no chair to which they can gravitate. Instead, they and their aids (the monitors) supervise students at their offices much as a foreman would supervise an assembly-line production.

Off in another corner is the testing station. A table that can seat up to eight students is kept completely clear except for students who are taking tests. Another area is reserved for reference books. The only feature that distinguishes the kindergarten–5th grade classroom is a "shop" that displays prizes (balls, coloring books, bubbles, etc.) which students can earn and a small cabinet for toys which students rarely are allowed to use.

While the student offices are restrictive (approximately two feet by two and one-half feet) with blinders extending an additional two inches on each side, the rooms give one a sense of space by being airy, light, and uncluttered. There is plenty of room to walk around offices and tables. Brightly colored Scriptural posters (often of pastoral scenes) and bulletin boards designed by teachers hang on the walls.

Individual pieces of students' work are not posted on the boards. Instead, the walls display charts that mark the successes (and by default, failures) of students in memorizing Scriptures, making the 100s Club, and performing certain duties. Thus, everyone is aware of *how* each student is doing, although they cannot judge *what* the student is doing. No display of work allows people to see what students have produced or to judge, if they so choose, the quality of work by their own standards.

A multi-purpose room serves as a cafeteria and auditorium. Church dinners, Bible studies, and Wednesday evening services as well as school assemblies, worship, and lunches are held here. Two-thirds of the room is an open area that is often filled with rows of folding chairs. A piano and lectern, framed on either side by an American and Christian flag, and a picture of an open Bible with an American flag draped across it and an eagle superimposed on it, occupy the front of the room. A ping-pong table sits in the back of the room. Five lunch tables fill the other one-third of the room, just off the kitchen. Sandwiches, potato chips, and candy are sold for those interested in buying lunch. The kitchen contains a sink, stove, and a refrigerator, the last of which is kept locked.

Teachers have separate bathrooms from the students. The upper-level students are responsible for cleaning the students' bathrooms.

There is no teacher's room; rather supervisors and monitors who are not on duty during lunch eat in the kitchen or at another table in the lunch room. During recess, they tend to retreat to the quiet of their own rooms. Teachers' meetings and prayer times are held in the cramped but cozy quarters of the pastor's study.

An asphalt playground, approximately twenty feet by fifty feet, is bordered by a street on one side and a lawn on the other two sides. Swing sets are the only permanent equipment. Students also play ball or jump rope; upper-grade children often hang out and talk. In addition, an old garage that was part of the church has been renovated into a gym which is small but functional. Here students play volleyball and basketball. The Baptist school also uses the fields and public school's gym that are just down the street.

Educational philosophy

> My major goals? Well, academics are high but not the highest. One day this will all pass away. Number 1 is to produce students who are all born-again, saved by grace and working on being the best Christians they can be—morally and academically. If they're saved, they know they're going to heaven and can witness to others. But to go and tell, you need to be educated. We want our education to be top-notch: well-rounded and well-grounded for the earth was made for God. We want students who will love the Lord; who'll take a stand—that's what it means to be good Americans. (Principal)

Being good Christians is equated with being good Americans. Educating people who can express themselves effectively is important to those at the Academy, for they will be the messengers of the good news that can restore America to its rightful dominion as God's nation. Therefore, the foremost concern is salvation. Beyond hopes that their students will come to love and serve the Lord, Academy teachers have little more to say about educational objectives, philosophy, or methodology. Part of the reason may be because there is little else left to say.

The Academy has adopted a modern, behavioral system of education whose curriculum is based on traditional values of Christian Americanism. Adopting a mass-produced system of education that resists (in fact, prohibits) modification, requires conformity and attention to detail. Continual revaluation of pedagogical goals and techniques subsides after the initial decision to adopt that particular system. Instead, energy goes into legitimating the decision and explaining the system, at least until a crisis point is reached and the decision itself is reevaluated. Therefore, teachers at the Academy would turn to the A.C.E. manuals to explain what they were doing—and not doing.

A.C.E., a highly structured and standardized system of education, dictates educational philosophy and policy. Perhaps the most distinguishing and controversial feature is the belief of founder Donald Howard, that "teaching is not important." No one teaches in A.C.E. schools. Rather teachers, who do not need to be certified or familiar with a particular subject, help students with their pre-packaged assignments; monitors check test scores, pray with students before they take tests, and help ensure discipline. Reverend Ron Caskey, principal of an A.C.E. school in Colorado states that, "This is the traditional approach to education in America. Originally education started with the preacher as teacher, and the Bible as textbook."

In fact, the Procedures Guide for principals and teachers conjures up images of old-time schooling in the rural past. The first pages depict a caricature of a farmer who sits in a cart swinging a big whip; in the other hand, he holds a bright orange carrot. He's smiling as the donkey pulls the cart. Underneath the picture, Five Laws of Learning lay out the basic pedagogical approach:

1. How heavy is the load?
2. How long is the stick?
3. How effective are the controls?
4. How big is the carrot?
5. How hungry is the donkey?

The load must be reasonable, and the student sufficiently controlled and motivated through the use of rewards and punishments. The guide stipulates that, "the pupil must be on a *level* of curriculum which he can perform; he must set reasonable *goals* that he can achieve in a prescribed period of time; and he must be *controlled* and *motivated* to use the material. Furthermore, the pupil's learning must be measurable and rewarded."

But while educators can design what they consider to be a good learning environment, responsibility for learning (as for sinning) and for success and failure lies with the individual student. The emphasis placed on individual responsibility translates into "minding one's own business." This philosophy permeates all facets of school life, from the physical arrangement of desks to being told not to share one's lunch with other students because "your mother made your lunch for *you*."

A.C.E., and therefore, the Baptist school advocate the merits of individualized learning. They value most strongly the importance of following directions, working independently without disturbing others, completing required work, and being able to establish goals and meet objectives successfully. In terms of personal and social development, they value their children being neat, courteous, self-controlled, respectful, and responsive to correction. Getting along with others and promoting church-school spirit are also important. Finally, at the end of the list comes the importance of being flexible and creative.

The introductory A.C.E. slide show emphasizes that children are different and that their program is geared to the individuality of each child. There are no grades, only twelve levels of achievement. Students work individually at their own pace, setting goals for themselves each day. Progress is then monitored by the staff. Since instruction is based on ability not age, each child works on a PACE that is suitable for his or her level. Thus, one might be working on 7th grade-level mathematics and 5th grade-level reading. The principal estimates that about 20% of the students have learning problems. According to the upper-level supervisor,

> a number of these students would probably have dropped out of high school but this way they don't have to be embarrassed because no one knows how they are doing. They aren't called on in class, nor are they forced to compete against other students.

The system is highly regularized; but they do not, as one supervisor said, "put the kids in lockstep" when it comes to the pace of learning.

By working individually, students do not waste much time waiting for other students to settle down or to catch on to the material, although they do wait for monitors and supervisors to respond to their questions or requests to score their work and take tests. But in general, there is always an ample supply of work to be done—as long as the PACEs are ordered and arrive in time.

Curriculum

Depending on where the student lives and the bus schedule, school begins at either 8:30 or 9:00 a.m., and ends at 2:00 or 2:30 p.m. The time difference does not disrupt the classroom since each student works individually. Students begin work immediately at their own offices, often before there is any interaction between them and the supervisors or monitor.

On Monday, Wednesday, and Friday, they work until chapel which lasts from 9:15–9:45 a.m. The whole school attends. Chapel begins much as church begins, with Mr. King greeting everyone and announcing the first song to be sung: "Gone, gone, gone are all my sins." Then students recite the pledge of allegiance to the American and Christian flags, and the Chrisian Bible. After this, the principal reads out the names of those who made 100s on their tests, and then of those who made in the 90s—in every subject. Certificates of excellent performance and attendance are handed out.

On a child's birthday, he or she is invited up front as everyone sings "Happy Birthday," including the second, adapted verse:

> Happy Birthday to you
> We don't have only one
> God give us salvation
> How many have you?

123

Reminiscent of the gifts given to visitors in the adult church service, the child is given a pen inscribed with Scriptures and his or her choice of a candy bar.

Then the principal begins to speak. On one occasion, he introduced his talk with mention of a *Time* magazine article that was negative about Christian education: "Of course the article's negative, it's ungodly. It just proves to you why it's important to listen to the wise counsel of your parents, to those mothers and fathers who are saved, and to your pastor." He illustrates his point by telling a story:

> There was a man who was selling hot dogs. He didn't have a radio to listen to, for he was hard of hearing, and he didn't read the newspaper for he couldn't see very well. But he could sell hot dogs. He advertised on the street, and his business prospered. He increased his bun and hot dog orders, and they kept selling. Then one day his son comes home from college to help him. His son listens to the radio and reads the newspaper. He tells his father that they are in the middle of a depression, that things won't sell. So the father cuts back on his bun and hot dog orders, takes down the ads on the street, and finally stops selling his hot dogs—well, his sales decrease rapidly. He says to his son, I guess you were right—we're in the middle of a great depression.

The principal concludes, "You have to be careful of what you read and who you listen to. Just because somebody's been to college, it doesn't mean they are smart."

On Fridays, there is often a guest speaker who preaches a sermonette. "We select men who avoid making favorable comments or endorsements of T.V., secular movies, mixed swimming, teen dating, social drinking, Halloween, Santa Claus, or the Easter Bunny. We want to avoid dragging the children's minds through worldly thoughts" (Pastor). On this particular Friday, a guest preacher from one of the area Baptist churches came to speak. He began his sermon with a verse from Isaiah (64:6): "We have all become like one who is unclean, and all our righteous deeds are like a polluted garment. We all fade like a leaf, and our inequities, like the wind, take us away." Then in a booming, deep voice, he exclaimed:

> All your *right-eous-ness-es* stink before God. You think
> they are pleasing. You think if you be good little boys and
> girls that you'll go to heaven. Wrong. It all stinks before
> God. It is like a dead mouse that you would find in the
> house. . . . What are you going to do with it? Throw it
> away, like a dead body in the sea. If you want to live, you
> must be saved. Jesus said, "I am the Way, the Truth, and
> the Life." Only through Him, by asking Him into your
> heart, can you be saved.

At the end, he looked over the rows of students, kindergarteners in the front and the senior high school students in the
back, and asked for a volunteer to read. When no one
immediately volunteered, he said: "Oh, I get it: The ones in the
back are too cool, and the ones in the front can't read yet." That
was enough to convince one junior high school student to
volunteer. Chapel ended with the preacher asking everyone to
close their eyes:

> Everyone close your eyes. Is there anyone who wants to ask
> Jesus into their hearts? [Pause] I see that hand. [Long
> Pause] Anyone who wants to recommit themselves to
> Jesus? I see that hand, yes, I see that hand, yes . . . Thank
> you.

Just before ushering the students out, the principal let them know
that if they wanted to talk to their teacher, the pastor, or himself,
they were all available. Then everyone filed out quietly, row by
row.

On Tuesdays and Thursdays, prayer and Bible recitations take
place in the classrooms and typically last for about fifteen
minutes. Part of the student's work involves reciting Biblical
passages which often are quite extensive. This gives students
practice in reading the Bible, memorizing and reciting long and
often complex passages, and public speaking. "It's a very good
example of practicing the basics."

Except for the kindergarten through 5th grade students who
occasionally gather for a story, this is the only "group work."

Afterwards, students return to work until 10:45 a.m. when they have a ten-minute break (if they have not lost the privilege). They then continue working until lunchtime which is staggered for the different classes. Lunch and recess last for forty minutes. Then students return to work until it is time for them to go home. Physical education and music classes are held three times a week; at present, students interested in art must teach themselves from the PACEs.

For each subject, students work through a series of twelve PACEs (Packets of Accelerated Christian Education), grading their own tests until they are ready for the final. When a student is ready to take the final test, a supervisor accompanies him or her to the testing station where they pray together:

> Thank you God for this child and for the test which can help us better understand Your universe and Your order in the world. Help bring back what ＿＿ has studied and help her to write neatly.

The final exam is marked by the supervisor; students must get 80% correct or else repeat the PACE. In addition to saving time and pride and being recognized in assembly for achievement, there is a monetary incentive to do well the first time around. Students buy their own PACEs. The first PACE costs $1.25; if a student must repeat the PACE, it costs $1.50.

In the lower levels, each PACE contains a Scripture (taken from the King James version) that must be memorized and "a character objective with character cartoons which inspire the child to live a quality of life consistent with the character traits of our Lord Jesus Christ" (A.C.E. pamphlet). For example, a Math workbook begins with the verse: "Be ye steadfast, unmoveable always abounding in the Lord" (1 Cor. 15:58). The character trait is "consistency." The character cartoon shows a mother shopping. As she pushes her cart down the aisle, she says to herself in the first two captions: 1) "Rejoice in the Lord always." 2) "I will rejoice even when I don't feel like it." In the third caption, she meets a friend, "It's a lovely day, isn't it?" In caption 4, she sings to herself, "Oh, how I love Jesus." This passage reinforces the message:

When you know it's right to do
And you know it's best for you
And the way you've done it has been working fine,
There's no need to make a change or try it some way strange,
Just continue on the good consistent line.

Obedience is a second major character trait that is emphasized in the PACEs. One cartoon shows a mother and daughter in the kitchen: Daughter: "The policeman came to school today. He told us how to be safe." Mother: "That is good news. We should obey the rules to be safe." Another cartoon depicts obedience to God's kind of music: Father: "Ace, will you find a good tune." (Loud rock and roll music blares out from the radio.) Ace: "It is a bad tune." (Radio is now playing the song, "Oh, How I Love Jesus.") Ace: "It is a good tune."

A 12th grade-level PACE teaches students that Jews and Roman Catholics "deny the power of the living God" and so lack "the inner power to live a truly Biblical, and therefore a truly free life." The same packet argues that "the free market economy diminishes rather than increases the amount of inequality in society" and insists that a wealthy class is important for motivating the poor to improve themselves.

Another social studies PACE, focusing on American history at the turn of the century, discusses Religious Liberalism, Territorial Expansionism, and Domestic Progressivism. The introduction focuses on social change, and the questioning of long-accepted views:

> The results of this reevaluation were cometimes good, but often bad. Social ills were corrected, but overreactions to these needs tarnished the legitimate reforms. Basic biblical and philosophical truths came under attack, and many people were led away into error. Christians, well-founded in their faith, however, need have no fear of the assaults of infidels.

The PACE goes on to discuss the conflict between evolution and creationism:

One of the above two versions [evolutionism and creationism] of the origin of animals and man has to be wrong. Both cannot be right. Is it logical to trust Darwinism or God? . . . It has been said that evolution, like Christianity, turned the world upside down. . . . [Darwinism,] however, did so for evil. In later years, men began to apply Darwinian thought to social relationships. The result of this extension of evolutionary thought was known as "social Darwinism." The survival of the fittest was applied to business practice and politics with disastrous consequences. Both the Nazism of the German Third Reich and Soviet International Communism justified their acts of terror, oppression, and racism with the theory of social Darwinism.

Pages later, the PACE discusses socialism and its major proponents:

The nature of Communism is atheistic, Satanic, and conspiratorial. World Communism began as an international conspiracy which was not limited by any geo-political boundaries. . . . In reality, Communism is not a social system or an economic system, but an international conspiracy which attempts to destroy the church, the family, and all legitimate governments.

The PACE presents readings, short answer exercises, and objective tests (matching, fill in the blank, true–false questions). Following each section, are a series of questions (see page 129). Students read and take tests on these materials. They are usually not open for discussion within the confines of the classroom; rather, the information is to be accepted as authoritative.

The curriculum consists almost solely of A.C.E. materials. Although the Academy has no library, each of the three classrooms has a collection of reference books. In grades 6–12, the most recent social studies text dates from 1961; most were published in the 1950s. Reference books that are used for reports or stories that are read to the younger children are censored.

Some supplementary materials are used. For instance, students read a pamphlet put out by the Institute on Basic Youth

---

Question:

(19) Even Darwin was not really sure his theory of
      evolution was true (True or False?)
(39) What is the three-fold nature of Communism?

    a. _____ b. _____ c. _____

Match these terms:

(42) _____ Karl Marx   a. natural selection
(43) _____ Ludwig Feuerbach b. dialectics
(44) _____ Georg Hegel   c. dialectical
                                    materialism
                                 d. materialism

Conflicts. In direct contrast to Covenant's position that world overpopulation, pollution, limited natural resources, and the energy crisis are real problems, this pamphlet posits that these are myths that are perpetuated by secular humanists (depicted as a serpent on the cover) who favor abortion, sterilization, and euthanasia. In response to "the destructive fallacy" of overpopulation, the pamphlet states,

> actually, the world is comparatively empty. There are 52.5 million square miles of land area in the world, not including Antarctica. If all the people in the world were brought together in one place, they could stand, without touching anyone else, in less than 200 square miles.

In response to the question of whether the world is running out of vital natural resources, it retorts:

> Projections of running out of energy or food are totally misleading. God gave to man the command and ability to fill up the earth with people and to subdue the earth for their own needs.

> Shortages of one product have always been a motivation to create a new product from existing and often overlooked resources.

129

Civilizations . . . have not been destroyed through lack of natural resources but by moral decadence which came by rejecting Biblical truth and devoting themselves to the passions and dissipations of perverted pleasure.

The A.C.E. curriculum models a behavioral system of controls. Students and teachers can gauge progress by the number of external rewards and punishments that are meted out to each student. For example, in the senior high school classroom one can see "Smiley Face" signs placed on a number of student desks. When I asked what these were, the monitor responded:

That means a student has detention. The last supervisor thought it was better to have smiley faces so that visitors wouldn't know that it was a punishment and embarrass the student. [Pauses and shrugs her shoulders] I think it's kind of like saying we're laughing at them.

Students set daily goals for themselves in each subject. When they achieve these goals, make a certain score on a test or memorize their Scriptures by a particular date, they receive gold stars, certificates of good work, more free time, or the chance to help teachers by running errands. The types of rewards and punishments depend to some degree on the age of the students. For instance, in the lower grades (kindergarten–5), a classroom store displays colored pens, bubbles, balls, toy cars, dolls, etc. Students earn points and can save up for the prize that they want—the goals are tangible and visible. In the upper grades, students may be permitted to help tutor the younger children or to have more free time. On the other hand, if they do not perform adequately, break times may be taken away and certificates withheld.

The Baptist service and school are regimented. Behavior is predictable because rules define when and where one should be. Students are fixed to their offices except for specified break times and lunch. They are to work individually without interacting with other students. If they need to go to the scoring table, they must raise their flag and get permission. When moving from one room to the next, everyone lines up single file, and begins marching in silence. This is true even in the upper grades, although they no longer need to be told to line up; by then, they naturally fall into line. Each student is permitted ten seconds drinking time at the water fountain. The older students often enforce this rule on the younger students, thereby continuing to conform to the system through a supervisory role.

Observing classes during the first weeks of the school year enabled me to see how kindergarteners are assimilated. Within a remarkably short period of time, these five- to six-year olds settled into school—a setting which allows them little opportunity to play and much opportunity to exercise "self-control."

Certain accommodations, however, were made for the first few weeks. For instance, one kindergartener was used to taking naps at home. The school day, lasting from 8:30 a.m. until 2:30 p.m. was too long for him. While his supervisor did not allow him to leave his seat, she did permit him to assume a modified sitting/sleeping posture by kneeling on his chair, stretching his torso over the cubicle top, and resting his head on a fluffy white pillow of Kleenex. When the comforts of home were not available, he accommodated—by the fifth week of school, he was no longer taking regular afternoon naps. In a similar vein, kindergarteners were expected to learn quickly that they must control their bodily urges. Bathroom runs were scheduled at 10:00 a.m. and at lunch time. One monitor explained, "They have to learn to control themselves. When they go to work, they won't be able to just get up and leave to go to the bathroom."

Certainly frustrating at first, the children learned quickly. With the exception of three or four students out of thirty-three in the kindergarten–5th grade classroom, they quickly conformed to the demands of the situation and appeared to be quite comfortable. In fact, the majority of students reported liking and feeling comfortable in school. There were, however, exceptions— especially in the beginning. For example, the same five-year old boy who took naps had a hard time sitting straight in his chair and "attending to his own business." Because of this, he was denied his morning break the first day of school. In protest, he called back to the teacher but was ignored. As the time arrived, he watched the rest of the children file out of the door for their 10:00–10:10 a.m. break. His eyes conveyed the disbelief and hurt he felt: "How could they do this to me? This has never happened to me before." But nobody stopped to say anything. The supervisor remained in the room but paid him no attention. Finally, when the rest of the class came back and settled into work, she went over to him and in a kindly manner looked at what he was doing with his coloring book. Although it took him longer than some of the others, he too quickly learned the rules and the appropriate ways of getting around them.

As with the adult worship service, children are expected to know the rules and to act with propriety. One should enter on time and not leave until the end; one should sit quietly; even a sneeze or cough is considered a disturbance. And as long as one conforms to certain external requirements, there is little prying into inner, that is private, thoughts and feelings.

Thus, within this rather rigid structure, students can exercise considerable control. For example, Academy students direct their teacher's attention by signaling them with one of three flags (the American flag summons supervisors for substantive questions; the Christian flag summons monitors for permission to score or to check goals and progress; and the school flag summons monitors for permission to go to the bathroom and has lowest priority). In general the flags are responded to within five to ten minutes. Students are very aware of the traffic flow of the classroom, and raise their flags accordingly. Even a kindergartener within the first two weeks discovered that he could manipulate the flags in such a way as to get quicker attention while avoiding negative consequences. After waiting for ten minutes for a monitor, the kindergartener realized that when the boy next to him raised the American flag, the supervisor responded immediately. With that "ah ha" expression lighting up his face, the kindergartener promptly replaced the Christian flag with the American flag. The supervisor responded immediately. Both parties were pleased: the supervisor, because the kindergartener was being conditioned and playing by the rules; and the kindergartener because he felt a strong sense of accomplishment in his first successful attempt at manipulating the rules so that he could get what he wanted.

Although the flags are meant to serve different purposes, students quickly learn to calculate how many flags of each sort are raised, and therefore, what their chances are of getting attention. Moreover, students show preferences for certain supervisors and monitors. They will wait until one monitor is nearby before raising their Christian flag; if they want to avoid the monitor who is approaching, they may take down the Christian flag and substitute the American flag.

Furthermore with the A.C.E. system, students do not have to worry about a teacher calling on them in class, embarrassing them in front of all of their classmates when they do not know the answer. As long as they are getting their work done, the five or ten minutes of intermittent daydreaming are likely to go unnoticed. In addition, school life—learning and discipline—is highly consistent and predictable. This gives students a sense of coherence about their world and security about themselves and others.

Predictability results from the high degree of formalization, and consistent enforcement of rules, procedures, and instructions. The degree of formalization is revealed through the parent–student handbook and the dress code. The Academy orients parents to the school by giving them a school handbook that describes the A.C.E. educational philosophy; it details a set of rules to be agreed upon and followed. Both parents and students receive the two pages of rules and regulations, including:

No pencil sharpening except during morning and afternoon
    breaks and lunch break.
Self-tests done. No asking for test scores.
No turning around in seat.
No gum chewing.
No candy. (Exception: sore throats.)
No getting out of seat without permission.
No leaning on chairs or partitions when standing.
No walking up to an adult conversation without an
    emergency.
No lying, cheating, stealing, or minced swearing.
Trying to get a monitor to let you do what you know you
    should not do will result in double the consequences.
Do not touch or read anything on any other students',
    supervisor's, monitors', principal's, or administrator's desk.

"No" most often begins the sentence. At the end of this list is the last dictate: "Love the *Lord* your *God* with all your mind, soul, and body. Supervisors and monitors will be striving for the same. Pray for them."

The dress code also illustrates the degree to which rules are laid out. Like the adults who wear conservative and formal attire to Sunday morning services, the Academy expects its students to dress neatly and conservatively. The Academy explicitly details its dress code: no dungarees or pants with contrast stitching for boys, no pants for girls. No sneakers. Girls must wear socks. Boys must wear long-tail shirts and keep all but the last button buttoned. The principal is encouraging uniforms (A.C.E. supplies red, white, and blue uniforms with American flags on the boys' ties), but he thinks it will take people a couple of years to get used to the idea. One page of the student handbook is devoted to grooming and dress. It begins with their interpretation of applicable Scriptures, among which are

> Don't be preoccupied with it (Matthew 6:23–5). Emphasize care and beauty of the inner person (1 Peter 3:34).

> It should be modest and not showy (1 Timothy 2:9). The purpose should not be to draw people to ourselves (how fashionable we are), but to draw people to Christ.

> We should seek to please "the many" even at the expense of our own rights. We should be careful not to offend "the many" in order that they might be won (1 Cor. 3:1–11; Romans 15:1–3).

> In light of these Scriptural principles and the purpose of the school, its relationship to other schools and the various levels of spiritual maturity of its students, we unashamedly feel we should HAVE standards of dress and grooming that are considered conservative in today's culture.

Indeed, the system is so highly structured and rules so clearly laid out there is little opportunity for a student to stray. Temptation is minimized. Everyone is kept in line—both metaphorically and literally—and to themselves. Except during recess where things tend to get out of hand.

During lunch, students sit chatting away in groups of similar age and sex. They either buy sandwiches heated up by a microwave or eat the lunches their mothers made for them. Most teachers, except those on duty, sit at one table and recount the events of the day and plans for the upcoming week: the Wednesday evening potluck or taking their children to the doctor.

After twenty minutes, the students are anxious for recess. While they line up in orderly fashion to go outside, they charge as soon as they are outdoors. The monitor, for the first time during the day, raises her voice: "Now boys, don't kick that ball into the street or you are going in. What happened to Jamie? Come here Jamie, that's OK. Boys, what did I tell you?" Daily, during recess, the monitor's patience is tested. Children continually kick the ball into the street "accidentally." Another child is pushed down—"accidentally." She breathes a sigh of relief when the whistle blows; the children line up again one-by-one, and walk without talking to the bathroom, past the water fountain for a ten second sip, and into the classroom.

Other than recess, there were few opportunities for children to test the limits of their school's rules. Students generally were very polite, responsive, and cooperative without being self-righteous. But once adults were not around, some students would bend school laws. For instance, without being outrightly rebellious, the senior high school girls would "rock" to religious songs. (This usually took place in the safety of the gym where we played volleyball without the supervision of any Academy adults. On occasion, I served as a "substitute"; otherwise, gym would have been cancelled for the day.) It was during rare times such as these and during recess that one began to sense the existence of a peer culture that was ready to emerge, one might say erupt, whenever adults were out of sight. While sex was never explicitly mentioned by students or teachers, and Health PACEs focused on Christian and civic responsibilities, anatomy, and hygenics— one could feel the tension of repressed libidos.

This kind of peer–culture testing was evident only among the senior high school students. As in any school, some teachers are better at handling the classroom than others. In the case of the senior high school, the relationship between teachers and students was problematic. Jim, the supervisor, and his wife Mary, the monitor, were new to the school and were constantly being tested by the students who had sensed their vulnerability and frustration. The more Jim tried to be understanding and helpful, the more the students would play with him. For example, when one student was reciting his Scripture for the day and had made a few mistakes, Jim interrupted him:

> I'm not trying to be picky, but if you don't have the
> right word, it changes the "meaning." Don't know what
> other clues to give—[nervous laughter—silence]—I'm
> not trying to confuse you.—You were doing good up until
> that point.

Defeated by the student's failure and his own inability to rectify the situation, Jim decided to have students return to their own work. But before they returned to work, students diverted their and his attention to a new topic:

> *Student A*:   When are the PACEs coming in?
> *Jim*:   I don't know.
> *Student B*:   Well, hurry up!

The students then engaged him in a discussion of rescheduling the day's activities:

> *Student A*:   We want an hour at the end of the day to play
>   volleyball.
> *Jim*:   Oh.
> *Student B*:   We had it last year.
> *Students*:   Yeah. [General laughter]
> *Student C*:   And for breaks—No level [of achievement]
>   gets five minutes; C level gets fifteen minutes;
>   and I level gets twenty minutes.
> *Jim*:   If you're on academic probation, no break.
> *Student B*:   How will you go to the "mercy seat"
>   [bathroom] then?

Completely frustrated and flustered by this time, Jim tells them:

> I think next time I'll have Mr. King [the principal] come in
> and make the announcements. Maybe, I didn't understand.
> If I'm wrong, I'll correct it. I'm not trying to be an ogre or
> anything.

He ends by suggesting that they take a slightly longer break than is designated by the A.C.E. manual. Two students respond:

Student A: [Unenthused] Wow.
Student B: I have work to do.

Other than the acting out described here, which tended to occur between work and other events (coming or going from chapel or missions day) and among approximately 40% of the students, the senior high school students generally focused on their work. Since they are settled into one classroom for the whole day, there is less opportunity to engage each new teacher or begin and finish each new class with diversionary tactics. And as time progressed from September into October, these students and their teachers reached a better understanding of classroom procedures, although this classroom was still not as well-controlled as the other two classrooms. A number of factors may have contributed to the more active assertion of student resistance: the inexperience and personality of the teachers; the age of students and composition of students in the senior high school. A number of them had failed or were thrown out of public school and had come to the Academy as their last resort.

During the two months I spent at the school, I witnessed few behavioral problems (other than those mentioned) and no corporal punishment. According to interviews with students, parents, and teachers, spanking was very rare. No one could remember anyone being spanked within the last two years, even though spanking is ideologically sanctioned and parents sign a form that permits the school to use discretion in such matters. One explanation is that other methods of control are so immediate, consistent, and effective that spanking is unnecessary —especially for the elementary school children who would be the only eligible ones for spanking.

Also, students initially are enrolled under a period of probation. This is problematic for Christian schools whose mission it is to win people over to Christ, and at the same time, protect those who are within the fold.

What does one do with the kids who were kicked out of public school for drugs, or prostitution, or delinquency?

Well, if they and their parents agree to live under our rules
and we sense the student is sincere, then we'll give them a
try. But if they do not adapt, they will be asked to leave.
We are not a reform school.

In many respects, the organization of the Baptist school
resembles a military model. In fact, the principal at the Academy
was pleased and proud that the United States Armed Services is
interested in recruiting A.C.E. students "because they are
disciplined." However, he did add that he would rather see his
students go on to Christian college and into the ministry rather
than into the military.

The question of how much control and conformity versus how
much autonomy and self-direction characterizes school life is
complex. While a high degree of supervision and routinization,
and a low degree of complexity characterize Lakehaven school
life, the question of autonomy is an interesting one. The degree
of autonomy is regulated, but within those limits students set
their own curricular goals. They choose what subjects they want
to work on and when to work on them. Students are granted a
fair amount of privacy. Unless a flag goes up, they may work for
long periods of time without interference by the supervisor. It is
the students, rather than the teachers, who decide when they
should be called upon. Therefore, if students are known to do
their work, then they generally will not be interrupted. The
Baptists are more concerned and content with external signs of
conformity and respect. They do not delve or challenge too far
below the surface. As Philip Slater suggests, the more progressive
types of childrearing may be more intrusive in wanting to know
and explore the innermost thoughts and feelings of children.

Thus, the A.C.E. system allows for greater individual choice
than does the traditional classroom where virtually all students
work simultaneously on the same subject for the same specified
period of time. And as long as students pass all the requirements,
they can graduate at any time during the year. If someone has
been ill, has recently moved from one school district to another,
or has dropped out of school for a period of time, he or she could
more easily enter and exit from an A.C.E. school than other

more traditional classrooms.

But what kind of education are students getting? A.C.E. is a model for *individualized* instruction, but it does not encourage *independent* learning. Curricular choices are made from fixed alternatives; supplementary materials are limited and censored. The curriculum allows little room for individuals to raise questions or to explore answers to the questions asked. Students are to read the unit (PACE), fill out the accompanying worksheet, and take the test. All of the answers can be found within the PACE—they need look no further.

The Baptists tend to avoid conflict if at all possible. Flight rather than fight characterizes their approach. The curriculum constrains the degree of interaction and reduces the need for intervention. Rules and regulations, rather than open discussion and prayer, serve as control mechanisms. Students have little opportunity to come into conflict with one another because they rarely interact with one another. When they do, conflict is often minimized and brushed away. For example, one 2nd grade girl complained about a boy who called her a bad name. The monitor at the Academy patted the girl on the shoulder and said, "That wasn't very nice of him, was it? Maybe you can pray for him."

While people report a high degree of value consensus, it is a consensus that has been agreed upon in principle rather than hammered out through practice. Because of this, it is more vulnerable to attack from within and people are less willing to talk about differences that do exist for fear that it will prove disruptive. For fear of offending anyone, Lakehaven Baptists tend to hide rather than confront issues.

The times for sharing concerns before bringing them to prayer, prayer itself, and worship are shorter, more rigid, and less intimate than at Covenant. Supervisors at the Academy often choose whom and in what order people should pray. Often two students will be chosen or solicited; just as in the teachers' meeting or adult worship, the two serve as representatives for the group. Both teachers and students share fewer personal concerns and less intimate details than do people at Covenant. Perhaps motivated by the presence of missionaries who were visiting the school one day, a senior high school student decided to risk sharing a personal concern of hers. She spoke about a relative who was being institutionalized. As she began to speak, some students began to laugh and make fun. The teacher ignored them for while, and then cut the concern time short. He prayed, "God, You care about all our concerns. You hear our prayers and understand even when others may not. Lord, help us to take prayer seriously." Neither the students nor the issue were ever confronted directly.

Student–teacher relations

The Baptist teachers are caring and loving but reserved; their emotions are kept in check. They do not want to "spoil" the children. When students arrive in the morning, they go immediately to their offices and begin work. If students seek out a teacher or monitor, then they will be greeted warmly (unless it is thought that the student is avoiding work). Since there is no "class," no collective ritual marks the beginning of the day. Likewise, when it is time for students to leave, they pack up and go.

Because of the nature and enforcement of a high degree of formalization, there is not much opportunity for personal interaction. Although supervisors make the rounds to student offices, the average amount of time per visit is fifteen seconds for the kindergarten–5th grades. In the upper grades, visits tend to be less frequent but longer. While supervisors and monitors often touch students on the shoulder (particularly common in kindergarten–5, sometimes in 6–8, and rarely in 9–12 grades), they are instructed not to talk to students or disturb them while working, but to answer their questions quickly and efficiently and move on to the next. "We respond to the needs of the individual student. When students need help, they ask for it by raising a flag. For the most part [i.e., with A.C.E. curriculum], students are quite capable of learning on their own." A.C.E. and the supervisors argue that A.C.E. students receive more individual attention than in public school where "children are thrown together. According to the *World Book Encyclopedia*, the average public school student gets only five minutes of personal attention from the teacher per day" (Principal quoting an A.C.E. pamphlet).

Teachers function as supervisors; outside of the classroom they have little involvement with students—not even for recess, extracurricular activities, or field trips. While teachers do see a number (one-third) of their students and their families in church, there are fewer informal encounters with the majority of students than there are at Covenant. Relationships tend to be friendly and cordial, but less intimate and intense than those between teachers and students at Covenant. As long as students comply with the rules, little more is demanded.

Teachers rated their relationships with students as more challenging, professional, warm, and sacred than did students. Students considered their relationships with teachers as more submissive. While both thought that their relationships with one another were not "closed," teachers thought that this adjective was less characteristic than did students.

Parent–teacher relations

Teachers are considered to be the servants of the parents; the school, the extension of the home. But parents have few opportunities to influence school decisions. Instead of overlapping networks, home and school tend to stand alone.

The network between teachers and parents is not as strong nor as entangled as it is at Covenant. Teachers are good friends with a few of the parents whom they know through church services and activities, but the majority (two-thirds) of the parents belong to other Baptist churches or are unchurched (5%). Communication between the school and the parents is more formal. Written notices are sent home with students or mailed. PTF (Parent Teacher Fellowship Meetings) are held four times a year, approximating the public school schedule. At these times, a speaker may address issues of nutrition, or parents may visit the classrooms of their children and talk with their teachers.

Monitors are mostly mothers from the congregation; approximately 20% of the mothers volunteer on a regular basis (usually once a week). The Baptist mothers do not volunteer in the same classrooms as their children because they feel they would show favoritism towards their own children. "Mothers, by nature, cannot do this [not show favoritism] with their own children" (Monitor and mother). Whether such favoritism would involve being more demanding or less critical of their own children, they believe that it is best to apply universal standards and treat everyone equally. They believe it is important to resist the temptation to "spoil" their children.

Baptist parents reported a lower degree of consensus between themselves and teachers than the charismatic parents, although both groups of parents report a relatively high degree of consensus. No significant differences were found between the values ranked by parents and teachers. Everyone ranked salvation as the most important value, and there was general consensus that wisdom, family security, and harmony followed as the next most important values.

Both the Baptist teachers and parents described their relationships as godly, supportive, warm, friendly, and meaningful. Parents and teachers described their relationships as least characterized by the adjectives: hostile, cold, and worldly. But there were some differences. Baptist teachers rated their relationships with parents as more colorful, cheerful, familial, and awkward than did parents. In contrast, Baptist parents described their relationships with teachers as more godly than did teachers.

Because of the high degree of formalization characteristic of the A.C.E. curriculum, there is less opportunity for parents to have input in the school. Innovation is neither needed nor wanted by A.C.E. programs. Participation is limited primarily to enforcing rules already established for the parents, as well as the teachers, administrators, and students. Although the school runs relatively smoothly, one can detect a certain defensiveness about its policies on the part of the school by analyzing the content and tone of its school documents:

> The regulations, standards, and principles of discipline that we feel are a necessity in fulfilling our purpose are not for everybody. . . . If a parent doesn't have the same goal or doesn't feel they agree with our approach, then it is best that they find a school that agrees with their philosophy.
>
> We do not expect every parent to agree with every "dot and title" regarding the school regulations. Over the years some of the standards have changed and they will continue

to change, to some extent. This is inevitable as the program develops and improves. However, we do expect parents to recognize that in light of the fact that we are co-workers together with them in the development of their child's character, we *must* support and encourage one another.

On our part it is essential that we inform the parents of what we expect, what we are doing, and why. On the parents' part, they *must* support the school staff—especially before the students. ("The Purpose of Regulations" given to Baptist parents; emphases in the original)

At the Academy, consensus primarily derives from the self-selection process of families and the school rather than being hammered out through collective discussions and decision making. Written documents respond to serious complaints that are made; if parents do not like it, they can leave. And, indeed, some have left while others have chosen not to enroll their children in the first place. Thus, the mutual voluntariness of choice is being exercised; only half of the children of the Lakehaven congregation attend the Academy.

Summary

Just as the Covenant school reflected the theological, class, and cultural orientations of the adult members of Covenant, so does the Academy reflect the orientations of the Lakehaven Baptists. Both adult services and school classrooms are highly regulated and predictable. Both the church and the school are characterized by a high degree of standardization, routinization, and tradition, and a low degree of complexity and experimentation.

The children of these working-, lower-middle, and agricultural-class Baptists are being trained to take over whatever jobs they can find, be they on the farm, in the factory, or in some kind of skilled labor. In order to prepare them for these roles, their parents and teachers stress obedience, respect for authority, conformity to external demands, and the ability to follow directions. Rules are used to regulate students' behavior.

It is not that the Lakehaven Baptists do not want more for

their children, but that they believe they have realistic expectations and cannot afford to dream away their children's futures. In fact, they pride themselves on being grounded in reality. They do not expect their children to revolutionize society or to become distinctive individuals in their own right. Rather they pray that they will become upstanding citizens and Christians, able to support themselves and their families in a reasonable manner.

The Lakehaven Baptists are transmitting their view of the world as a place in which individuals need to conform to certain prescribed behaviors and expectations in order to get by. These Baptists are pleased that their system is well-suited to preparing disciplined, punctual, obedient, conforming, and self-instructed students who will grow up to be "good workers."

7

Spheres of Influence

The school can never be defined as an institution apart from the parents who are represented in it. The school is an arm of the church and an extension of the family. Together, they represent a "trinity." It is like a three-legged stool—unless all legs are balanced, the stool will not be stable.[1]

A major reason for establishing separate Christian institutions that require financial sacrifice and additional time commitment is to enhance the control of the church and family. Parents have greater choice, support, and participation in educating their children; teachers are able to express their beliefs and values more freely and to form more intimate relationships with their students; and religious leaders are able to exercise greater influence over their flock. With mutually reinforcing institutions based on consensus and dedicated to similar goals, one can expect more consistent results in socializing both adults and children.

Evangelicals, who are particularly adverse to government intervention in the family, do not want to lose control over the moral and spiritual development of their children. While they advocate a "pro-family" stance, they lobby and vote against legislation in favor of women's and children's rights (E.R.A., shelters for battered women, child abuse laws, family planning clinics), believing that it would undermine the "traditional" and godly American family they are trying to preserve.[2] They have supported the introduction of such legislation as the Family Protection Acts of 1981 which sought to preserve the "traditional sex role norms as traditionally understood in the United States" by monitoring funding for educational materials.[3] They resist reliance on secular agencies for psychological, social, and educational services. Instead of playing the managerial role typical of the modern family, they want to establish their own authority and networks without relying on outside professionals.

Otto Pollack writes that, "The function which truly has been taken away from the family by other institutions is not education, health care, or homemaking, but the autonomy of setting its own standards."[4] It is this autonomy over setting and living up to standards that evangelicals are seeking when they establish their close-knit networks of family, church, and school. George Ballweg points out in his study of Christian schools, that the major underlying reason for parents enrolling their children in Christian schools is "to exercise their *right* as parents to free their children from an educational environment which is perceived to be in direct conflict with the value system which they wish to instill in the lives of their children."[5]

Family–school relations: allies or enemies?

We're not afraid of difficulty. God uses it to test us. We will confront it. Furthermore, our greatest strength is that we are a people, a community—we're not alone—we're a family. (Covenant mother)

Members of Covenant and Lakehaven consider themselves to be part of a large family. Built on value consensus rather than political consensus,[6] Christian school parents and teachers have come together, in large part, because of a common value system. They agree, at least rhetorically, that teachers are the servants of parents who have ultimate responsibility for training their children.

Teachers are selected (and self-selected) on the basis of Christian character more than on professional credentials or expertise. In sharing a commitment to evangelical Christian values which uphold the traditional, patriarchal family, teachers reinforce parental roles, authority, and values. Suspicion and competition is minimized.

> When the community is homogeneous in culture and the
> teacher is drawn from that same culture and thoroughly
> imbued with it . . . the teacher will be a fairly exact parent-
> surrogate, faithfully transmitting both the overt and covert
> content of the culture with a minimum of conflict.[7]

Both parents and teachers at Covenant and the Academy
describe their relationships with one another positively, as being
godly, supportive, warm, friendly, and meaningful.

This contrasts with much of the literature on public schools
which reports the negative, hostile, distrustful, alienating, and
defensive feelings that often characterize relationships between
parents and teachers.[8] Parents and teachers are often portrayed
as competitors, pitted against one another as adversaries rather
than allies. Sarah Lawrence Lightfoot, in her book *Worlds Apart:
Relationships Between Families and Schools*, observes that

> [Teachers] are, however, intent upon excluding families
> from school life. They seem to want to establish an
> exclusive, isolated environment, free from the intrusions of
> parents.[9]

While there is much variation within and between schools, the
fact that public education is based on political consensus means
that many public school parents and teachers do not necessarily
share much of a common ground.

When asked about their relationships with public and Christian
school teachers, a majority of the Christian school parents
reported being less defensive, more objective, and more
empowered in their relationships with their children's Christian
school teachers. Trust is developed through agreement over
common goals and values; because they are engaged in a
common mission, they can support one another in their
respective roles.

On the other hand, such close relationships and the sharing of
family concerns through prayer in school makes family life more

public and vulnerable. Thus, some parents reported being more sensitive to interactions with their children's Christian school teachers than they did with their children's public school teachers. Although teachers are supposed to defer to parents who are invested with the ultimate responsibility of educating their children, the teachers, by virtue of their office, often feel it is their responsibility to point out certain behaviors and attitudes to the parents. As professionals who see children in contexts outside of the home, they point out that they may see things that parents do not see in their own children. Although their goals may be similar, their interpretation of a child's behavior may differ and this can create tension in family–school relations at Christian schools as well as public schools.

Another factor to consider is the expectations that Christian school parents may have towards interactions with public school teachers. As the Covenant transition study indicates,[10] most parents did not continue to make contact with their children's school after their children made the transition from Covenant to public high school. Both implicit and explicit messages coming from the school indicated a more formal structure into which parents were "invited" but not made overly welcome. On the other hand, parents stated they did not want to interfere, put teachers on the spot, or make their children stand out by drawing too much attention to them. They felt that their children needed to learn to stand on their own, to tackle problems independently. This was not a stance taken after initiating contact and being rebuffed, but rather a posture taken before the students made the transition. What is not discernible at this time from the data is whether parents were somewhat relieved from this responsibility or whether they felt disempowered. The data do show that what both students and parents missed most about the Christian school was the informal, caring relationships with teachers. But it is also clear that they thought they were gaining in other areas, specifically their children's independence. Time and again, Covenant parents and teachers referred to the public school as "a good testing ground" for their adolescent children. By letting their children negotiate the public school system by themselves, their children's maturity was being tested while they still lived at home and had the support of their family and fellowship.

For many Covenant teachers who had taught in public school

and then chose to teach in Christian school, the quality of their relationships with students and co-workers was central as well. They cited being able to establish close, intimate relationships with their students and to feel that they were supported by the parents as one of the most important and rewarding aspects of their job.

For the majority (two-thirds) of Academy parents, it was not so much the close contacts with teachers that were significant since contacts were infrequent (generally four times a year) and relatively formal. Rather it was the assumption of a common commitment to Christian values that provided the security, assurance, and reinforcement of parental authority that they were looking for in a school.

Although Academy teachers felt there was greater distance between themselves and most of the parents than Covenant teachers, there was a generalized sense that parents supported them in their mission as teacher. And sometimes there was direct positive reinforcement. For example, a mother of one of the Academy students talked about how much the A.C.E. program and the Academy teachers had done for her son. She described her son as having had "personality problems, and sometimes bad moods":

All we got from the public school—and he had some excellent teachers—was "Alan doesn't do this, and Alan doesn't do that." He had a very bad self-image. I figured if this went on 'til 6th or 7th grade, he'd finally say, "I've had enough." So we put him into Christian school and things are much better. He's working better. Teachers here [at the Academy] were willing to work with him individually, at his own pace. They could discipline him and give him a lot of attention. He doesn't get as frustrated now.

Furthermore, by learning to set and achieve his own goals, he was better able to make lists of chores to be done at home and to check them off by himself without his mother "nagging" him. In return, his mother praised the school for helping to discipline him in such a way that generalized to the home, benefitting the whole family.

149

Parental power

Parents have a certain amount of power in the very fact that they choose to send their children to a particular Christian school, and therefore, can decide to withdraw them at any time. This power, however, is couched in a network of relationships that encourage them to participate in and make a commitment to the ministries of the fellowship. Commitments to one's Christianity and to the church and school become enmeshed. Indeed, it can be difficult for many parents to question school policies. This is especially true at the Academy, where to question too much is to doubt; and to doubt is to sin. The administration's ultimate stance was: "If you don't like it, leave it."

But even though Lakehaven parents and educators have less input in the educational structure and process than do Covenant parents and educators, they still argue that they have exercised choice in creating a Christian environment for their children. They feel as though the primary institutions in which they are involved are no longer working at cross-purposes. As a group of like-minded people, the Baptists have joined together to preserve a social environment that is consistent with their way of thinking. The community is meant to protect their lifestyles and ideologies —and their children. It serves as a sanctuary where sacred values are preserved. The community exists to protect individual freedom by securing consensus on fundamental beliefs and norms.

In the case of the charismatics, a group of diverse people with similar values joined together to create a social environment in which they could grow and perfect. Parents at Covenant have more opportunity to express their opinions and participate in the operation and direction of the school. Decisions are collectively made and beliefs, attitudes, and values continually worked through. Here the community models itself on group therapy techniques, where process rather than rules and content are emphasized. But although Covenant parents are more actively involved in school decision making, everyone is expected to be involved in the process. Everyone is expected to send all of their children to Covenant. Thus, both groups exercise power and influence over the individual but in different ways.

Impacts: the church

Religious leaders increase their control over the lives of their congregations when members have multiple ties to the church. By establishing schools, ministers are reclaiming territory they once surrendered. As Sidney Mead notes, "perhaps the most striking power that the churches surrendered under religious freedom was control over public education."[11] Of course, this was an unintended consequence. C. Eavey, discussing the evangelical perspective on the disestablishment of churches and the creation of public education, explains:

> [Evangelicals] were seeking to provide freedom of religion, not freedom from religion. What they wanted to rule out was sectarianism—not faith—and special advantage for any one religion—not God. Although men did have the same views, they were not asking that public-supported education be wholly secular, having no religious content, but that governmental authority should not give preference to any religion or denomination. Yet the unforeseen result of this amendment [The First Amendment separation of church and state] was the complete secularization of public education.[12]

One consequence of the separation of church and state was that religion came to play a more specific role in American society.[13] Evangelicals who are integrating the church, home, and school want religion to permeate all—or at least more—aspects of daily life. And for those involved at the Academy and at Covenant, religion has become more pervasive.

Impacts: parents

Many of the parents talked about themselves as having lacked confidence, positive self-esteem, and a sense of control over their lives before being converted. While they are adamant about having no control or power on their own, they strongly believe that they now are able to affect greater personal, and even social change through the power that God has invested in them. Current locus of control measures[14] thus miss the essential part of what is going on in this evangelical subgroup. While responses would suggest that these evangelicals have an external locus of control placed in Powerful Others,[15] specifically supernatural others, they nonetheless perform their roles with a greater sense of self-efficacy. They explain that God, their Powerful Other, manifests Himself through their own lives; the Powerful Other lives within. God is consistent; while they cannot control Him, they can depend on Him. This is part of the Covenant bargain. As long as they are faithful, God will support and direct them. Furthermore, although they "are nothing but specks of dust," God cares for and loves them—they are worthwhile because they are God's children.

On the surface, before-and-after conversion measures of self-esteem, self-efficacy, and locus of control may be surprisingly consistent. The conversion experience of radical transformation may not so much change how one evaluates oneself, but how one interprets such evaluations. Unlike some secular therapies, evangelicalism does not attempt to contradict one's previous beliefs about control and self-esteem, rather it puts them into a different context. No man has control; that is the heretical belief of secular humanists. Only God has the power, and man can be successful only by totally surrendering his life to Christ. Moreover, a person feels inferior because he is. As sinners, all men are imperfect. But God forgives and loves you; only He can make you whole again. You can make that happen by surrendering control and judgment to God; good works are neither sufficient nor necessary.

Many parents reported feeling empowered because they had acted on their beliefs; others believed they were supporting the wishes of the religious community by sending their children to Christian school. Their perceptions and evaluations all depended on what role they individually played in conceiving, establishing, and participating in the school.

Both out of feelings of personal empowerment and/or out of identification with a group project, the majority of parents believed that they had been successful in establishing a viable alternative to secular, public education for their children. This sense of accomplishment was more strongly expressed by Covenant parents, in part because of their greater involvement in school life, and in part because all the children of Covenant community attended the school. In the case of the Lakehaven Baptists, people believed that they had created a positive alternative but not necessarily a substitute for public school. Many children of the congregation attended public school rather than the Academy, and in a few families, some siblings attended public school while others attended the Academy. But parents in both communities believed that Christian education *validated* and supported them in their role as parents.

Impacts: teachers

Each school environment structures the lives of both students and teachers in ways that reinforce the value and class orientations of the respective fellowships. For example, at Covenant teachers are expected not only to be committed to the community but also to express themselves and their talents in ways that enable them to continue to grow and develop as individuals. Teaching at Covenant is characterized by a high degree of complexity, autonomy, and self-direction. There is no limit, except time and energy, to the amount of creative and intellectual energy that teachers can put into teaching and relating to their students. In fact, most teachers feel pressured by such high expectations. They feel "stretched to their limits" by the number and the complexity of jobs they are asked to perform. But they also feel exhilarated and challenged. They describe themselves as professionals. Believing that they are "called to teach," they also believe that the Holy Spirit will direct and empower them to do what they need to do.

These descriptions are characteristic of "undermanned work environments." According to Barker's study of work environments, people in undermanned work settings tend to work harder and longer to support the setting and its functions; get involved in more difficult and important tasks; participate in a greater diversity of tasks and roles; have a greater functional importance as individuals within the setting; become more responsible in the sense that the setting and what others gain from it depend on the individual occupant; and have more frequent occurrences of success and failure depending on the outcome of the setting's functions than their counterparts.[16]

What is revealing is that although the Academy has approximately the same number of students with 60% fewer teachers than Covenant, they do not define their work environment as "undermanned," while Covenant does. This can be attributed to the different conceptions of teaching and professional responsibility and the degree of technical control that define each environment. At the Academy, the standardization of teaching materials is thought to relieve the work load of teachers who need not be "professionals." A.C.E. does relieve teachers of many of their responsibilities. It takes away the creative and self-directed responsibilities commonly associated with the profession of teaching,[17] and reduces the teacher to completing the unskilled tasks of paper sorting, distributing, and checking. Such standardization functions as a form of "quality control"; it is meant to be "teacher proof."

But the A.C.E. system of education does not relieve teachers of their work load. Teachers at the Academy race around the room, responding to flags and trying to keep up with the paperwork (remember there is no chair at the teacher's desk). The teachers report that they have less time and fewer rewards than they had had in other teaching situations. Although they still support the A.C.E. system because of its "efficiency" and its support of Christian values, they personally do not feel very professional. While they monitor quality control, they have no hand in defining it. Rather than being creators of curriculum, they are executors of procedures defined by people they have never met.[18] In comparison with the "relatively autonomous nature of teaching . . . which has been partially resistant to technical and bureaucratic control,"[19] A.C.E. represents a loss of autonomy, power, and professionalism. In introducing a more affordable and efficient model of schooling, A.C.E. has contributed to the "deskilling" of labor, and at the same time, has caused work speed-ups for teachers.

In contrast to Covenant teachers working within what they defined as an "undermanned work environment," the Academy teachers do not feel as involved in the life of the school or in the lives of their students. Both the structure of the curriculum and the emphasis on individual privacy and responsibility sets the stage for this. In comparison with Covenant teachers, their jobs are more routine, less complex, and less rewarding. Although they feel "called to teach," they do not feel as personally responsible for the successes of their students (nor do they feel as responsible for their failures).

It is important to remember that socialization and education is not just preparation for a particular kind of life; it is, in the words of Dewey, "life itself." Schooling not only influences students' orientations and chances for the future, but also structures the daily lives of millions of teachers, students, and administrators. More precisely, teaching is the work of teachers.

Organizational studies indicate that when there is a high degree of professionalization, there is likely to be a low degree of formalization and standardization.[20] Formalization, or the use of rules in an organization, involves control over the individual. If members of an organization are thought to be capable of exercising superior judgment and self-control, formalization is likely to be low. This was true at Covenant where teachers are considered professionals and formalization and standardization are minimized. For both students and teachers at Covenant, the degree of supervision and routinization tends to be comparatively low and the degree of complexity high; this in part reflects the perfectionistic theology of the Covenant people.

On the other hand, if members of an organization are thought to be unqualified to make decisions and in need of explicit rules and regulations to guide their behavior, or the administration is unwilling to relinquish control, formalization is likely to be high.[21] This represents the situation at the Academy where teachers do not need to be highly qualified; here, the emphasis is placed on individualized instruction, not on quality teaching. Because the A.C.E. curriculum is designed for an unlimited number of schools operating under varying conditions, the degree of standardization and formalization is very high. The dynamics of an ideology that distrusts the individual, the reliance on ritual to regulate affairs, the need for inexpensive schooling with a low teacher–student ratio (3:76), and a relatively low degree of professionalization among the staff, make the highly standardized and formalized A.C.E. program attractive to the Lakehaven Baptists.

Impacts: students

Both the Academy and Covenant are too new to determine the impact of their schooling on students' lives and their life trajectories. Furthermore, trying to disentangle the multiple effects of home, school, church, and class backgrounds is virtually impossible, particularly with cross-sectional data and a sample of two schools. Additional research on Christian schools would help. For example, have any working-class Christian schools developed their own curricula? Have any middle-class schools chosen to use A.C.E.? If so, how are they similar to or different from Covenant and the Academy, and why? These are questions I cannot answer at this point.

A longitudinal panel study would yield more information on the schools and students five years after they have graduated from high school. But one way of roughly measuring the effects of socialization on students is to examine their lives now. Are they currently leading the kinds of lives their parents, teachers, and pastors would want them to be living?

This section examines the values, beliefs, activities, and behaviors of Academy and Covenant students, and how they feel about their respective schools. I was not able to obtain exactly the same kind of information, or with as much detail about the Academy students for a variety of reasons: test scores were not available for the Academy, only the national A.C.E. scores were presented; since students did not transfer as a body to public high school but rather remained, with individual exceptions, at the Academy, the kind of comparison that the transition study offered for Covenant students was not possible for Academy students.

Both schools consider their systems of education to be humane, or more precisely in their terms, Christian. In the case of the Academy, school life is highly routinized and predictable; both students and teachers can anticipate the day's events. Because the parameters of classroom behavior are so clearly defined, people feel in relative control of their environment. Because lines are clearly drawn, students know where they stand in relation to the rules; because they are aware of expectations and the consequences of deviant behavior, they feel responsible for their actions. The result is a sense of security. In fact, when asked to rate how comfortable they felt in school with teachers and with other students, and how much they liked school, the Academy students were more positive than Covenant students.

Table 2   Students' ratings of adjustment to school life

	Baptist (n = 40)		Covenant (n = 20)	
	Mean	Median	Mean	Median
How much do you like school	4.39	4.00	6.42	6.80
How comfortable do you feel				
– in school	4.32	3.81	6.15	6.87
– with teachers	4.19	3.49	6.00	6.25
– with students	3.64	2.81	5.47	5.66

Note: Scale ranged from 1 (Very Much Like/Very Comfortable) to 10 (Do Not Like at All/Very Uncomfortable).

Covenant students, on the other hand, are required to be intensely involved in school life, to explore their relationships with themselves, their God, their fellow students, and their teachers. Such high expectations and the sense of continually being challenged, of always striving for perfection, prove to be exhausting and frustrating at times. This may be an important reason why Covenant students reported feeling less comfortable in school and liking school less than their Academy counterparts. In talking with Covenant students, they had more to say about school life and were both *more positive* and *more negative* about school than Academy students. Academy students, who were left alone as long as they did the required amount of work and followed the rules, had little argument with the school but also expressed no excitement about it.

Students from both schools reported feeling more comfortable with their fellow students than with their teachers. And for all of the students, school generally "remained school—something one had to put up with" given one's destiny as a child in contemporary American society.

Peer pressure

Psychologist Urie Bronfenbrenner argues that joint activity between adults and children is crucial to the process of learning and human development. It can enhance parental control and the solidarity between parents and their children *if* it is mutually rewarding. The Lakehaven and Covenant people want their children to be family and church oriented. By reuniting the church, school, and family they hope to encourage interdependence. (It is worth noting here that the church is the only major social institution, other than the family, that is intergenerational.) They well recognize the consequences of increasing specialization and segregation that sociologist Robin Williams describes:

> As parents' and children's activities become segregated, interdependence diminishes, which further decreases loss of parental control over interactions and sanctions.[22]

Students at both schools do spend the greatest amount of time out of school with their families. Following family, they spend the greatest amount of time with Christian friends, and then on homework. In contrast, a nationally representative sample of high school students spent the greatest amount of time with friends, then with family, and third at work (some kind of paid employment).[23] Both Covenant and Baptist students spend more time on homework and at religious services than the average American high school student, and less time on dates or social activities, working after school, or in athletics. None of the groups spend much time on community activities.[24] These findings do not tell us whether the Covenant and Lakehaven children are voluntarily choosing to spend more time with their families or not, but they do suggest that the evangelical families exercise greater supervision over the activities of their children.

One major reason parents give for enrolling their children in Christian schools is to avoid the drugs and drinking that are considered prevalent in public schools. Both students at Covenant and the Academy report virtually no exposure to alcohol or marijuana. (Given the rapport I established with Covenant students during the fieldwork and the anonymity of my questionnaires at both schools which assured students their responses would be seen only by me, I expect that these self-reports are valid.) But the interesting finding, given the concern and publicity about drugs and alcohol in the public schools, is how low the means and medians are for a nationally representative sample of American high school students. The average American student reports that friends suggested they drink or smoke marijuana with them only once or twice in the previous three months; moreover, when one examines the medians, we find that the majority of American high school students reported that not once in the previous three months did friends put pressure on them to go drinking or to use drugs.[25] The differences were not large, even though the samples represented different age groups. Since the mean grade for the national sample was 11th grade; for Academy students, 9th grade; and for Covenant students, 6th grade, one would have anticipated greater experimentation among the older students, who would have had greater opportunity to be exposed to drugs and pressured by peers.

It may be that students feel they are voluntarily drinking or taking drugs, that they are not "pressured" from friends. But it is also important to remember that the presence of drugs does not necessarily imply pressure to indulge, as students making the transition from Covenant to public high school (in the 9th and 10th grades) found. In fact, the majority of students (eight out of nine) did not report greater peer pressure to party, drink, take drugs, or swear in public school, although all reported that the pervasive "foul language" bothered them.

The study of the transition and adjustment of nine Covenant students to public school sheds greater light on the context of the home school, Covenant. When interviewed in May 1983, in anticipation of the transition, parents listed their number one concern as greater peer pressure to party, to drink, and to swear; this was the students' second greatest concern (first was making new friends, moreover, the "right" friends). When interviewed in late September (during the transition) and again in January (after the transition), pressure to drink and party were not mentioned as concerns by either students or parents. Swearing, however, continued to be bothersome. Students reported that the lack of respect for authority; the lack of trust; and the more formal, less-involved relationships with teachers are what distinguish the public school most from their Christian school experience. While students expressed greater confidence in who they were and stronger convictions in what they believed as a result of being exposed to public school, most students did not think that public school was as bad as it had been made out to be. The following quotation from one student represents the views of the majority:

> Things were not as bad as I expected. I had a picture of
> public school as a bad and horrible place where you got
> beat up and you always were forced to take drugs—this was
> from hearsay. It really isn't like that at all if you hang out
> with the right kids. It all depends on who you associate
> with.

The Covenant community stresses interdependence among age groups and incorporates the energy and enthusiasm of its youth into the mission of the community. The youth are given responsible and therefore, meaningful roles. Their religious experiences as children are legitimated and they actively participate in worship services, testimonials, and the Body Life Groups which meet in the homes of members. A strong peer group exists but the prevailing philosophy is that adolescents need not rebel against their elders if they all join together in a crusade against a powerful spiritual enemy. At Covenant, students are incorporated into rather than separated from adult groups in ways that encourage them to identify with their elders and to join in a community resistance against demonic forces.

Thus, the nature and degree of resistance and accommodation depend upon the person, the cultural/organizational context, and the process. The possibility of resistance is deliberately minimized at the Academy by isolating individuals. Although students do learn to manipulate the flags, and therefore their teacher's attention or non-attention, they resist as individuals rather than as student groups. While Paul Willis's lads found ways of resisting middle-class culture by "goofing-off" in school,[26] the Academy students have little opportunity within the context of school to form any kind of peer group, and therefore, to resist in any collective way. The one exception here is recess where control breaks down. One gets the sense that the situation is volatile, that it would not take much for these students to rebel—and this may be what their parents and teachers are afraid of.

The mere word "adolescence" can send tremors up the spine of many American parents. Many view the adolescent years as a test of their own success or failure as parents. Will the peer group usurp their power as parents? How will they and their children handle the potentially seductive teen years?

Underlying the adult concern for control is the sexual energy of adolescents. In our culture, one of the greatest tests of parental success is whether their children have learned enough to "keep out of trouble" and to restrain or protect themselves until the "proper" moment, however this may be defined. In the case of Covenant and the Academy, it is defined as the moment of marriage. The two communities deal with their own and their children's sexuality in ways that reflect both their cultural and class backgrounds. Covenant teachers and parents talk about sex as a gift from God. Although they believe sex is a treasure to be saved until marriage, they consider it a natural and beautiful part of life that can be talked and fantasized about.[27] Frustration is made noble through sublimation. Not only adolescents but all single people of the fellowship are expected to abstain until marriage. So it is not sexuality, *per se*, that is feared but rather the improper and premature expression of it.

Moreover, my sense is that the middle-class charismatic parents are not so much afraid of their daughters' blossoming sexuality and the evils that might involve (i.e., pregnancy) as of their daughters not becoming "feminine" enough. Their fear may be that their girls and women will choose to pursue jobs and positions of power and leadership which are not "natural" for women to pursue. The exercise of control rests more with assuring the femininity of their women and therefore, the authority of men, than with premature sexuality. This is where we see the convergence of gender and class.

The Baptists do not talk about sex let alone sexuality. Health packets discuss civic responsibilities and hygiene. They do not fear, like the charismatics, that their women will not become feminine enough; rather, they fear that their girls will become too feminine too early. By flaunting their femininity, they may get themselves and their boys into trouble. In this working-class culture which elevates romantic love and the traditional family, the subject of sexuality is repressed.[28] By ignoring the libido, the Baptists hope to bury sexual feelings which they feel are unbecoming to anyone. The hope for these working-class Baptists is that their girls will have a proper marriage.

Thus, both communities stress the virtues of the traditional, patriarchal, American family for similar reasons—to secure the authority of men—but they have different means and motivations. The middle-class charismatics fear that women may become too independent and powerful, thus disrupting family commitments all together, while the working-class Baptists fear that their women may become seduced too early by the temptations of bodily urges and the secular world, and thus destroy the morality of the legitimate family. Are they succeeding in controlling their children?

It is difficult to say. In general, students in both schools were friendly, polite, and generally well-behaved without being self-righteous. But given that the Baptists stress privacy, it was difficult to talk with students or adults about very personal—especially sexual—matters. But they all had known girls who had become pregnant. In fact, in their rural communities they had known of a number of girls who had become pregnant. Three of them were Academy girls who had become pregnant and dropped out of school within the last three years; one of the girls currently enrolled at the Academy had come there after leaving public school to have her baby.

Because I did not "hang out" with students after school, I do not have a good understanding of their social life outside of school. My observations suggest, however, that many of the senior high school girls at the Academy are very boy conscious. Although they sing traditional Christian hymns, they tend to "rock" with the songs in ways that communicate very strong sexual messages. The "rocking" not only is lively but is very much against the prescripts of the church, which denounces rock music as the music of the devil. Therefore, while there is no "fraternizing" going on in school, there is evidence that the idea and lure of sex is not foreign to these students.

At Covenant, the junior high school boys and girls are interested in the opposite sex and teasing certainly occurs. But there doesn't seem to be as much distance from and romanticization of the opposite sex nor the sense that they see each other as different species. Rather, my impression is that there is greater understanding and friendship between boys and girls at Covenant than at the Academy, at least within the confines of the school.

When I asked students about their views of the opposite sex, I received more stereotypical and traditional views from the Academy students than from the Covenant students, who tended to talk more about friendship, caring, and supporting one another. Nonetheless, there were plenty of comments from both Covenant and Academy boys about "silly girls" and from girls about "stupid boys." And both groups of girls would talk about "cute" guys, although Academy girls would tend to be a little more explicit. On the other hand, neither in my presence nor in informal conversations did the boys talk about physical characteristics of the girls.[29]

Students did respond, however, to specific questions about sex-role norms and responsibilities. The vast majority opposed women's rights and supported the separation of spheres of influence (the home for women, and work and government for men). They also distinguished female and male sensibilities: women were valued as "keepers of the heart," and men, as "guardians of the mind."

Both fellowships stressed the importance of the traditional patriarchal American family and adherence to traditional sex-role norms. To test whether the Christian school students espoused more traditional sex-role norms than the average high school student, I compared my data with the National Youth sample. In contrast to the National Youth sample, the combined sample of Christian school students thought that

1. Fathers should have greater authority in disciplining children.
2. Men are more reliable than women in emergencies.
3. It is the man's responsibility to earn the money for the

family.
4.   Women are physically weaker than men.
5.   Women cannot do most jobs as well as men.[30]

The only significant difference between the Baptist and charismatic school students on the ten items was that Baptist students more strongly (p = .03) agreed that "a wife should submit to her husband."[31]

Like their families and fellowships, both Covenant and Academy students expressed general support of the traditional, patriarchal family and opposition to E.R.A., shelters for battered women, mandatory child abuse reporting, and aggressive women. They believed that men were the "natural leaders" and that women should know their place, even though they recognized (like their parents) that some girls and women were stronger and smarter than men and that some men had very nurturing feelings towards young children.

Academic achievement

The Lakehaven educators want their students to be trained in the basics. They are task and content oriented, wanting their children to know specific pieces of information. This is manifested in the emphasis on recitation rather than interpretation and in the objective testing (multiple choice, true–false, fill-in-the-blank) that characterizes the A.C.E. materials. The Covenant educators are more process oriented, wanting their students to explore ideas and express their creativity. They believe that interaction and discussion is crucial to learning and development. These orientations tend to reflect those commonly attributed to the working and middle classes.[32]

I do not have comparable data on the Academy, Covenant, and public school students, but the available data do suggest that the quality of education that Academy students are receiving is not lower than that of the average public school student, *given the criteria commonly used to test academic achievement* in the United States. (How good the measures of academic achievement are is another question.) Andrew McDearmid's 1979 study found higher S.A.T. mean scores for A.C.E. graduates than for the general population in Pennsylvania, and 16% more A.C.E. grads enrolling in college than public school graduates.[33] In May of 1983, CTB/McGraw-Hill conducted a major testing survey of 7,500 A.C.E. students. The results indicate that the average student using A.C.E. materials scored higher than 65% of the students in the control group, a nationally representative sample of students. These figures are commonly cited by A.C.E. advocates, including the principal at Lakehaven; however, specific statistics for Academy students were not available. Given their training, A.C.E. students should be well prepared to digest "how-to-manuals" but less well prepared to write essays and ask critical questions. In fact, in a comparison of essays that I asked the 6th and 7th graders at both schools to write, the essays of Academy students were significantly shorter, less detailed, less well organized, and more restricted in vocabulary. A superintendent of children's education in a large Christian organization indicated that A.C.E. students had difficulty making the transition to other curricula, whether Christian or secular, because they could not handle the breadth of material.

But the Academy did service a number of "problem" students from area schools. A number of students who were considered "problem learners," "emotionally disturbed," and or "delinquent" were enrolled in the Academy. In fact, the principal estimated that a number of students would have otherwise dropped out of school except for the fact that the Academy was able to give them the kind of instruction and space that they needed. Therefore, while the majority of Academy students would probably do well academically in public school, a minority of them would most likely otherwise have dropped out. One of the oldest students in the school was reading at the 4th grade level.

A.C.E. has picked up on this success with "problem" students. Recent brochures, distributed by the national headquarters, are turning a perceived weakness into a potential advantage. The literature reflects a shift in thinking from the 1970s:

In the early years conventional Christian educators
counseled A.C.E. not to take the slow learners—that the
A.C.E. program would be overrun with problem kids and

that it would hurt the reputation of A.C.E. By the 1980s A.C.E. became known as "a school system for problem kids." Most of the problem kids came from conventional schools. . . . How can you practice Christianity if you reject those who need help most?[34]

At Covenant, students are scoring above the national average on the Stanford Achievement Tests (S.A.T.) And all of the students who transferred to public school during 1982 did above-average work academically. Although the sample is too small (nine students) to draw any reliable conclusions, a number of them entered New York State Regents classes and all of them were placed among the more advanced classes in their grade. Interviews with their public school teachers and inspection of their public school report cards indicates that they were academically well prepared for public school, regardless of which of the three public schools they attended. In fact, a number of the public school teachers wished that they had more students like those transferring from Covenant primarily because they were well behaved and intellectually curious, taking initiative to ask interesting questions both during and after class.

Summary

Both fellowships established schools in order to provide a more controlled Christian environment for their children. As we have seen, the meaning and types of "Christian" environments can differ radically, depending on the conceptions and resources of the adult leadership.

At Covenant, parents, educators, and administrators are actively involved in questioning the purpose and practice of schooling and in experimenting with the design of the curriculum. Teachers feel that they are better able to express their creativity and caring through teaching in a Christian school, and parents feel that they are better supported in their roles as Christian parents. Everyone values the intimacy of their relationships, although they realize that it exacts a certain price. Maintaining intimate relations takes energy. Combined with the high expectations that come with a perfectionistic theology, such an intense and intimate environment can be both invigorating and exhausting; it certainly is demanding. At the Academy, the Lakehaven Baptists have adopted a system of education that enables them to operate a school and provide a more controlled Christian environment for their children. While they realize that it has its limitations, once the decision was made to go with A.C.E., there was little discussion about the pros and cons and how they might adapt the system better to their needs and interests. Neither administrators, teachers, parents, nor students have much input in decision making or curricular design. All are constrained by the rules and regulations of A.C.E. which they tend to follow faithfully. But in comparing their situation with the alternatives they have, parents, and especially church and school leaders, believe they have more power and influence than they would (and in some cases do) have with the public schools.

And while teachers at the Academy do not have the autonomy and power that many teachers have, it must be remembered that for many of them, it was not a matter of personally "giving up" their own sense of professionalism. Only two of them had been teachers in other settings; the other supervisor/principal had been a truck driver, and the monitors had all been either secretaries or housewives. In their view, although they felt harried and preoccupied with paperwork, they were proud to be in the field of education. The rhetoric of the profession lived on, if not the realities.

The relationships among parents, teachers, and students at Covenant and the Academy are embedded in a network of relationships that are couched in a theology of evangelical Christian belief and behavior. Both communities emphasize the Christian duty to care for and love one another. The differences in the nature of their relationships lie in their conceptions of what it means to care. The Baptist version of the Golden Rule "to not do unto others as you want them not to do unto you" suggests that one cares by "being there," by being dependable without intruding. Support is tied to comfort and legitimating what is and what always has been. The good rules are universal; the characteristics of the "good man," timeless. In the face of change—be it personal or social—one comforts by reaffirming the continuity of past traditions.

For the charismatics, caring involves the kind of support that encourages people to explore their own potential and the possibility of relationship. People should comfort one another, but they should not feel too comfortable. If one is not changing, one is stagnating. Instead people should challenge themselves and one another to strive for perfection.

As this chapter suggests, the Baptists are seeking to preserve a sense of community that has existed for generations. The charismatics are attempting to build a sense of community that they have found lacking in contemporary American society. The next chapter explores interactions between the collective and the individual and the ways in which class and culture find expression in communication in each community.

8

Rhetoric and Reality:
Two Views of the World

Ideologies [are] . . . most distinctively, maps of problematic
social reality and matrices for the creation of collective
conscience.[1]

The last five chapters have examined the philosophy, social
organization, and demographic characteristics of two evangelical
fellowships and schools. This chapter explores the relationship
between philosophy and social organization and rhetoric and
reality.

Meaning systems reflect the positioning of complex and
contradictory values, attitudes, and beliefs. Dialectical values are
held in dynamic tension as people attempt to make sense out of
the real worlds they experience and the ideal worlds they
envision. It is here, within the complex of the meaning system,
that the ideal and the real mingle and define one another.

The fact that the real does not perfectly reflect the ideal does
not imply that the meaning system has lost its potency. In striving
for perfection, the ideal is often disappointed by reality.
Although evangelicals adhere to their particular religious worldview *because* it provides them with meaning and a sense of
coherence, discrepancies and contradictions still exist. They too
find themselves falling short of their expectations and highest
values. In the principal's office at Covenant School, the following
inscription by Derek Prince helps to sort this out for them,

There are two things, the actual and the ideal. To be
mature is to see the ideal and live with the actual. To fail is

to accept the actual and reject the ideal. And to accept only that which is ideal and refuse the actual is immature. Do not criticize the actual because you have seen the ideal. Do not reject the ideal because you see the actual. Maturity is to live with the actual but hold onto the ideal.

Slippage between the promise and the practice of values and norms does not necessarily lessen the importance or the potency of these values. Robin Williams says,

> values make a difference; they are not epiphenomenal. . . . We cannot safely underrate any value merely because it seems characterized by lip-service, or more honored in the breach than in observance, or is advocated primarily by hypocrites. For all of these activities serve to maintain the value as valid currency or acknowledged benchmark— whereupon it can be used at any time to praise or blame, to honour or bring into disrepute. We must never lose sight of the fact that values continually are used as weapons in social struggle.[2]

Both the people at Covenant and Lakehaven are engaged in a symbolic crusade. They are struggling to achieve a greater sense of personal and social coherence in a world that appears chaotic and unpredictable—that appears out of control, at least out of their control. In order to achieve greater mastery over their own lives, they recognize the need to exercise greater influence on the world that in large part defines their lives. They want Christianity to have a more powerful influence in contemporary society. It is no longer a question of manifest destiny, of how to spread Christianity to other countries, but primarily of how to "restore" America to a Christian nation.

Both communities perceive men as sinners who need to be saved and the United States as a country that needs redemption. They share core evangelical beliefs and cherish similar values. Members of both communities unanimously ranked salvation as the most important value and consistently ranked wisdom and family security among their top four values. Recognition, an exciting life, a comfortable life, pleasure, beauty, and peace were consistently ranked at the bottom of Milton Rokeach's value survey.[3]

Although their worldviews—their meaning system, definition of morality, and description of the world—are relatively similar, the ethos of each community—their aesthetic sense, their judgment of people and situations, the "tone" of their institutions are quite different. By examining their respective statements of faith, we can learn a great deal about the two fellowships. Each statement explicitly reveals a view of human nature. And each implicitly reveals a view of man's relationship to God, to nature, and to other people—both within and beyond their religious community. The tone, the date or lack thereof, and the use of "we" versus "I" likewise represent critical differences.

Covenant Fellowship

We believe that man was created in the image of God as the crowning work of His creation. Man stood in a unique relationship with his Creator and was commissioned to rule the earth under God's headship. Through the temptation of Satan, man transgressed the command of God and fell from his unique relationship to God; thus, all his descendents inherit both a nature and an environment twisted by sin. Because of sin, man is separated from God and is without hope of reconciling himself to a just and holy God through any of his own efforts. Only the grace of God can restore man to his original calling: to live in fellowship with God and to fulfill the purposes for which he was created. (A Statement of Faith, Covenant Fellowship, undated)

Baptist Congregation

I believe man was created in the image and likeness of God (Gen. 1:26–27). I reject all theories of evolution, including Theistic. Man was created in innocence, but by voluntary transgression fell from his sinless state, (Gen. 3:1–6) and is lost in sin and separated from God (Rom. 3:10) except he be born again (Jn. 3:7). All men, without respect of condition or class, are sinners before God (Rom. 3:9–10). This universal sinful condition is vitally connected with the sin of Adam (Rm. 3:19). Unregenerate men are regarded as children of the devil (Jn. 8:44), and not sons of God, in helpless captivity to sin and Satan (Eph. 2:3). Man is totally

depraved, and of himself, totally unable to remedy his lost
condition (Rom. 7:18, 23; Eph. 2:1–3, 12). (Doctrinal
Statement, Baptist Church, October 2, 1974)

The Baptists believe that man is inherently evil and "totally
depraved"; blame and responsibility are placed on the individual
who is considered guilty from the start. "Man was created in
innocence, but by *voluntary* transgression fell from his sinless
state" (emphasis mine). In order to be a good Christian, one
should abstain from indulgences (alcohol; drugs; dancing;
movies; mixed swimming for teens; cards; rock music) and mind
one's own business. One helps others by not tempting or
offending them. Baptist institutions tend to protect people (by
restraining individuals) and to offer comfort and consolation. A
Sunday bulletin warns and comforts them: "The Christian is not
ruined by living in the world, but by the world living in him."

The charismatics believe that men are sinners but that man's
nature is twisted, in part, by external forces. Responsibility is
shared by the individual, the environment, and demonic forces.
Charismatics attribute sin more to the temptation of Satan: man's
"nature" and "*environment*" are "*twisted* by sin," it is not
inherently evil (emphases mine). Men therefore need to support
one another actively by joining together to combat evil forces.
Rather than minding one's own business, people should positively challenge one another to grow stronger. A Covenant
sermon asks,

we are God's army. Look at the person next to you. Do you
trust him? Are you ready to go into combat with him? We
have to strengthen one another.

The active version of the Golden Rule applies: "Do unto
others as you wish them to do unto you." The charismatics tend
to challenge and confront people to become stronger and more
active in their pursuit of perfection: "Don't be members of the
white knuckle club, holding on to religion for your dear life. Let
go, jump into the middle of things, get beat up" (Covenant
sermon).

For the charismatics, both blame and credit are attributed to
supernaturally powerful others; for the Baptists, blame is

attributed to the individual and salvation to supernaturally powerful others. This has important implications for individuals (regarding self-control, guilt and shame, self-esteem, self-efficacy, and empowerment) and for the organizational styles of their institutions.

The Baptists place a high value on privatism and individual responsibility. But in distrusting the individual, they also tend to limit the range of acceptable behavior, beliefs, and values for adherents. The tension between the belief in man's sinfulness and the value of individual liberty is manifested in the norm that people should attend to their own affairs, neither corrupting nor being corrupted.

In contrast, the charismatics place a strong emphasis on community, believing that people need to support and challenge one another. Trusting the individual, the charismatics teach discernment and encourage people to explore their Christianity within the context of pluralistic values and beliefs. While the Baptists tend to emphasize training, the charismatics tend to emphasize testing. In simplified terms, the Baptists are oriented more towards notions of corruption, constraint, and consolation; the charismatics, more towards notions of perfection, discernment, and challenge. These orientations derive from the interaction of both their religious and class orientations.

Class and religion

> Religion is created not by one great man, but [is] a
> cumulative product of many persons making their religious
> interpretations in a specific cultural and social
> environment.[4]

Religion, by providing meaning for life, is intimately connected with one's class position in a particular society. It may serve different functions for different people, depending in part on their life circumstances.[5] Objective distinctions of class (including most commonly education, occupation, and income) strongly influence how we assess our life situations. Like religion, class helps define needs and expectations; it affects both how we view the world and how we choose to respond within that world.

While the Lakehaven Baptists and the Covenant charismatics share similar values and beliefs, they differ dramatically in their expectations of life, their views of human nature, and their views of education. These differences are grounded in the realities of these peoples' lives—in their personal, family, religious, and class backgrounds. The Baptist congregation is largely composed of farmers; skilled and unskilled laborers; factory workers and truck drivers; and some teachers and secretaries. The Covenant people are oriented more towards the arts, social work, teaching, middle-management, and engineering; a number of members are secretaries and skilled laborers. The differences in income levels and occupational titles, however, are not what primarily distinguish the two communities. In fact, the average salary range for both congregations in 1983 was between $15,000–25,000. More critical are the substantial differences in educational and cultural background, the degree of geographical mobility, and the age of their members.

The Baptist congregation is primarily a working, lower middle-class, agricultural community living in a rural area that is politically and socially conservative. Some of the members attended college, primarily Christian colleges, but the majority started working after high school on the farm or in a trade. Academic education is not a high priority; in fact, they are somewhat distrustful of education and intellectual endeavors. What is important is doing a good job at work and being responsible for one's family.

Most grew up within a twenty-mile radius of the church and have experienced the security and watchfulness of a small-town environment. People know one another and one another's families. They are aware of "Uncle Joe's" drunkenness and "Aunt Sally's" faithfulness. Weaving in and out of the familiar institutions of the family, farm, church, shop, and school, they understand one another well enough to depend on one another. There is no great need to analyze or articulate what someone thinks or feels, or what they do and why.

Understanding this system of relationships in positional terms, where power and authority are invested in a person (because of his or her position as mother, father, teacher, etc.), Lakehaven Baptists tend to use a restricted language code in their family, church, and school communities.[6] Because much is tacitly understood, little elaboration is needed. Out of an expansive common ground of similar experiences grows the respect for individualism and privacy. The mysteries and meanings of life lay in the universe of shared experiences and symbols, not in the explorations of men's minds and souls. Self-exploration and expression are likely to be considered frivolous obsessions in contrast to the seriousness of making a living. The Lakehaven Baptists are more concerned with whether there will be enough rain for the crops to grow or enough money to patch the roof or buy new tires for the truck. The coherence of their lives has to do with "getting by" not "getting it all together." Their perception of the good life is to be grateful for a warm home, the comforts of daily living, and a good measure of inner peace and grounded wisdom.

In contrast, the Covenant people's desire for community comes out of their diversity and pursuit of individual fulfillment. Covenant is a diverse community drawing people from all classes and many different geographical regions. The majority, however, come from the middle class and are primarily college graduates of secular colleges. Many retain connections to academia through teaching or working (especially in computers, accounting, agriculture, or secretarial work) at nearby universities. A high value is placed on education and the arts.

The religious backgrounds of the Covenant people are also diverse. Many grew up in Protestant or Catholic families that they describe as "non-Christian"; others report no religious training. A few came from fundamentalist families. Many of the early members of the community participated in the counter-cultural movement of the late 1960s and experimented with drugs, sex, alternative lifestyles, and secular therapies. As a group, they are quite well aware of popular culture and contemporary theories of psychology and sociology.

Their struggle is an internal one. It involves an often excruciating search for self—a preoccupation with psychological processes and the meaning and attainment of significance. Many of them grew up in middle-class families which they then rejected. In their minds, materialism is something that contaminates social relations. Many feel that if they had been brought up in more loving and traditional families, they would have become more responsive and responsible people.

The Covenant people are energized by struggle. They welcome challenges which assure them of their humaneness and intimate connection with others. Their community serves to connect them as individuals to one another in meaningful ways and to challenge them to new heights of experience and enlightenment. While the Baptists yearn for a sense of inner security and groundedness, the charismatics yearn for inner flight.

Culture and communication

These orientations interact with how these two groups of evangelicals communicate with one another and how they socialize their children. According to Basil Bernstein, a restricted code arises where social relations are based on common expectations and assumptions, and on closely shared identifications. "It emerges where the culture or sub-culture raises the 'we' above the 'I' " (Bernstein, p. 146).

The Baptists tend to use restricted codes. People do not need to elaborate verbally because the most important things are tacitly understood; the most important understandings are commonly shared. Common and literal interpretations of the Bible are presumed (in fact, only the King James version is used). It would be too embarrassing to emphasize one's own views, for that suggests too much pride and indulgence in oneself. For Baptists, the "I" is communicated more in the "tone, volume, and nonverbal expressions than in the language they use" (Bernstein, pp. 34–35). Bernstein's analysis of working-class speech applies well to the patterns of communication of the Lakehaven Baptists:

> Speech is played out against a background of communal,
> self-consciously held interests which removes the need to
> verbalize subjective intent and make it explicit. (p. 77)

Moreover, the subjects open to inquiry are limited. In part, this helps to maintain a sense of community consensus. Thus, the

Statement of Faith sits nestled in the pastor's drawer and there is little discussion about religious belief or pedagogy.

We have established that within the Baptist context the sense of community is more pervasive than the sense of the individual. Why then do they proclaim "I" rather than "we" in their statement of faith? How do we reconcile this with the elevation of the community over the individual within the restricted code? I would suggest that the rhetorical emphasis on the individual compensates for the lack or loss of individuality in reality.

The use of "I" in the Lakehaven statement of faith stresses the importance of the individual's allegiance to Christ. Given that the community of believers can be assumed, it asks for people to individually espouse their beliefs. Within the working-class Lakehaven community, the value of individuality is cherished but threatened; thus, it becomes all the more salient. Conversations, sermons, and church and school literature frequently refer to the primacy of the individual in a way that suggests its precarious or problematic nature within the church and larger community.

In contrast, the charismatics tend to use an elaborated code and to make explicit verbally their subjective meanings and intentions. With the elaborated code, especially one oriented to persons as it is with the Covenant people, the self becomes a subject of inquiry (Bernstein, p. 151). The "I" is raised above the "we." Bernstein argues that this is characteristic of middle-class patterns of speech:

> If the restricted code facilitates the construction and exchange of "social symbols," then an elaborated code facilitates the construction and exchange of "individuated symbols." (p. 78)

The Covenant people tend to see the individual as the primary actor: the one who rebels against authority, who challenges commonly held assumptions, who goes in search of the lost or undiscovered self. But they are aware that too great an emphasis on the individual can lead to the disintegration of community. Moreover, it can entrap the individual in loneliness and despair. Perceiving the dangers of too much individualism, they glorify the community, the unity of individuals, which they struggle to achieve. Assuming individual interpretations of the Scriptures,

Covenant people stress the community of believers by using "we" instead of "I" in their statement of faith.

Both are rhetorical responses to the realities of their lives. The Lakehaven Baptists, whose lives are grounded in an expansive common ground, emphasize the individual; the Covenant people, whose lives are grounded in individual experience, emphasize the community. In the balance, both the individual and the collective are recognized—but in different ways. The Baptists grant their members greater individualism through privacy; the charismatics grant their members greater individuality through self-expression. In the process, both systems engender social solidarity:

> The use of a restricted code creates social solidarity at the cost of the verbal elaboration of individual experience. The type of social solidarity realized through a restricted code points towards mechanical solidarity, whereas the type of solidarity realized through elaborated codes points towards organic solidarity. (Bernstein, p. 147)

The application of the A.C.E. curriculum, where teachers do not encourage nor entertain controversial questions, becomes one way of ensuring social solidarity and the perception of a high degree of consensus. There is little opportunity to question to what degree the common ground is an illusion or a reality.

For the charismatics, an extensive and pervasive common ground is not assumed. Instead, much work has gone into hammering out a philosophy that people can agree upon. The process is a continual and interactive one. Given peoples' diverse experiences, a common ground had to be created. People's understandings needed to be articulated in order to discover where there was agreement and disagreement, and finally, to discuss why there were differences and similarities. Their use of an elaborated code is expressed through extensive classroom discussions and the complexity of their curriculum.

Curriculum, class, and control

People at the Academy not only use, and therefore, reproduce a restricted code, but also select a curriculum that inherently favors the use of a restricted code. As Bernstein argues:

A restricted code contains a vast potential of meaning. It is a form of speech which symbolizes a communal culture. It carries its own aesthetic. (p. 152)

It is direct and straightforward in its simplicity. And for congregations like the Lakehaven Baptists, this serves a particular purpose.

The intent of those using A.C.E. materials is to control the thoughts and articulations of students and to censor the kinds of information they are exposed to. A.C.E. manuals instruct teachers and students alike that all the answers lie within the text—no discussion is needed. Furthermore, the curriculum is classified into a clearly defined (boundaried), limited, and fixed array of subjects (see Bernstein, postscript).

At one level, this suits the aims of the Lakehaven Baptists quite well. They are familiar and comfortable with this form and articulation of knowledge, and they do not want to "broaden their students' horizons." On the contrary, they want to purify the curriculum and weed out what they consider to be corrupt ideas. Rather than expose their students to all sorts of ideas and teach them to analyze their validity and weigh their merits, they prefer to censor the curriculum strictly and protect their children from conflicting, confusing thoughts. The irony is that by purifying the curriculum, they are also simplifying the curriculum in ways that may make it difficult for their children to be able to question and evaluate ideas that they may be exposed to later on.

Furthermore, although Academy parents have greater control over what ideas their children are exposed to than they do in the public schools, they nonetheless have adopted a curriculum produced by a for-profit corporation in Texas. While A.C.E. produces a fundamentalist, pro-American curriculum, and thus reinforces many of the values most important to members of Lakehaven, it involves a significant compromise. In separating the conception of education from its execution, the degree to which parents and educators have achieved a greater autonomy over the education of their children is open to debate.[7] More generally, the degree to which individualism as a value is manifested in institutional life, needs to be explored.

The working-class Baptists are oriented to a meaning system that values tradition and the individualism of self-reliance and privatism. The rhetoric of individualism compensates for the reality of their lives. The organizational style that characterizes their work, church, and school life demands conformity, and enforces a high degree of supervision and routinization. But the Lakehaven Baptists are willing to adopt a universalistic perspective, a system of rules and regulations that clearly defines a framework of authority in which they can know the rules and then operate as much as possible as "individuals" with little additional interference.

Their sense of coherence and autonomy comes from adapting to a set of rules that demands their allegiance but not the exposure of their innermost feelings and thoughts. The emphasis on external conformity to rules allows individuals to pursue their own inner lives privately. For example, in order to protect children's privacy and their right to equal education, Academy mothers volunteer in classrooms other than those of their own children. They want to treat everyone equally and are afraid that as mothers, they would give their children preferential treatment (whether positive or negative). They avoid this by not interfering. Furthermore, parents are not called in to witness the spiritual conversion of their child, but they are called in to witness a spanking. Concern rests more with the external control of behavior than with internal motivations and feelings.

The more middle-class charismatics, on the other hand, are oriented toward a meaning system that emphasizes the values of community, cooperation, change, and diversity. Their organizational style emphasizes self-direction, autonomy, and flexibility. They stress the special talents and roles of each individual and the power that a diverse group of individuals who complement and cooperate with one another can have in building community. Their sense of coherence and autonomy comes from acting as individuals who have already internalized group values. There is a greater sense of autonomy and self-direction but also a greater degree of censorship over internal motivations and attitudes. While the Covenant people are less oriented to rules and regulations and are more particularistic in their treatment of one another, they must be open to sharing their private thoughts and feelings with the community. Parents are not called in when their children are spanked, but they are involved when a child feels ready to accept Christ. Concern is with internal motivations rather than external control.

At Covenant, parents choose to work in the same classroom as their children. The primary objective is to spend more time with their children; to come to understand their children better by seeing them interact and perform in environments other than the family; to acquire a better sense of what is going on in the classroom; and to increase parental involvement and empowerment. Children's privacy is compromised for parental understanding. Perhaps as a result of their particularistic orientation, Covenant people tend to rate their school environment as more familial than do the Baptists.[8] But with that comes the pressure to perform, to be distinctive.

Both groups value the uniqueness of the individual but the emphasis is different. Lakehaven Baptists claim that they place the individual student at the center of their philosophy and educational system. Agreeing with the founder of the A.C.E. system, they argue that

individualism is theistic and must be re-established as a basic philosophy of education and philosophy of life for Christian education in this time of reform. . . . The conventional classroom is based upon a philosophy of conformity to the group. It forces an equality of teaching upon an inequality of learners. The uniqueness of the individual is sacrificed for the expediency and convenience of grouping. A.C.E. begins with the individual. All curriculum, placement testing, motivation, measurement, and progress are charted and graded on an individual basis.[9]

But while students are allowed to work at their own pace, universalistic criteria are used; the rules and regulations apply to everyone equally. Students are not encouraged to express themselves nor to explore their individuality or the individuality of others. The individualistic orientation of A.C.E. allows individuals to keep their own company with little interference from others; it stresses self-reliance. In fact, teachers are not considered central to learning for students can instruct themselves.

In contrast, Covenant considers the teacher–student relationship to be the most important factor affecting students' learning.

> The teachers are of vital importance in Covenant. . . .
> Because it is through them that the students are exposed to
> a tangible expression of the Holy Spirit, they are
> indispensable and cannot be replaced by any methods,
> textbooks, or materials. The vibrant life of the classroom is
> created by the teachers who establish the atmosphere in
> which the students operate. (Covenant handbook)

For Covenant people,

> success or failure rests on whether or not the students'
> hearts are opened. It has been learned that this comes
> through loving relationships, sensitivity to their [children's]
> needs, and much prayer. (Covenant handbook)

Positive relationships are at the center of their philosophy of education and of life:

> Jesus is an example to us of a holistic educator. He did not
> read the disciples a list of rules to follow in order to be
> godly men; He taught them by living and sharing His life
> with them. Christ's school was life itself. (Covenant
> handbook)

What this implies is that teachers should know their students personally and respond to them as individuals. The charismatics often refer to a child's disposition and how best to deal with a particular student. While the emphasis is placed on relationships, individuals are encouraged to express themselves and to explore their own identities. As Basil Bernstein suggests, an orientation towards the person rather than his or her position or status, means that the concept of self is more differentiated and more open to inquiry.

Thus, while each school recognizes and values both the

(universal) standard and the (particular) individual, they balance them differently. The Baptist rhetoric of individualism and the charismatic rhetoric of community serve to balance their respective use of universalistic criteria and particularistic criteria in educational practice. The rhetoric both helps to explain reality, and at the same time, compensate for it.

The ethic of individualism has been central to American thought, especially to evangelical thought. It finds expression in the centrality of the individual conversion experience: the most effective way to transform society is to save individuals, one by one. Throughout American history, evangelicals have focused on the sins of the individual rather than on the conditions of the society. This is one of their strong points: they do not reify "society." Rather they see society as nothing less than individuals coming together to agree upon certain norms of conduct and belief. What they tend to neglect, however, is that society may also be something more.

I too have argued that individuals have the potential to transform society and penetrate the boundaries of institutions that people have constructed. But it is naive to ignore the realities of institutional and structural forces (the environment, the economy, the polity, for instance) that strongly limit and resist the power of individuals and shape the parameters of their actions. Both institutional forces and the potency of socialization, whose primary goal is to prepare people to "fit into" society, powerfully define our lives and our perceptions. Basil Bernstein argues:

> Socialization is the process for making people safe. The process acts selectively on the possibilities of man by creating through time a sense of the inevitability of a given social arrangement, and through limiting the areas of permitted change. (p. 174)

Individuals are actors but they *negotiate* the realities of life which are defined by the interaction of material, ideological, organizational, and demographic factors.

In the next two chapters, we will explore what kinds of negotiations people at Lakehaven and Covenant have made. Chapter 9 examines issues of control and autonomy from a micro perspective. It focuses on the meaning and significance of the individual conversion experience and how it relates to the choices and anxieties of evangelical parents in contemporary American society. Chapter 10 likewise explores issues of control and autonomy, but from a macro perspective. It examines Christian education as a form of collective accommodation and resistance to the dominant culture of contemporary American society and speculates about its possible consequences.

9

Teaching Discipline: Socializing Disciples

> Train up a child in the way he should go, and when he is old he will not depart from it. (Proverbs 22:6)
>
> As the twig is bent, so is the tree inclined. (Virgil)

Keeping their children out of the hands of Satan is serious business, for in the words of Bob Dylan, "he who's not busy bein' born, is busy dyin'." In order to save them from Satan and prepare them for this life and the next, parents must teach their children how to submit to authority.

Disciplining in love is central to the child-rearing philosophy of evangelicals. Like their evangelical ancestors,[1] contemporary evangelicals believe that "children who learn to yield to the loving authority of their parents, will learn to yield to the loving authority of their Heavenly Father" (Covenant principal). The goal is for their young people to grow into disciples of Christ, being obedient to His higher Authority and spreading His Word. To prepare them for this ultimate submission, they teach their children to obey their parents, teachers, spiritual leaders, and civil authorities, but they warn against those who are not saved and who therefore are not considered legitimate authorities.

Members of both Lakehaven and Covenant are quick to point out that the word "disciple" derives from the same root as "discipline." They consider discipline to be essential to developing self-control and character in the child. Both communities refer to the Scripture that "to spare the rod is to spoil the child," but they also believe that if preventive measures are successful, there will be no need to use corporal punishment. The challenge, therefore, is to exercise enough control over children that they will not "force" the parent into reprimanding them with physical punishment.

Authority and control are central to both the socialization process and the conversion experience.[2] In order to feel in control of their own lives, parents need to exercise control over the lives of their children. Moreover, in order to protect their children from evil, evangelicals believe that they must act quickly before the secular world seduces their young.

In order to be saved by the grace of God, evangelicals believe that a person must understand the difference between right and wrong, the nature of sin, and the meaning of accepting Christ as one's personal Savior. In colonial America, this meant that most conversions occurred in people's late twenties and thirties, when they had achieved a certain personal and spiritual maturity. With each great awakening, however, the average age of conversion dropped; today, conversions among children are commonly reported. This represents a shift in theological thinking about the meaning, nature, and conditions of conversion and in the socio-psychological thinking about human development.

In American society, the transformative experience of conversion has been associated historically with adolescents' search for identity during the crisis years that bridge the passage from childhood to adulthood.[3] Embedded in a time of role uncertainty, religious conversion represents a break from childhood patterns and a stepping into new, unanticipated roles, that is, a rite of passage.[4] Today, a new pattern is developing; conversions are being reported much earlier in the lifecycle, among children as young as ages three to nine. In this case, conversion as a response to uncertainty may well represent parental anxiety more than the anxiety of the individual convert.

In her study of a fundamentalist community in New England, Nancy Ammerman reports that approximately 50% of conversions were among children or teenagers, although she does not specify the ages or percentages by age.[5] In my sample of 100 children at Covenant, approximately 50% of the children under the age of ten either reported or were reported to have had a conversion experience. Age five is a pivotal age, although a number of three-year old conversions were reported. Age five is considered to be a ripe time for childhood conversions since the child is considered old enough to understand the difference between right and wrong, and therefore the meaning of sin. Furthermore, it coincides with the transition of children from home to school, a rite of passage that is meaningful to both children and parents.

While my research did not focus on conversions, time after time people mentioned that their children had been "filled with the Holy Spirit." This intrigued me for the following two reasons: 1) I had found no record of such a pattern of early conversions in American social and religious history,[6] and 2) since the act of "being born-again" by their definition means that an individual understands and accepts Christ, the parents, teachers, and religious leaders must believe that young children are capable of understanding and committing their lives. The study of pre-teen conversions, then, became a rich area for the investigation of contemporary socialization goals and processes and the legitimation of the roles and religious experiences of young children by adults. Set against the background of the earlier history of the phenomenon, these precocious conversions have particular meaning.

I suggest that the interaction between uncertainty about parenting in the dominant society; current conceptions of child development; anxiety over children entering adolescence; and the direction and support that evangelical parents find through their church–home–school networks, have contributed to the relatively new phenomenon of pre-teen conversions and the proliferation of Christian schools.

Contemporary authors, writing books with such titles as *The Disappearance of Childhood*, *The Erosion of Childhood*, and *Children Without Childhood* argue that childhood is disappearing,[7] or at the least, hurried.[8] Evangelicals would agree; they place the blame, however, on secular humanism and the secular world. Therefore, they encourage and legitimate conversions among pre-teen children in order to protect them from "loss of innocence" and its negative consequences. At the same time, they seek to preserve that childhood and "to keep their children from the world."

Before moving into a final discussion of socialization at Covenant and the Academy, I want to take a short diversion into the history of conversions. I think this will provide some useful background for thinking about the issues of control which are central to the socialization process.

Control, conversions, and the life course

During each of the Four Great Awakenings, the majority of converts has been drawn from the ranks of adolescents. The transforming experience of conversion interacts with other transitions that are taking place in the life of the adolescent, as well as in the larger culture. The early studies of Edwin Starbuck[9] and William James[10] analyzed the "natural relationship" between youth and religion, a relationship that had been observed during previous awakenings. These studies defined adolescence as a life-stage. Characterized as enthusiastic, idealistic, and impressionistic, American youth throughout the nineteenth century was most ready to experiment with religious movements.

The processes involved in assessing self and society are the very ones that characterize adolescence as a dynamic "life-stage." The young, then, are particularly susceptible to religious experimentation, for one of their main tasks, searching for meaning, is essentially a religious one. Their involvement in identity formation encourages them to question and redefine social norms as well as personal values. Nancy Cott draws from Erik Erikson's theory of identity formation to explain the relationship between role uncertainty and religious experimentation in the Second Great Awakening: the less secure people are about the roles they are to fill, the more likely they are to turn to an ideological framework that makes sense out of the situation and offers them a guide to behavior.[11] Suspended between childhood and adulthood, adolescents are more occupied *searching for* rather than *living up* to standards and roles. They are caught in a transitional period marked by relative deprivation because society's uncertainty about expectations and roles renders adolescents incapable of fulfilling them. Thus, the study of conversion experiences throughout the Four Great Awakenings provides one way of examining critical disjunctures in the lives of individuals and society.

The First Great Awakening (1730–1760)

Prior to the First Great Awakening, the average convert was thirty years of age.[12] According to spiritual autobiographies and ministerial tracts of the seventeenth century, the conversion experience of the "middle-aged" convert was considered to be a mature experience, the result of a long, lonely, painful, and often terrifying journey. Sudden "crisis conversion" experiences were seen as suspect.[13] By the First Great Awakening, however, slow, torturous rebirths tended to be replaced by immediate, radical "crisis-conversion" experiences. This theological shift implied that the less spiritually developed could experience rebirth, and indeed they did: the average age at conversion declined with the revivals of the First Great Awakening.[14] Philip Greven argues that demographic factors contributed to the declining ages at conversion and also to the predominance of male converts. In a study of converts in eighteenth-century Andover, he discovered that earlier conversion experiences accompanied declining ages for marriage and property acquisition. During the period 1711–1719, men usually married and acquired property late and rarely became full members of the church before the age of thirty. In the period 1729–1749, all of these indicators dropped and, concomitantly, public professions of faith were found most frequently among those aged fifteen to twenty-four.[15]

Building on the premise that conversion is in part a religious response to uncertainty, Patricia Tracy offers an explanation as to why conversion was especially common among males. While his Colonial brothers had received land from the community or inherited it from their fathers, the young man of the First Great Awakening found that both land and capital were scarce. Furthermore, the First Great Awakening encouraged men by offering ministerial opportunities that were not contingent upon financial or land resources or established clerical offices.[16] Thus, people were inclined to conversion at younger ages because of theological legitimation of younger converts, life-stage susceptibility, and social and economic conditions that created uncertainty among young males.

The Second Great Awakening (1790–1840)

In the years after the First Great Awakening, the number of conversions decreased and the average age at conversion increased. The revivals of the Second Great Awakening once again reversed these trends; they not only attracted but often started among young teenagers.[17] Joan Brumberg states, "It is a simple fact of antebellum life that the youth of America provided the raw material of the Second Great Awakening."[18]

The younger age at conversion was consistent with the First Great Awakening. However, a gender shift had occurred: girls now outnumbered boys. Nancy Cott describes the economic situation in New England which led to a shifting of the uncertainty from men to women, and consequently, the greater susceptibility to conversion among young, unmarried women. Between the First and Second Great Awakenings, the shift from household to market economy was well underway.[19] These developments increased both opportunities and uncertainties for young women. Leaving home for the factory often meant working and living with strangers in unfamiliar towns, as well as stepping into roles for which women had not been socialized. To add to the unpredictability of the future, there was, in this period, a surplus of women of marriageable age and a shift from parental to "couple control" over the arrangement of relationships. Thus, neither the young woman's work within the home nor her marriage was as secure as it had been during the First Great Awakening.

The Second Great Awakening offered liberating opportunities to women, just as the First Great Awakening had to frustrated young men.[20] Female seminaries flourished by 1850; teaching, foreign missions, and charitable societies provided work and volunteer opportunities; and many of the denominations granted important and often equal roles to women.[21]

The Third Great Awakening (1890–1920)

The First Great Awakening belonged predominantly to young, middle- and lower-class men of New England and the Southern poor; and the Second to the small-town, rural middle class—especially young, unmarried women. The Third Great Awakening largely involved young, rural, middle-class Americans who immigrated to the cities.[22] White, Anglo-Saxon, Protestant, rural Americans arrived in the urban areas finding that they had to compete with recent immigrants of various ethnic and religious backgrounds for space, jobs, and influence. The more liberal Social Gospel Movement and the Christian Socialists who concentrated on the needs of the lowest immigrant classes failed to reach "a vast, undigested middle class transplanted from the farm."[23] For them, evangelicalism responded to and reinforced traditional values associated with the Protestant work ethic: respect for authority, patriotism, and the supremacy of Protestantism. Evangelicalism emphasized individual salvation, independent of the state of society and the sins of other men; its focus was on individual character, not social conditions.

According to Edwin Starbuck, the majority of converts during the Third Great Awakening fell between the ages of thirteen and seventeen. Thus, he argues, *"conversion is a distinctively adolescent phenomenon."*[24] In his study of 1,265 converts, Starbuck writes, "We may safely lay it down as a law, then, that among the females there are two tidal waves of religious awakening at about thirteen and sixteen, followed by a less significant period at eighteen; while among the males the great wave is at about sixteen, preceded by a wavelet at twelve, and followed by a surging up at eighteen or nineteen."[25] In explaining why conversions fell within the range of ten and twenty years of age, Starbuck concludes that *"the child of very early years is impressionable, to be sure, but before it can attain spiritual insight it must have a certain degree of mental grasp, some capacity to see in abstract terms, and an ability to feel deeply."*[26]

The Fourth Great Awakening (1960–the present)

Converts of the Fourth Great Awakening continue to be young, with females being disproportionately represented.[27] A study of Billy Graham crusades indicates that the majority of converts are white, middle-class teenagers of Anglo-Saxon or Northern European ancestry brought up in mainstream denominations. In the Knoxville crusade of 1970, over half were less than sixteen years of age and came from families with higher levels of education than the general area population. They came disproportionately from professional and managerial families and from the Southern Baptist church rather than from low-status sects or high-status churches. Ninety-three percent were church members.[28] For many Southern Baptist youth, a severe disjuncture between their religious upbringing and their conversion experience did not exist.

The experiences of Southern Baptist youth provide an interesting contrast with those young people involved in the countercultural movement of the 1960s who later became involved in evangelical religion. For many of these counter-cultural youth, the "born-again" experience was preceded by intermittent experimentation with a variety of secular and religious forms. Many flocked to conservative, evangelical sects after experimenting with drugs, secular therapies, and individualized forms of psycho-religious expression.[29] However, many of the Southern Baptist and countercultural youth shared a sense of disorientation and disillusionment in a time of personal transition and cultural crisis and an affinity for an evangelical response and resolution. Thus, these adolescent conversion experiences are still common today, representing a continuous thread through all of the Awakenings. But there appears to be a new phenomenon peculiar to the Fourth Great Awakening: *the frequent born-again experiences of pre-teens*.

In previous Awakening periods, the community and church were more closely aligned and had greater control over the socialization of the young. With increased secularization in the public schools and larger society and greater privatization of religion,[30] many evangelical families have taken on more of the responsibility for the moral development of their children. But they often feel overwhelmed in their task. Looking for support, evangelicals are attempting to return to a time when families and schools provided consistent environments for their children. Barbara Finkelstein's description of urban schooling in the nineteenth and twentieth centuries would surely appeal to them:

> In the midst of diverse world views and expanding
> possibilities, [schools] sought to circumscribe the lives of the
> young—to enclose them in constant and close-knit
> affiliations in a universe of shared symbols.[31]

Evangelicals are attempting to recreate this in the Fourth Great Awakening by establishing their own organizations. But they do so in the context of a secularized and diverse society. Finding the competition from secular sources to be strong, they realize that they cannot "enclose" their children forever.

The evangelical response is to secure their children under God's mantle before they are seduced by the secular world and secular humanism. By establishing Christian schools in which they can shelter their students and censor materials according to their own guidelines, evangelicals are attempting to preserve the "innocence" of childhood. They borrow the phrase from contemporary psychology, "It is easier to build children than to rebuild men," for "if we don't train them, the world will."

Many contemporary evangelicals believe that children are old enough to understand their sinfulness and the need to commit themselves to Christ. But a child's "spiritual insight" and conversion experience is likely to be seen as qualitatively different from an adult's.[32] For example, one Covenant mother talked about the conversion experience of her son at three years of age:

> He asked Jesus into his heart. He knew the difference
> between right and wrong, and he knew that he had done
> wrong and therefore was a sinner. So Jesus came, and he
> knew Him—in his three-year old way. As he has gotten
> older, he has come to know Jesus better and more fully.
> Something very special happened over Christmas. He had a
> vision of God [the boy is now age eleven].

Another father explained that children can know the difference between right and wrong at an early age. Although it depends on the temperament of the child, the religious maturity of the parents, and their commitment to Christ, he argues that they can be ready by around the age of three, although age five is more common:

> I give communion to my children, and I say to them, "*As much as you know Christ*, take this and eat . . ." The child will then grow in his understanding of the Lord, just as adults are babes upon their second birth and need to be nurtured and raised in the Lord.

Both child and adult converts are viewed as babes who must be nurtured by Christians more mature in their spiritual walk with God. Spiritual development is viewed as progressive and continual. To be saved, people need to recognize themselves as sinners and open their hearts to Christ, but they do not need much formal preparation or instruction. The conversion secures them in Christ, and *begins* rather than *completes their spiritual journey*.

For Sarah, baptism in the Holy Spirit was a first, and very important, step. In fact, when she announced in her 3rd grade class one day that she was to be baptized the following day, the teacher expressed some surprise. The teacher, however, did not question the decision which was Sarah's and her parents', but she did ask how she had prepared for it. Sarah responded:

> Well, the past few weeks I've been battling the devil and have had a hard time being nice to everyone and stuff like that, so my Mom said if I were baptized, then I would have more help and power to fight off evil. I wanted to be baptized in water, but Mom said in the Holy Spirit.

For many adults, baptism in the Holy Spirit and in water happens simultaneously; for children the process is more likely to be a step-wise progression and their transitions slower and more distinct.

The radical conversion experience is more likely to be

experienced by an adult; *for the child, conversion is part of the socialization process rather than a form of re-socialization whereby one breaks from one's past and establishes a new self, lifestyle, and reference group.* In recreating a conversion experience for their children, parents want to save their children from going through what they went through and to shelter them from the mistakes that they made. In this sense, the childhood conversion may be seen as a preventive rather than a corrective measure. This is not to say that the childhood conversion experience is artificially manufactured by parents; if it is to be valid (in the short run and in the long run), it must be real and meaningful to the child. It must represent a genuine commitment.

At Covenant, parents are contacted immediately if the child feels he or she is ready to accept Christ. "We do not convert students; that would be like adopting them. If a child is readied and feeling the Spirit, we call the parents" (Covenant teacher). Believing that the responsibility for training children lies with the parents, they consider it the right and privilege of parents to be with their children when they undergo "the most important and significant experience of their lives."

At the Academy, if a child is inspired through worship or a missionary's talk to receive Christ, then the faculty will pray with that child, encouraging him or her to accept Christ on the spot. Altar calls are a regular part of school worship but the conversion is considered an individual experience whose time cannot be controlled by man: "We don't want to jam it down their throats" (Academy principal). At the end of the school day, the child is free to go home and tell his parents about his "born-again" experience, but the school does not necessarily or systematically inform parents.

This reveals important distinctions between the two groups in how they define the conversion experience and in the arenas in which parents exercise control. For the Baptists, being "born-again" involves a conversion experience that centers around the individual and God; if it's time, it's time and no human can interfere. Moreover, once saved, one is saved forever. The charismatics' treatment of childhood conversion suggests that they believe the timing can be directed to some extent—"wait until you're home with your parents." Although it is a personal experience between the individual and God, it can be and should be shared collectively.

Theories of socialization have focused on social requisites; on individual potentialities; and on the experiences, competencies, and actions—both conscious and unconscious—of the socializing agent. A comprehensive model of socialization needs to incorporate all of these factors, for the process of enculturation responds to and shapes individual and social needs and values, and operates at both conscious (deliberate) and unconscious (unintentional) levels. In investigating the process of socialization, it is important to consider the interaction of personal, psychological, biological, cultural, social, and historical factors. One needs to consider "the person, process, and context."[33] In the next chapter, we examine the cultural and social contexts of Christian education from a more macro perspective.

10

Re-creation or Re-production?
A Critique of Christian Schools

> Neither the life of an individual nor the history of a society
> can be understood without understanding both. Yet men do
> not usually define the troubles they endure in terms of
> historical change and institutional contradiction. The well-
> being they enjoy, they do not usually impute to the big ups
> and downs of the societies in which they live. [They are]
> seldom aware of the intricate connection between the
> patterns of their own lives and the course of world history.[1]

In this passage, C. Wright Mills discusses the difficulties and
hence, the challenges that we all encounter as people trying to
make our way in this world. The dilemma is all the more
poignant for parents who serve as mediators between society and
the individual. Their repertoire as socializers comes from their
own upbringing and experiences, as well as from their anticipation of their children's future roles and experiences. But parents
are not alone in this task; other sources compete for influence
over the young. The structure and requisites of our society
powerfully frame our possibilities and desires for action in ways
that may often transcend our awareness.

Parents are negotiating their way in this world, and they are
trying to prepare their children to become, in Vandenburg's
terms, "at home in the world." They want them to be able to
function "successfully," however they may define the term. The
difficulty for parents often is in anticipating what kind of world
their children may enter and what kind of roles they should
prepare them for—be they part of the dominant culture or
resistant to it.

The establishment of Christian schools in the midst of a society that values educational conformity requires energy, confidence, and resourcefulness. It represents both an act of rebellion and commitment. Yet the form that these schools take also reveals that it is an act of accommodation. While evangelicals are challenging the established order of American public education, in many ways they are also reproducing the social structure of American society.

My primary interest in writing this book was to give the reader an in-depth look at two evangelical Christian fellowships and schools. The book has been largely descriptive in an attempt to understand better "Christian" education from as neutral a perspective as possible. Now I want to offer a critique of the schools: the possibilities they offer and the limitations they suggest.

Throughout the book, we have discussed the intentions of evangelical parents and educators and how they have attempted to enact their values and commitments. It is now time to question what some of the unintended consequences of Christian schools may be. The following discussion raises some hard questions— questions that should be asked by evangelical and non-evangelical alike. What is it that "we" want for our children and how do we best go about achieving it? What are the requisites of our society and to what degree do they shape our decisions; to what degree do our questions and decisions need to evaluate and reshape those requisites?

It is clear that the "we" here presumes a consensus that does not exist.[2] In fact, the rhetoric of imagined consensus represents attempts to cover up the conflict that exists in the educational arena. Schools are loci of conflict because people come from different backgrounds, have different interests to protect, and therefore, different ideas about how to educate their children. Moreover, people have different ideas about how to educate different groups of children dependent upon class, color, creed, and gender. Schools are not equal in the United States, either qualitatively or quantitatively. The inequalities and conflict in the educational arena are just as real, poignant, and political as they are in the economic, labor, and political arenas precisely because all these arenas are embedded in the same interactive system.

This point is clearly understood by evangelicals involved in "Christian" education. In the context of the symbolic crusade that they are waging, they continually confront questions of value, power, status, influence, and economics. They are both resisting the dominant cultural ideology which they call "secular humanism," and at the same time, are trying to maintain and strengthen evangelical Christianity. Once again we are reminded of the quotation by Rushdoony: "The battle for the Christian school is the battle for the faith."

Christian schools represent the mobilization efforts of evangelicals to establish greater control over the socialization and education of the young, and therefore, over the future of society. These parents and educational leaders of the Christian school movement want to protect their children from the degradation of modern, secular life—although they attempt this in very different ways. How successful they are depends upon the criteria by which one judges success. In the creation of Christian schools, we see neither total rejection of secular processes (can we even envision what this might mean?) nor a total acceptance of traditional, patriarchal, evangelical ways. This act of compromise involves myriad contradictions as they selectively reject, accept, and appropriate modern ideas, conveniences, and lifestyles.

Success for the people of Lakehaven and Covenant means keeping one's integrity and faithfulness in the midst of a corrupt and corrupting world. It means, in the older version of the American work ethic, that to be a good businessman, you must also be an honest businessman and a good family man and citizen. Both groups are trying to resist, in their own ways, the mass commercialization of culture, blatant materialism, and the erosion of ethical guidelines. They value the ability to trust one's neighbors more than the ability to exploit and profit from them. But they are not naive. They also know that they need to provide for their families, to find and keep decent work, and to prepare their children for future roles. They also know that this has become increasingly difficult.

The skills and values they want their children to possess are the same ones that good Christian men and women were supposed to have possessed throughout the other awakenings. In holding on to their faith and resisting cynicism, they teach their children the "old" biblical and republican ethic of success that was embedded in civic responsibility.[3] They pass on their belief, or at least their hope, in the mythic hero of Horatio Alger—before he was seduced into becoming the "Happy Hooker" who would sell anything, including himself.[4]

This the two communities share, although again their definitions of success reflect their different class interests and life chances. The Baptists tend to define success as "not becoming a bum or going on welfare." Parents and teachers emphasize obedience and the importance of respecting authority. In working-class fashion, they stress the value of doing what one is told to do in the context of institutional life. Even though you may realize that the person in charge is not wiser or more competent than you, you should keep your opinions to yourself, do the work you are supposed to do, and keep your own good counsel that is grounded in the wisdom of God. Only then you will receive your reward.

The Academy boys want to find jobs, preferably ones that are not too confining or boring, and most of them eventually want to marry. While most of the boys want to learn a trade, some of them plan to go on to college. The girls want to marry a good Christian man: someone who has an even temper and does not drink too much. (These descriptions are strikingly similar to those presented by Lilian Rubin in her study of working-class families.) Increasingly, the girls want to go to college and work before they marry—and more of them are doing just that.

Parents and religious and educational leaders at the Academy are very proud of the fact that the majority of Academy students are now going on to college. (The percentage of students going to college has increased since 1983; between 1983–1986, ten out of twelve graduates went on to college.) The vast majority enroll in Christian colleges (including Pensacola, Bob Jones University, Liberty Baptist, Grace, and Practical Bible College); the remaining few tend to enroll in Community colleges. For them this represents a major advancement; most are first generation college-bound. But the fact that many of these students are not likely to be economically or occupationally better off or more upwardly mobile than their parents, limits the "real" advancements that they once may have made by earning college degrees.

Their families are aware of this, reporting that now to get a skilled job or sometimes even unskilled labor, one needs a college degree. Nonetheless, they are proud of the fact that their children are able to attend and perform in college.

In contrast, the middle-class charismatics define success as "living a happy, rich, and full Christian life." When asked, they say they want their children to live meaningful and happy lives. While they teach respect for authority, they stress good communication skills and the importance of personal discernment.

The majority of children and their parents assume that Covenant students will enroll in some sort of higher education (because the first group of students is just now graduating, it is impossible to compare the rates of college enrollment.) The majority of both girls and boys say that they want to find meaningful, challenging, exciting work which pays well; marry good Christians; and have a family. The major difference between the boys and girls is that girls anticipate either discontinuing or interrupting their work when they decide to have children.

Every society offers certain opportunities to its citizens and blocks others; moreover, these opportunities are usually stratified in some fashion. Because of their cultural and class backgrounds, the opportunities perceived to be generally available by the Covenant people are quite different from those perceived by the Lakehaven people. This, I would suggest, affects the kind of schooling they consider reasonable and feasible for their students.

Both schools have attempted to structure their schools to realize their goals as best they think they can; and both realize that the actual operation of the school does not match the ideal visions they may have. In fact, like most of us they are not exactly sure what that "ideal" educational system would involve even if they could operate without restrictions. But they do feel that they have had the power to establish their own schools and to improve in some ways on systems that had been available to them previously.

But in separating their children, Christian schools not only may be resisting mainstream public education, but also may be reproducing more effectively a stratified society than their public school counterparts. This is not to say that they are intentionally

201

doing such or that there is a one-to-one correspondence between the world of school and the world of work and economic relations. But it is to say that we need to examine the ways in which they are interrelated. How will these children's Christian education serve them as they enter the work world of the 1990s, and how might it serve the capitalist, political economy of contemporary American society?

Although theories of reproduction can be too economistic and reductionistic, they are important and central to understanding the process of schooling in American society. Therefore, this chapter focuses on the processes of cultural production and reproduction in order to raise questions about the kinds of bargains evangelicals may be forging as they negotiate their way in contemporary American society.

Samuel Bowles and Herbert Gintis have argued that schools are conservative institutions that reproduce the consciousness of the dominant ruling class:

> How does the educational system reproduce consciousness? In a very general way, schooling fosters and rewards the development of certain capacities and the expression of certain needs, while thwarting and penalizing others, and by tailoring the self-concepts, aspirations, and social class identifications of individuals to the capitalist division of labor.[5]

Melvin Kohn concurs:

> Bowles and Gintis are essentially correct in their observations . . . that schools teach children to value conformity to authority, or in the higher grades to value self-direction, not by preaching at them, but by organizing their lives in ways that are conducive to their valuing one or the other.[6]

According to "correspondence principle" and "post correspondence" theory,[7] schools reflect the hierarchical relations of production and prepare students for the world of work. The public school, a socializing institution invested with the responsibility of transmitting social values to the masses of individuals, in some ways serves to reproduce the values, beliefs, and behavior of the dominant society. But it does more than that. As Michael W. Apple argues in *Education and Power*, schools are also producers of culture; students and teachers are actors as well as the "acted upon." Socialization is a reciprocal process.

Such complexities are revealed in the ethnographies of Covenant and the Academy. Both schools are resisting the cultural hegemony of commercial culture and the liberalizing influences of the women's and civil rights' movements. By appropriating the values, expectations, and roles of the working and middle classes, they are maximizing the economic and cultural capital which they have achieved or been given.

Thus, the two schools, one operated by a church of working-class, rural Baptists and the other by a middle-class charismatic fellowship, are doing more than preparing their students for a proper Christian life. They are both resisting and reinforcing the values of the secular world. While the schools provide alternative education, they also reinforce the social hierarchy of our society by socializing their children to adapt to certain class roles.

Studies of public schools have shown that lower-class and minority schools and curricula tend to emphasize conformity to external rules and exhibit a high degree of discipline.[8] This kind of training prepares them for the kinds of jobs they are most likely to find after graduation: jobs characterized by greater conformity, routinization, and supervision than those their upper middle-class counterparts will be getting.[9]

> This socialization pattern corresponds with the needs of the unskilled workers who need primarily to defer to authority; to respond passively to orders; to accept alienation from work and to become one of the faceless multitudes at the bottom of the work hierarchy.[10]

In contrast, upper middle-class schools and curricula tend to emphasize the internalization of values and self-direction over conformity to rules, adopting a model of decision making that involves negotiations among the students, faculty, and administration.[11] Specialized study groups, individual projects, and flexible scheduling are more characteristic of upper-class schools than lower-class schools. Just as middle- and upper-class parents tend to value self-direction in their children, a reflection of their own work experience,[12] their schools (or upper-level classes within the schools) tend to enforce this philosophy. The flexible curricula and schedules and the negotiation of the rules prepare these students for work in which they are likely to experience a relatively high degree of autonomy and non-routinization; a need to make choices among alternative strategies and to supervise others; and the need to engage in negotiations between co-workers and clients.

Rather than utilize the "tracking system" which separates the different social classes within a heterogeneous public school, Christian schools tend to select a relatively homogeneous student population, most often drawn from the ranks of the sponsoring congregation. The majority of members of a specific church tend to share similar class backgrounds, interests, lifestyles, and aspirations for their children. When the church, family, and school join together to create a mutually reinforcing socializing network, values and beliefs may be more efficiently transmitted to their children than in those public socializing institutions which are ambiguous or contradictory about their goals. While elite private academies have long been seen as socializing children for appropriate roles, lifestyles, and social networks of the upper class, and military academies as providing the needed discipline and adherence to authority required of military men, this kind of analysis has seldom been used to examine the socializing functions of religious schools.

My findings indicate that the working/agricultural class Baptists have organized a school that stresses conformity to external demands and relies on rules to regulate students' behavior. They are transmitting their view of the world as a place in which individuals need to conform to certain prescribed behaviors and expectations in order to preserve themselves as *good* Christians. With their highly standardized form of Accelerated Christian Education (A.C.E.), they are pleased that their system is well suited to preparing disciplined, punctual, obedient, conforming, and self-instructed students who will make "good workers." Recall the words of the Academy principal:

> The military is pleased with A.C.E. students because they
> are disciplined, obedient, and respect authority—they make

good workers. And that's not all that easy to come by these days. Not that I want all of them going into the military—I'd like to see some of them going into Christian ministries.

The parents and educators of the Academy students are making compromises that have elements of what Michael W. Apple calls "good and bad sense." They realize that their own and their children's opportunities are limited. Therefore, they "create" an educational environment that better insures their students learn the basics and become well-disciplined workers. Moreover, by reproducing an environment that relies on a restricted code and traditional values, many of the children tend to feel quite comfortable and secure. Their most fundamental values and beliefs are not challenged, nor is their self-esteem put on the line by teachers who may devalue their working-class, fundamentalist culture.

In the case of the Academy, the teachers come from the same background as the parents, and the children do not experience any great disjuncture between the language and values of their working-class, fundamentalist homes and the school. In this sense, the Academy and A.C.E. may have something to offer the working-class and problem students; they may escape much of the humiliation and devaluation that they are likely to experience in the average public school. In fact, Academy students report feeling quite comfortable with the structure of their schooling.

The contradiction, however, is that by resisting what Academy parents and educators often think of as the "snobbish intellectuality" of the public schools (where their children are disproportionately tracked into the "slower" classes), they reproduce patterns of communication and thinking that are likely to limit their children's possibilities in the future. The children of the Academy may become "good workers," but they may not become full citizens.

In contrast, the middle-class charismatic parents and educators challenge their students to think more critically. Like all parents, they want to instill their values and beliefs but the process of instruction is more important than the specific content. Group work, discussions that examine a spectrum of values and beliefs, and various strategies for formulating and resolving problems characterize school life. Challenge and interpretation rather than conformity and security are stressed.

Covenant people are communicating their view of the world as a place in which individuals are actors who, in cooperation with one another, can transform the world. In contrast to the Baptist emphasis on individual discipline, the middle-class charismatics stress self-directed and cooperative work in their children's education. The charismatics anticipate their children entering roles that will enable them to act on the world. As John Meyer and David Kamens explain:

> The allocation function of schools . . . affects their socialization capacity via the mechanism of anticipatory socialization.[13]

Charismatic parents encourage their young people to explore possibilities and then to obtain the best training they can in that particular field. If it takes attending a secular college to do this, that's okay. "If Christians are going to work effectively in this world, then it is important that they get the best possible training" (Covenant school principal). None of the Covenant students has yet reached the age to enroll in college, but the high school students are considering a variety of possibilities (mostly secular), from Ivy League schools to small liberal arts college to state universities; a minority are considering Christian colleges. Most of the Covenant parents expect their children to be competitive in the professional job market—"not in order to be successful in worldly concerns, but to be able to influence society from a position of power and strength."

The economics of schooling

What role are Christian schools playing in contemporary American society? Are Christian schools the vanguard of a new educational structure, or will they continue to present merely one alternative to the mainstream educational system in America? Could they be the forerunners of a kind of social reproduction that better serves a society which has become, and shows every sign of continuing to be, increasingly dominated by the needs and values of large corporations? Are these schools the testing ground for direct reproduction of a less egalitarian and more self-consciously stratified society?

Public schools prospered in the United States at a time when the economic prospects of most Americans were being affected for the better. The 1930s and 1940s were the only years in the twentieth century when income was redistributed from the well-to-do to the rest of society. This period of increasing economic equality was followed by a long period of prosperity, the 1950s and 1960s, during which the relative incomes of all social classes were increasing.[14] Many people's expectations were high: schools were to be the great equalizers that would usher in a truly democratic society, and eliminate poverty and crime.[15] Although "tracking" and differential drop-out rates belied the supposed egalitarianism of the public school system and supported the implicit ideology of perpetuating existing social divisions, the contradictions inherent in the slippage between the promise and process of education were tolerated. The premise that "universal, compulsory, and free" education would benefit everyone persisted because people actually were becoming better off economically.

Most people did not improve their economic status in the 1970s and 1980s. This can be confirmed by a number of economic measures: weekly earnings for wage-earners actually dropped; the proportion of middle-income families declined sharply while the number of poor increased; wealth and income have been steadily redistributed to the upper classes. Between 1969 and 1982, the income share of the bottom 70% of the population slipped from 43% to 38%; almost all of this was gained by the top 10% whose income climbed from 29% to 33%.[16] The average full-time wage earner today has a weekly income of $176 when adjusted for inflation, compared to $184 in 1967. Figures from the United States Bureau of Labor Statistics indicate that the "middle class" (those earning between $17,000 and $41,000 per year) is shrinking fast: it dropped from 53% to 42% of American households between 1978 and 1983.

There is every indication that the economic expectations of many or most Americans will not improve in the 1990s. Manufacturing jobs are being lost to robots or are being transferred abroad to Third-World countries where wage rates are extremely low. The projections for future jobs indicate significant growth in areas which require low levels of skill and offer low pay: according to the Bureau of Labor Statistics, by 1995 the top three employment categories generating jobs will be building custodians (779,000 new jobs), cashiers (744,000), and secretaries (719,000).[17]

It is in this era of economic decline that Christian schools have prospered. The explicit ideology of the Christian schools states that they are withdrawing students from the sinful and undisciplined atmosphere of the public schools and resisting the "worldly" practices of the larger and dominant secular society. The irony of their educational practice, however, is that they may come to serve better the educational needs of late twentieth-century American society. The A.C.E. Baptists are creating a controlled educational environment appropriate to the economic prospects of their children. They are, in effect, choosing to institute a system of education that limits the social status and employment expectations and opportunities of their children. They are adapting to an era of diminished economic expectations. Given robotization and employment projections of increasing numbers of service jobs, it is likely that their children will have even fewer opportunities for interesting work than they have had—that is, for successfully operating a small farm, taking up a mechanical or construction trade, finding employment as a skilled factory worker, or operating a small store or service shop. Low levels of skill and cognitive development will be required for the jobs which the Baptist children are likely to enter.

Harry Braverman, in *Labor and Monopoly Capital: The Degradation of Work in the Twentieth Century*, has demonstrated the progressive devaluation of skill and aptitude required of workers in modern corporate enterprises. Part of the process of creating a malleable and cooperative work force is dependent upon continually simplifying the work process and limiting the individual human control over complicated fabrication or assembly. Because a working person is easily replaced by another unskilled or de-skilled individual, the corporate production rate cannot be disrupted as easily as in the past, when disgruntled skilled workers could show their displeasure with working conditions by engaging in a work slowdown or strike. These "over-educated" workers were often irreplaceable, thus less manageable. The education offered at the Baptist Academy appears to anticipate the future of efficient, corporate-oriented instruction. The emphasis on orderliness and discipline at the "office" learning station realistically mirrors the working stations of many present and future jobs. The increasingly automated and computerized clerical or office job requires someone who is willing and able to sit at a word processor or computer terminal for an entire day with little or no interaction with fellow workers. Progress in the factory means more automated or robotized machinery operated or watched by solitary people who are attentive to sporadic requests from the control board.

The A.C.E. program stresses the extreme self-discipline and isolation required of each student at his or her "work-station." The pre-packaged learning program of A.C.E. creates a monologue of instructions rather than a dialogue; no longer is the teacher needed to communicate knowledge to or engage in joint activities with students. Thus, A.C.E. is keeping up with the times. It uses a system of transmitting information through manuals under the direction of adults who are more like supervisors than teachers, who are not as well educated or well paid as public-school teachers. This correlates nicely with the standardization of production and procedures now practiced by many large corporations in the service, manufacturing, insurance, and banking fields. Low- and middle-level managers all over the country (and all over the world) use extensive operations manuals to instruct and govern the smallest procedures performed by the employees they supervise; the manuals even severely limit the kinds of decisions the managers themselves can make. The A.C.E. methods reflect, in a more extreme form, the de-skilling and re-skilling process which is taking place in curricular reform in the public schools.[18] As Michael W. Apple observes:

> The encroachment of technical control procedures is
> exemplified by the exceptionally rapid growth in the use of
> pre-packaged sets of curricular materials . . . that include
> statements of objectives, all of the curricular content and
> material needs, prespecified teacher actions and appropriate

student responses, and diagnostic and achievement tests coordinated within the system.[19]

A.C.E. takes pre-packaged curricular systems and teaching models, such as the one Madeline Hunter[20] presents, to their extreme. What are the consequences? Apple argues,

> With the large scale influx of pre-packaged material, planning is separated from execution. . . . As procedures of technical control enter the school in the guise of pre-designed curricular/teaching/evaluation "systems," teachers are being deskilled. . . . While the deskilling involves the loss of craft, the atrophy of educational skills, the reskilling involves the substitution of the skills and ideological visions of management. . . . As teachers lose control of the curricular and pedagogic skills to large publishing houses, these skills are replaced by techniques for better controlling students.[21]

The Academy and other Christian schools that use A.C.E. or similar educational systems are providing an alternative that may help to restructure the educational system of the United States in conformity with the needs of advanced capitalist society. A.C.E., initially used by two-thirds of the Christian schools established in the last decade, is cheap, about one-third the cost of public school education. And it is spreading around the world. A.C.E. reports having close to 600 schools in eighty-six countries. It also produces diligent, unquestioning workers.

> Studies of industrial and office settings suggest that: Increasing rationalization and a more sophisticated level of control tend to encourage people to manifest: a "rules orientation," where workers are aware of rules and procedures and the habit of following them; greater dependability . . .; and the internalization of the enterprise's goals and values, where conflict is minimized and slowly, but surely, there tends to be a homogenization of interests between management and employees.[22]

It is unlikely, at this point in our history, that an elite upper class could openly impose the bottom tier of a two-tiered education system upon working-class people. Parents would be outraged if A.C.E. methods were proposed as an alternate education for students with lesser prospects in the public schools; or if school boards were to say they could no longer afford to spend the money and effort which they currently spend on "universal" education; or if corporations were to suggest that they had much cheaper and more efficient ways to educate a large part of the workforce which would never be needed for professional or skilled jobs in the future. Parents and communities would object that this was an unfair and un-American proposition. Yet by combining the A.C.E. format with the goals of small fundamentalist congregations, the working-class children have effectively been separated from middle-class, college-bound students. This is a much cleaner method of selection than the "tracking" programs used for public junior and senior high school students. In fact, because of the nature of the education, A.C.E. students are unlikely to challenge the kind of education they are receiving or to question whether or not they have been "educated." Given their isolation in work stations, they are much less able as a group to create patterns of "resistance" of the type Paul Willis observed in working-class youth.[23] Indeed, they may be getting the best preparation possible for the army, the factory, or the automated office.

The very reproduction of A.C.E. programs is modeled on the corporate franchise through which one buys the package that simultaneously makes one an independent purveyor of culture and an agent of corporate culture that blankets the nation. A.C.E. is a for-profit corporation operating out of Texas with a nationwide network of approximately 5,000 entrepreneurs who pay for the use of the A.C.E. system. A.C.E. began in 1970 with forty-five students. By 1972, there were 4,000; by 1974, 30,000; by 1976, 80,000; by 1978, 160,000; by 1980, 275,000 students. As of 1986, A.C.E. operates some 5,900 schools throughout the United States and in eighty-six foreign countries. The average school size is thirty-five to seventy students. Moreover, they provide curriculum to 1,600 families in the United States and 300 families in foreign countries who are educating their children at home. A booklet, "Facts About Accelerated Christian Education: Christian Education on the Forefront of Reformation," declares A.C.E.'s goal of having ten thousand schools with one million

211

children by 1989.

A.C.E. has been so successful in this country that recently they have broadened their ministry to reach students outside of the fundamentalist movement and beyond America. They publish a new curriculum under the neutral academic label of Basic Education which now provides materials in English, Spanish, and French. Acutely aware that many of their constituency may disapprove or at least question whether they are "selling out," they are careful to explain that Basic Education represents A.C.E.'s outreach ministry and as such, is a "fulfillment of the Great Commission."[24] A.C.E. proudly proclaims itself to be on the forefront of educational research and innovation. How is this innovation distributed?

If we consider the Baptist school as a corporate franchise, the minister is the educational entrepreneur in the modern corporate sense; he brings A.C.E. to his community the way someone else brings a McDonalds or Wendy's fast food franchise. The minister may get some financial rewards for his efforts, but his major gain is his increased control over the spiritual and educational lives of his congregation. The owner of a McDonald's can feel like an independent businessman at the same time he is purveying the same low quality food that thousands of others are feeding to millions of Americans on behalf of the same corporation. So too, the independent Christian school can feel as if it is breaking free from the "secular humanist" stranglehold on education—only to buy a repetitive, programmed meal of knowledge which fits the needs of corporate society (or the military–industrial complex) much more efficiently than do the public schools.

Perhaps this is one of those moments in history when progress means deterioration of culture. Just as fastfood and the rule of McDonald's over the American eating culture seems like a parody of culture—or the triumph of commercial non-culture—so the development of A.C.E. and its counterparts seems like the ascendancy of religious non-education. Yet McDonald's may serve the needs of families strapped for time and money, torn between the need of keeping two parents in the workforce and the duties of raising their children; it feeds people too busy to take time for a "civilized" meal. So, too, do the new Christian schools meet a pressing social need: some American parents, many of them working class, are asserting their right to control their children's education—at a price they can afford. Their sense of empowerment should not be lightly dismissed, even if their real control is limited to the degree that they purchase a franchised corporate product. In ten or twenty years, it may be evident that their "sacred" schools were the experimental testing grounds that preceded a massive invasion of the education business by corporate America. (If any observers doubt that this is possible, they should contemplate a present-day phenomenon: the extraordinary rate of conversion of public and non-profit hospitals to private facilities owned or operated by giant hospital corporations. Who twenty years ago would have conceived of their impact on health care systems today?)

This kind of speculation does not mean to suggest a level of conscious intentionality on the part of Baptist parents, for they may truly believe their children are being protected from the "worldly" influences of the modern era. Remember the statement made by a Baptist mother:

> Some people say we are protecting them from the world,
> sheltering them. Well, that's right. I don't want them in the
> world. I want them to go into Christian service. [Besides]
> it's like tomatoes in a greenhouse; you have to protect them
> and nourish them until they grow big and strong before you
> put them in the garden.

Nor does this suggest that multinational corporations have generated a masterful educational conspiracy which will be sure to meet their future needs for a manageable and loyal workforce. As Roger Dale observes:

> Institutions of cultural preservation and distribution like
> schools create and recreate forms of consciousness that
> enable social control to be maintained without the necessity
> of dominant groups having to resort to overt mechanisms of
> domination.[25]

But there is an underlying rationality to the system of education which A.C.E. provides; it is a cold rationality which may

213

represent the revival of "scientific management" in schools. It pushes out its rival, "secular humanism," which is encumbered by the "messiness" of tolerating diverse values and diffuse ideas of education. With the state absented, these schools can resist the democratizing influences of many public schools.

While public schools do reproduce the inequalities of the economy and workplace,[26] in some ways they also challenge the legitimacy and practice of such discrimination. By operating within the political arena, they have to contend with the pressures of a variety of interest groups. The participation in government at the school board level is probably more accessible and democratic than anywhere else in the American system. In many respects, the public school is more democratic than the workplace.[27]

The charismatics at the Covenant School have created another rational alternative for education in the coming century. They have also created a more homogeneous population of children than is present in the public schools. The middle-class or professional aspirations of Covenant parents for their children are actualized in the educational environment. The elite classes of American society have always managed to provide a similar environment of educational superiority for their children by isolating them in special preparatory schools—schools where children of the elite hold similar expectations of the place they will assume in adult society. Covenant parents are not the elite but rather the middle strata who value educational excellence and worry about the chances of their children finding secure and purposeful work and achieving meaningful lives. The "Christian-ness" of Covenant students is their bond of homogeneity and superiority, just as wealth and status constitute the bonds of students in elite preparatory schools. Such identification is created for the Covenant children in the form of Christ as one's personal savior and the cohesiveness that their parents labor to produce within the church–home–school community.

The Covenant school emphasizes many of the learning values stressed in progressive public schools; in some ways it may be implementing them even better. Covenant parents grew up in an era when many high school and college students questioned the basic values of American society. Many young people protested the ever-increasing power of corporations to control economic and cultural life; and the efforts of the "military-industrial complex" to reach its global goals. But "corporate culture" has predominated, and most members of the 1960s "protest" generation have accommodated themselves to it.

To Covenant parents, the liberal notions of "secular humanism" are too vague to offer security to themselves or their children, especially in this era of diminished expectations. They have constructed a unique blend of secular and religious institutions: their own version of an elite school—one which can help their children find enriching "upscale" jobs in the future, while at the same time ensure the Lord is there as protector, as legitimator of each child's existence and potentiality. Even if the children do not live up to their own or their parents' expectations, Jesus will have guided them to their appropriate place.

The Covenant parents are acting as practically as the Baptists but with the added determination that their children will have their best chance of "making it" into the shrinking middle class. They not only protect their children from the "evil" influences of the secular school; they prevent them from slipping into the mid-range of students in the public schools who may have become disinterested in learning and pursuing promising careers; who are disrespectful of authority; undisciplined; and increasingly uneducated.

The evidence of economic indicators and social attitudes points to a marked increase in social stratification; the creation of a less-equal American society; an increase in the numbers of people living in poverty; a degradation of the skill levels and wages for working-class jobs; a decrease in the proportion of middle-income families; and a successful resurgence of the wealthy, whose efforts to revamp tax laws and federal spending in their favor have been very successful. One would expect to find, then, groups of people who are changing their approach to socializing their children for a different kind of America.

The irony is that many evangelicals may be educating their children in ways that reinforce what they say they want to resist. For example, while evangelicals react against the commercialization of culture, many develop, sell, buy, and use mass-marketed curriculum packages which dictate virtually every aspect of school life; moreover, they are exporting these packets abroad.

Also, both communities believe in the traditional patriarchal family and the "natural" submission of women. Yet, because of their size and curriculum, the schools have not segregated boys from girls, nor do they offer different curricula to them. Especially at the Academy, the education for boys and girls is similar, although traditional gender roles are reinforced in the texts themselves, and adult men clearly have more status and authority than adult women within the school.

In many respects, school life is less segregated than the future adult lives these boys and girls can anticipate. Both at the Academy and Covenant, the girls are being prepared for the dual labor market: unpaid labor in the home and either part- or full-time paid labor in the workforce. While the Academy boys are being prepared for jobs and the Covenant boys largely for careers, most of the girls anticipate working in the secondary or tertiary labor markets (especially in the service sector). While some of the Covenant girls are contemplating professional careers as teachers, most think that they will work until they have children and then stay at home with their children. The Academy girls, on the other hand, would like to stay home once they have children although they realize that this may be unlikely. Thus, we have a double contradiction. Although women are supposed to stay home and be supported by their husbands, most expect to work at some point during their married lives. Secondly, although boys and girls are receiving the same educational instruction and thus developing the same skills, they are being socialized for different kinds of family and work lives. Given job clustering (which is still closely related to gender and the lack of equal pay for men and women), even the Covenant girls who enter professional jobs are likely to earn less than the Academy boys who are working in a trade.

Finally, while Christian schools are theoretically open to all children (as part of the inclusive Christian ethic), they tend to be very self-selective on the basis of color and class as well as creed. Their students tend to be from the middle and working classes, white, and Christian; their sense of elitism is one of moral superiority. When asked on a questionnaire what class they belonged to, more than one parent responded: "We belong to a saved class."

Will Christian schools serve as models for future social reproduction and increasing polarization of different class, religious, and ethnic/racial groups or will they simply continue to be an historical alternative among many public and private schools? The answer remains to be seen. Today, they represent 20% of the private school population, or about 2% of the total American school population. While their numbers are not staggering, their unprecedented growth and influence have been significant.

The Christian schools represent experiments in cultural production as well as social reproduction. They represent the efforts of many evangelical parents and educators who care enough about the education of their young to envision and test out alternative forms of education. As such, they present a challenge to all of us to question what kind of education we want for our children. Even more critically, they challenge us to examine what kind of world we want to prepare our children for, or more precisely, what kind of world we want to fashion for our children.

Evangelicals have withdrawn their children from public schools for a variety of reasons, ranging from differences over philosophy to disappointment in the practice. Some evangelicals have resisted public education because of what the public schools promised to do (integrate the student body, make the curriculum more secular) and promised not to do (teach Christian values as Truth). But some have withdrawn their children from public schools because they have realized that public education does not deliver on the promise of providing an equal, quality education for all children. They believe that they could do as well, if not better, than the public schools, while at the same time providing a Christian environment for their children.

Finally, many parents, religious leaders, and teachers want to have greater influence over the education of their children. In many ways, even in the highly standardized Academy, both the parents and teachers feel as though they are appreciated for the roles they respectively play, that the teachers and administrators are more accessible to them, and that they can participate more meaningfully in their children's education. While the public schools *are* more democratic than most other public institutions, the range of players (students, parents, and teachers) often feel shut out. In response, evangelicals have established their own schools.

Conclusion

In both deliberate and unconscious ways, people at Covenant and the Academy are preparing their children to live in this world. Most of them truly believe that they are doing their best to secure their children by enrolling them in the new Christian schools. As discussed throughout the book, there are positive interactions and instructions taking place in these schools which are likely to contribute to the children's well-being and to the empowerment of parents, teachers, and religious leaders. Both the people at Covenant and the Academy are proud of their schools, although the people at Covenant appear more confident in their system of education than do parents and teachers at the Academy.

Much energy and thought has gone into offering alternative education to the students of Covenant and the Academy. But what may the consequences be? For whom are these schools working and why? Are they in the end supporting or undercutting the religious motivations of their organizers, the well-being of their children, and the common good of society?

This chapter has focused on the "macro" world and the ways in which A.C.E. Christian schools conform to the new requirements of American society and the demands of its economy. As experimental models, these new schools have flexibility; they are not entrenched in an older tradition or a self-perpetuating bureaucracy. But even though the new Christian schools are constructed as fortresses to protect children from unhealthy "worldly" influences, their unintended effect on future education may be far different. They could be the forerunners of a new kind of social reproduction which offers commercial solutions to the educational needs of American consumers, all neatly tailored to the means, expectations, and fears of different social classes. The product could be far more "secular" than any educational system ever imagined by the founders of the "sacred" schools.

The people who participate in these schools are not mere puppets but actors who interact with other actors in the process of defining, conforming to, and resisting various institutional norms. There is pride and there should be pride in the Academy. Students are doing relatively well on standardized tests and are enrolling in college after graduation. From the parents' point of view, their children are being better protected at the Academy from "evil" ideas, drugs, and alcohol than they would be in public school and this is a comfort to them. Furthermore, their children do not seem to be suffering from (in the words of Emile Durkheim) "the malady of unlimited aspirations." In many ways, frustrations seem to be kept at a minimum at the Academy. There is a noticeable lack of complaining that "life is not fair." Many of the Academy students have learned early on that life is not fair—they know from the beginning that it is hard. When talking about their futures, both boys and girls talk of "wanting jobs that pay well and that are not too boring." One boy adds that, "if possible, I'd like to work outdoors, somewhere where it's not too boring or confining. And I'd like to marry a nice girl—it would help if she were pretty." Is this so much to ask? Is it surprising that Academy parents may want to protect their children from teachers who may consciously or unconsciously treat the lower and working classes differently from the middle and upper classes; or from movies and television shows that frustrate so many people by inviting them to judge their lives by unrealistic, unattainable standards of wealth and luxury?

The egalitarian rhetoric of "making it" still infuses our efforts to bring equal education to the masses. If this rhetoric is no longer acceptable, perhaps it is because public education so seldom delivers what it promises. Should twenty working-class children suffer humiliation so that one can go on to receive an elite college education?

Although people at Covenant and the Academy have established alternatives to the American public educational system, they are still operating within the traditional structures of American society. They are doing for their children what they believe public education should be doing but is not. In the case of the Academy, we have working-class parents who are teaching their children to be disciplined and obedient workers. The fact that some parents selectively choose which of their children they will enroll in Christian school and which in public school suggests that they evaluate their child's abilities and which environment is best suited for their particular child. Two mothers described the children they send to public school as being more "academically inclined" and "socially adaptable" and those they send to the Academy as being "a bit slower and more shy" and "temperamental." This also indicates that religion is not the only motivation for parents to enroll their children in Christian school. By and large, the Academy is successful at getting their students to finish high school without dropping out and increasingly is successful at preparing them for college. They are, in their evaluation, teaching their children the "basics."

Afraid that their children will be corrupted by exposure to different views, the Academy Baptists have choosen to shelter their students and censor the values and ideas to which they are exposed. In giving their children a Christian education, the Academy Baptists believe they have given them a fair and disciplined education.

Both of these Christian schools argue that public education fails because it attempts to be value-free or value-relative, and they agree that Christian education remedies this problem. But in the case of Covenant, we have middle-class parents who believe that public education does not teach students to reason things out enough and therefore to be able to discern what is a good or bad idea. The Covenant leaders are afraid that their children may be too easily seduced by secular forces and ideas because of both the content (secular humanism) and the process (not teaching critical thinking skills well enough) of public education. In response, Covenant attempts to expose their students to various ideas, simultaneously exposing the faults of the ideas with which they disagree. They believe that in giving their children a Christian education they also are giving them a more challenging and humane education in an environment where people care about one another.

It is no doubt clear to the reader by now that I am not allied with Christian schools; in fact, I find many of their practices and beliefs to be reactionary impulses in a time of social change and to be limiting rather than liberating. But I respect those who have become actively involved in something they deeply believe in; they have had the courage, energy, and resourcefulness to change their children's and their own lives in substantial ways.

I would rather see the parents of Academy and Covenant students preparing their children for full participation in a more egalitarian, progressive society. We need to take seriously the desires of all people—of all classes, colors, creeds, and genders—to be engaged in meaningful work at home, at school, and at the workplace. Yet, I cannot fault them for recognizing that most public schools—despite the long-standing myth that educational opportunity is the agent of equality in the United States—do not offer their children very good chances of upward mobility or even maintaining a solid working-class livelihood.

As Jean Anyon argues, acts of accommodation and resistance are played out in response to particular sets of conditions, structures, and ideologies. Ultimately, power lies not only in coping with the conditions set before you but in questioning how valid and healthy those very conditions and demands are. Education in a free and democratic society should encourage people to exercise their ability to analyze how and why their lives are the way they are, and to envision and revision the way life may be. The "basics" should involve not only basic reading, writing, and arithmetic skills, but also the skills of critical thinking that enable one to question, to observe, and to act—reasonably as well as faithfully.

Notes

Series Editor's Introduction

1. Michael Omi and Howard Winant, *Racial Formation in the United States* (New York and London: Routledge and Kegan Paul, 1986), pp. 214–15.
2. Marcus Raskin, *The Common Good* (New York and London: Routledge and Kegan Paul, 1986).
3. Omi and Winant, *Racial Formation*, pp. 215–16.
4. Omi and Winant, *Racial Formation*, p. 220.
5. This loss of legitimacy is discussed in greater detail in Michael W. Apple, *Teachers and Texts: A Political Economy of Class and Gender Relations in Education* (New York and London: Routledge and Kegan Paul, 1986). See also, Stephen Arons, *Compelling Belief: The Culture of American Schooling* (New York: McGraw Hill, 1983).
6. Allen Hunter, "Children in the Service of Conservatism: Parent–Child Relations in New Right Strategy and Rhetoric," unpublished paper, University of Wisconsin, Madison, 1986, p. 1. Hereafter cited in the text as Hunter.
7. See Omi and Winant, *Racial Formation*, p. 214.
8. Walter Dean Burnham, "Post-Conservative America," *Socialist Review* 72 (November-December 1983): 125.
9. Michael W. Apple, *Education and Power* (New York and London: Routledge and Kegan Paul, 1982).
10. On this matter, see Apple, *Education and Power*.

Preface

1. Passage quoted in Joan Brumberg, *Mission for Life* (New York: The Free Press, 1980).
2. Passage quoted in William Martin, "God's Angry Man," *Texas Monthly* (April, 1981).

3. This is the paradox that Peshkin highlights in his book *God's Choice: The Total World of a Fundamentalist Christian School* (Chicago: University of Chicago Press, 1986). The paradox, however, may be more problematic for researchers such as us than for evangelicals themselves.

Introduction

1. Rousas Rushdoony quoted in Daniel Gleason, "A Study of the Christian School Movement," Ph.D. diss., Indiana University, 1980, p. 17.
2. James Robison quoted in William Martin, "God's Angry Man," *Texas Monthly* (April, 1981): 226.
3. See Urie Bronfenbrenner, *The Ecology of Human Development* (Cambridge: Harvard University Press, 1979).
4. See Richard Quebedeaux, *The Worldly Evangelicals* (New York: Harper and Row, 1978); James Hunter, *American Evangelicalism* (New Brunswick: Rutgers University Press, 1983).

1   A Search for Coherence

1. Clifford Geertz, *The Interpretation of Cultures* (New York: Basic Books, 1973), p. 5.
2. Geertz, *Interpretation of Cultures*, p. 218.
3. Glen H. Elder, "Adolescence in Historical Perspective," in Joseph Adelson, ed., *Handbook of Adolescent Psychology* (New York: John Wiley and Sons, 1980).
4. Irvin Child in John Clausen, ed., *Socialization and Society* (Boston: Little, Brown and Company, 1968), p. 1.
5. See Aaron Antonovsky, *Health, Stress, and Coping* (San Francisco: Jossey-Bass, 1979).
6. William McLoughlin, *Revivals, Awakenings, and Reform* (Chicago: University of Chicago Press, 1978).
7. Milton Yinger, *Countercultures: The Promise and Peril of a World Turned Upside Down* (New York: The Free Press, 1982), p. 9.
8. Yinger, *Countercultures*. This phrase, part of the subtitle of the book, is mentioned frequently in his text.
9. Research on socialization suggests that parents seek information and advice from a variety of sources, including books on childcare, the media, teachers, physicians, and neighbors (Urie Bronfenbrenner, *The Ecology of Human Development* [Cambridge: Harvard University Press, 1979]; Urie Bronfenbrenner and Maureen Mahoney, *Influences on Human Development* [Hinsdale, IL: The Dryden Press, 1975]). With the diffusion of cultural

pluralism and greater secularization, the diversity of opinions on childcare has increased. The extent to which this has occurred, however, is an historical judgment. One must be careful not to paint too halcyonic a view of parenting in earlier times. For instance, it is well-documented that immigrant children, especially in urban areas, received many mixed messages from their families and work and school experiences. I do argue, however, that a higher degree of consensus and greater consistency existed between the primary socializing agencies during the first three Awakenings (that is, up through the early part of the twentieth century).

10. James Richardson, "The Active vs. Passive Convert: Paradigm Conflict in Conversion/Recruitment Research," in *Journal for the Scientific Study of Religion* 24, no. 2 (1985): 163–79.

11. Antonovsky, *Health, Stress, and Coping*, p. 123.

12. J. Rotter, "Some problems and misconceptions related to the construct of internal versus external locus of control of reinforcement," *Journal of Consulting and Clinical Psychology*, 43 (1975): 56–67; Herbert Lefcourt, ed., *Research with the Locus of Control Construct*. Vol. 1, *Assessment Methods* (New York: Academic Press, 1981); Hanna Levenson, "Activism and Powerful Others: Disjunctures within the Concept of Internal–External Control," *Journal of Personality Assessment* 38 (1974): 377–85; Christopher Peterson, "The Sense of Control Over One's Life: A Review of Recent Literature." Prepared for the Social Science Research Council on The Self and Personal Control over the Life Span, New York, October 1980.

13. Antonovsky, *Health, Stress, and Coping*, p. 155.

14. To what degree people actually confront and actively support one another in their parenting depends on the individual fellowship and its organization. Parents of the charismatic group are much more actively involved in reciprocal parenting than the Baptist parents. Reciprocal parenting includes discussing and confronting one another with parenting issues and behaviors; conducting family life workshops; holding intergenerational meetings in individual homes in addition to Sunday services. Both parents and teachers in the Baptist school tend to avoid confrontation. Nonetheless, both Baptists and charismatics reported that the high degree of consensus and the relatively closed network between church, family, and school was a strong source of support for them as parents and educators.

15. Clifford Geertz, 1973, Ch. 4.

16. See Charles Glock and Rodney Stark, *Religion and Society in Tension* (Chicago: Rand McNally, 1965); and Clifford Geertz, *Interpretation of Cultures*.

17. Geertz, 1973: 19.

18. McLoughlin, *Revivals, Awakenings, and Reform*, p. 2.

19. See McLoughlin, *Revivals, Awakenings, and Reform*.

20. See Joan Brumberg, *Mission for Life* (New York: The Free Press,

1980).
21. See Sidney Mead, *The Lively Experiment* (New York: Harper and Row, 1976).
22. According to Bernard Weisberger (*They Gather at the River: The Story of the Great Revivalists and Their Impact Upon Religion in America* [Chicago: University of Chicago Press, 1958], p. 13), the number of churches increased from one per 1740 inhabitants in 1800 to one church per 895 inhabitants in 1850.
23. See Brumberg, *Mission for Life*.
24. Mead, *The Lively Experiment*, p. 120.
25. Martin Marty, *The Righteous Empire* (New York: Dial Press, 1970).
26. Whitney Cross, *The Burned-Over District: The Social and Intellectual History of Enthusiastic Religion in Western New York, 1800–1850* (Ithaca, NY: Cornell University Press, 1950).
27. See McLoughlin, *Revivals, Awakenings, and Reform*.
28. Weisberger, *They Gather at the River*, p. 163.
29. Weisberger, *They Gather at the River*, p. 163.
30. Andrew Greely, *The Denominational Society: A Sociological Approach to Religion in America* (Glenview, IL: Scott, Foresman and Co., 1972).
31. Michael W. Apple points out that the reorganization of school curricula had begun five years before the launching of Sputnik. Although the increasing emphasis on science education and the need for higher standards is often attributed to Sputnik, there is evidence that it did not initiate such reorganization but rather was used to legitimize and intensify the pace of curricular change that had already begun to respond to the needs of reindustrialization (personal correspondence with Michael W. Apple).
32. See Seymour Lipset, *The First New Nation* (New York: W. W. Norton, 1979).
33. For a definition and discussion of evangelical groups, see Richard Quebedeaux, *The Worldly Evangelicals* (New York: Harper and Row, 1978), and *The Young Evangelicals* (New York: Harper and Row, 1974); George Marsden, *Fundamentalism and American Culture* (New York: Oxford University Press, 1980).
34. Max Weber, *The Sociology of Religion*, trans. Ephraim Fischoff (Boston: The Beacon Press, 1963).
35. Marsden, *Fundamentalism and American Culture*, p. 127.
36. For reference to the influence of wealthy elite during previous awakenings, see Brumberg, *Mission for Life*; McLoughlin, *Revivals, Awakenings, and Reform*; Liston Pope, *Millhands and Preachers* (New Haven: Yale University Press, 1942). For a discussion of the role of wealthy businessmen in the Fourth Great Awakening see Robert Liebman and Robert Wuthnow, *The New Christian Right* (New York: Aldine, 1983).
37. See Harry Braverman, *Labor and Monopoly Capital: The Degradation of Work in the Twentieth Century* (New York: Monthly

Review, 1975); and Richard Duboff, "Wealth Distribution Study Causes Change of Discomfort," *In These Times* (Dec. 11, 1984).
38. Jerry Falwell, *Listen, America* (New York: Bantam Books, 1980).
39. See Brumberg, *Mission for Life.*
40. See Marvin Harris, *America Now* (New York: Simon and Schuster, 1981), Chap. Eight.

2 Morals and Quarrels

1. Milton Yinger, *Countercultures* (New York: The Free Press, 1982).
2. Diane Ravitch, *The Great School Wars: New York City 1805–1973: A History of Schools as a Battlefield for Social Change* (New York: Basic Books, 1974).
3. Barbara Finkelstein, "Cultural Transmission and the Acquisition of Identity: Learners and Learning in American Educational History." Paper presented at the Meetings of the American Educational Research Association, New York, 1982.
4. David Tyack and Elizabeth Hansot, "Conflict in American Public Education," Special Issue: American Schools: Public and Private, *Daedalus* (Summer, 1981).
5. Otto Kraushaar, *American Nonpublic Schools: Patterns in Diversity* (New York, Basic Books, 1972).
6. "The Consolidation of Schools," quoted in David Tyack, *The One Best System: A History of American Urban Education* (Cambridge: Harvard University Press, 1974), p. 277.
7. Sidney Mead, *The Lively Experiment* (New York: Harper and Row, 1976).
8. Lawrence Cremin, *Traditions of American Education* (New York: Basic Books, 1977), p. 50.
9. Tyack, *The One Best System*, pp. 129–31.
10. William Herberg, *Protestant, Catholic, and Jew: An Essay in American Religious Sociology* (Garden City, NY: Doubleday, 1955).
11. Paul Kienel, *The Christian School: Why It Is Right for Your Child*, forward by Paul Harvey (Wheaton, IL: Victor Books, 1980).
12. Jerry Falwell, *Listen, America!* (New York: Bantam Books, 1980), p. 17.
13. Martin Marty, *The Righteous Empire* (New York: Dial Press, 1970).
14. For a discussion of Christian women at work, see Patricia Ward and Martha Scott, *Christian Women at Work* (Grand Rapids: Zondervan Publishing House, 1981).
15. George Ballweg, "The Growth in the Number and Population of Christian Schools Since 1966: A Profile of Parental Views Concerning Factors Which Led Them to Enroll Their Children in a Christian School." Ph.D. diss., Boston University School of

Education, 1980.

16. Ballweg, "The Growth in the Number and Population of Christian Schools"; Gerald Carlson, "Christian School Growth Continues," *American Association of Christian Schools Communicator* 2, no. 6 (1982).

17. Ballweg, "The Growth in the Number and Population of Christian Schools."

18. Peter Skerry, "Christian Schools, Racial Quotas, and the IRS," Ethics and Public Policy Center, Washington, D.C., December 1980; Bruce Cooper, "The Changing Demography of Private Schools," *Education and Urban Society* 16, no. 4 (1984): 429–42; James Carper, "The Christian Day School," in J. Carper and T. Hunt, eds., *Religious Schooling in America* (Birmingham, AL: Religious Education Press, 1984).

19. Ravitch, *The Great School Wars*, p. 240.

21. Kraushaar, *American Nonpublic Schools*, p. 17.

22. Daniel Gleason, "A Study of the Christian Day School Movement." Ph.D. diss., University of North Dakota, 1980; Henry Becker, "The Impact of Racial Composition and Public School Desegregation on Changes in Non-Public School Enrollment by White Pupils," Report no. 352 (Center for the Organization of Schools, The Johns Hopkins University, June 1978).

23. Ballweg, "The Growth in the Number and Population of Christian Schools," p. 3.

24. Mead, *The Lively Experiment.*

25. NAIS stands for the National Association of Independent Schools.

26. Dennis Brown, "An Investigation Into the Philosophy of Education of Christian Elementary and Secondary Schools." Ph.D. diss., Indiana University, 1977; Ballweg, "The Growth in the Number and Population of Christian Schools"; Cooper, "The Changing Demography of Private Schools"; Carper, "The Christian Day School."

27. Brown, "An Investigation Into the Philosophy of Education of Christian Elementary and Secondary Schools."

28. Christian school students tend to come from families with an average income of $25,000 or more. In general, their parents tend to be more highly educated than the general population of public school parents; almost all have completed high school and many are college-educated (Donald Erickson, "Private Schools in Contemporary Perspective," Report No. TTC–14 [Stanford: Institute for Research on Educational Finance and Governance]); Virginia Nordin and Wiliam Turner, "More Than Segregation Academies: The Growing Protestant Fundamentalist School," *Phi Delta Kappan* 61, no. 6 (1980): 391–94.

29. Robert Liebman and Robert Wuthnow, *The New Christian Right* (New York: Aldine, 1983), p. 2.

30. It is difficult to assess the degree to which the Christian School Movement's growth can be attributed to the Supreme Court's 1954

Brown v. Board of Education decision to desegregate schools, but the two are clearly connected. Some schools, such as Jerry Falwell's Christian Academy publically advertised themselves as "for whites only." In a study of a Baptist-affiliated southern segregation school, John Wood found that seven of the eleven nearby Christian schools were established at least partially to resist integration (John Wood, *Ridgewood School: An American Revitalization Effort* [Chapel Hill: University of North Carolina, 1983]). David Nevin and Robert Bills (*The Schools That Fear Built* [Washington: Acropolis Books, 1976]) link desegregation and the proliferation of Christian schools. Before the *Brown v. Board of Education* ruling in 1954, 0.9% of the children in eleven southern states were enrolled in private schools; by 1971, 6% of them were enrolled in private schools (see James Palmer cited in Corrine Glesne and Alan Peshkin, "The Christian Day School" in Patricia Bauch, ed., *Private Schools and Public Concerns: What the Research Says.*) But a number of schools were not established as "segregation academies," and proliferated in places where desegregation was not an issue (see Skerry, "Christian Schools, Racial Quotas, and the IRS"; Nordin and Turner, "More Than Segregation Academies."). And some that initially were established "for whites only," are now integrated, including Falwell's Christian Academy.

31. A. A. Baker, *The Successful Christian School* (Pensacola, FL: A Beka Book Publication, 1979), p. 36.
32. Kienel, *The Christian School.*
33. Richard DeCharms and Gerald Moeller, "Values Expressed in American Children's Readers: 1800–1950," *Journal of Abnormal and Social Psychology,* 74 (February, 1962): 136–42.
34. DeCharms and Moeller, "Values Expressed in American Children's Readers."

3 To Live in Fellowship: Covenant Community

1. Peter Berger, *The Sacred Canopy* (New York: Doubleday, 1967).
2. Philip Greven discusses this phenomenon among earlier generations of evangelicals in his book, *The Protestant Temperament* (New York: Alfred A. Knopf, 1977).
3. Greven, *The Protestant Temperament.*
4. For a more detailed discussion of the negotiation of gender within the Covenant community, see Susan Rose, "Women Warriors: The Negotiation of Gender in a Charismatic Community," *Sociological Analysis* 48, no. 3 (1987): 245–58.
5. David Gordon, "Dying to Self," *Sociological Analysis* 45, no. 1 (1984): 41–45.
6. James Richardson, Mary Stewart, and Robert Simmonds, *Organized Miracles* (New Brunswick, NJ: Transaction Books, 1979); Dick

Anthony and Thomas Robbins, "Spiritual Innovation and the Crisis of American Civil Religion," *Daedalus* (Winter, 1982); Steven Tipton, "The Moral Logic of Alternative Religions," *Daedalus* (Winter, 1982), and *Getting Saved from the Sixties* (University of California Press, 1981).

7. Claude Nunn quoted in N. J. Demerath, *Social Class in American Protestantism* (Chicago: Rand McNally, 1965).

8. Milton Yinger, *Countercultures* (New York: The Free Press, 1982); Richardson, Stewart, and Simmonds, *Organized Miracles*; Takie Sugiyama, "Millenarian Movements and Resocialization," in R. Lauer, ed., *Social Movements and Social Change* (Carbondale, IL: South Illinois University Press, 1976).

9. Edward Hindson quoted in Joan Brumberg, *Mission for Life* (New York: The Free Press, 1980), p. 224.

10. See Barbara Ehrenreich and Deidre English, *Complaints and Disorders* (Old Westbury, NY: Feminist Press, 1973); Kathryn Sklar, *Catherine Beecher: A Study in American Domesticity* (New York: Norton and Co., 1973).

11. "Milk meetings" refers here to classes that are held for the newly born in Christ. Newly committed members are thought of as babes in Christ; in order to grow, they need to be nurtured in the ways of the Lord, thus the reference to "milk." The classes consist of lectures, discussions, and Bible study.

4 School Life: Covenant School

1. See Susan Rose, "From Sacred to Secular Schools: The Transition as a Methodological Tool." Paper presented at the Eastern Sociological Meetings, Boston, 1984.

2. Charles Cooley, *Human Nature and the Social Order* (New York: Scribner's, 1909), p. 199.

3. Lewis Coser, *The Functions of Social Conflict* (New York: The Free Press, 1956), p. 75; emphasis mine.

4. Victor Turner, *Image and Pilgrimage in Christian Culture: Anthropological Perspectives* (New York: Columbia University Press, 1978).

5. Émile Durkheim, *The Rules of the Sociological Method*, trans. by Sarah Solovay and John Mueler (1896; reprint, New York: The Free Press, 1964), pp. 68–69.

6. Rose, "From Sacred to Secular Schools."

5 To Live in Fellowship: Lakehaven Community

1. For a discussion of the differences between sects and churches, see

Max Weber, *The Sociology of Religion*, trans. Ephraim Fischoff (Boston: Beacon Press, 1963); Charles Glock and Rodney Stark, *Religion and Society in Tension* (Chicago: Rand McNally, 1965); N. J. Demerath, *Social Class in American Protestantism* (Chicago: Rand McNally, 1965).
2. See Lilian Rubin, *Worlds of Pain* (New York: Basic Books, 1976).

6 School Life: The Academy

1. The immediate willingness of this Baptist principal contrasts with the hesitation to and later rejection of the proposed study by another area Baptist school.

7 Spheres of Influence

1. This idea was repeated over and over again by people at Covenant and the Academy, and is often referred to in the Christian school literature.
2. James Hunter, *American Evangelicalism* (New Brunswick, NJ: Rutgers University Press, 1983); Stuart Rothenberg and Frank Newport, *The Evangelical Voter* (Washington: The Institute for Government and Politics of the Free Congress Research and Education Foundation, 1984); Beth Hess, "Protesting the American Family: Public Policy, Family and the New Right," in Rosalie Genovese, ed., *Families and Change: Social Needs and Public Policy* (South Hadley, MA: Bergin and Garvey, 1984); Jeffrey Hadden, "Televangelism and the Mobilization of a New Christian Right Family Policy," in William D'Antonio and Joan Aldous, eds., *Families and Religions: Conflict and Change in Modern Society* (Beverly Hills: Sage, 1983).
3. See Hess, "Protecting the American Family."
4. Robin Williams, *American Society* (New York: Alfred A. Knopf, 1970), p. 557.
5. George Ballweg, "The Growth in the Number and Population of Christian Schools Since 1966: A Profile of Parental Views Concerning Factors Which Led Them to Enroll Their Children in a Christian School." Ph.D. diss., Boston University School of Education, 1980), p. viii.
6. J. McPartland and E. McDill, "Control and Differentiation in the Structure of American Education," *Sociology of Education* 55, no. 2/3 (April/July 1982).
7. Williams, *American Society*, p. 329.
8. Sarah Lawrence Lightfoot, *Worlds Apart: Relationships Between Families and Schools* (New York: Basic Books, 1978); William

Waller, *The Sociology of Teaching* (New York: Wiley and Sons, 1932); John Ogbu, *The Next Generation: An Ethnography of Education in an Urban Neighborhood* (New York: Academic Press, 1974); Ray Rist, *The Urban School: A Factory for Failure* (Cambridge: M.I.T. Press, 1973); M. Wax, S. Diamond, and F. Gearing, eds., *Anthropological Perspectives on Education* (New York: Basic Books, 1971).

9. Lightfoot, *Worlds Apart.*

10. An evaluation of the transition of the 8th and 9th grades (n = 9) from Covenant school to three area public schools was conducted in 1982–83. Since Covenant only ran through 9th grade in 1982, and 8th grade in 1983 these students needed to relocate in public school. Students and their parents were interviewed and administered surveys in May 1982, prior to the transition; in late September as they were undergoing the transition; and in late January, 1983. Their Christian school teachers were also interviewed and surveyed in May and January. I visited the three public schools they attended in January and interviewed and surveyed their public school teachers and guidance counselors in January as well.

11. Sidney Mead, *The Lively Experiment* (New York: Harper and Row, 1976), p. 16.

12. C. Eavey, *History of Christian Education* (Chicago: Moody Press, 1964), p. 209.

13. Seymour Lipset, *The First New Nation* (New York: W. W. Norton, 1979), and "Religion and Politics in the American Past and Present," in R. Lee and Martin Marty, eds., *Religion and Social Conflict* (New York: Oxford University Press, 1964).

14. Hanna Levenson, "Activism and Powerful Others: Disjunctures within the Concept of Internal-External Control," *Journal of Personality Assessment* 38 (1974): 377–85; Christopher Peterson, "The Sense of Control Over One's Life: A Review of Recent Literature." Prepared for the Social Science Research Council on "The Self and Personal Control Over the Life Span," New York City, October, 1980.

15. Levenson, "Activism and Powerful Others."

16. Barker, "Ecology and Maturation," in M. Jones, ed., *Nebraska Symposium on Motivation*, no. 8 (Lincoln: University of Nebraska Press, 1960).

17. As Michael W. Apple has pointed out, "the large scale influx of pre-packaged material" is encroaching upon the professionalism of teachers in the public schools as well, where de-skilling is becoming more and more a reality. See Michael W. Apple, "Curricular Form and the Logic of Technical Capital," in Michael W. Apple and Lois Weis, eds., *Ideology and Practice in Schooling* (Philadelphia: Temple University Press, 1983), pp. 143–66.

18. Apple and Weis, *Ideology and Practice.*

19. This quotation is taken from Apple, "Curricular Form and the

Logic of Technical Control," p. 148. Apple further qualifies this statement, arguing that the "relative autonomy of teaching (usually one can close the door and not be disturbed) . . . at the level of actual practice," has persisted "until relatively recently."

20. Jerald Hage and Michael Aiken, "Organizational Interdependence and Intraorganizational Structure," in Merlin Brinkerhoff and Phillip Kuny, eds., *Complex Organizations and Their Environments* (Dubuque, IA: William C. Brown, Co., 1972); Richard Hall, *Organizations: Structure and Processes*, 3rd ed., (Englewood Cliffs: Prentice-Hall, 1982).

21. Hage and Aiken, "Organizational Interdependence"; Hall, *Organizations*.

22. Williams, *American Society*, Chap. 4.

23. These data are taken from the National Youth Survey (1980) conducted by the Behavioral Research Institute in Boulder, Colorado. I replicated items that they used in their 1980 survey on my two Christian school samples. The data provide interesting comparisons, but they should be taken only as suggestive since there is a wide variation in sample size (Covenant: N = 20; Academy: N = 41; National Youth Sample: N = 1511) and in the average age and grade of students in each sample (Covenant: mean grade = 6th; Academy = 9th; National Youth Sample = 11th). These confounding factors are likely to influence the findings and will be accounted for in the comparisons I draw in the next few pages.

24. There is an age difference among the student samples which may be confounding the results. The sample of Covenant students is on average younger (mean grade = 6th) than the Academy (mean grade = 9) and nationally representative (mean grade = 11) samples.

25. See 1980 National Youth Survey.

26. Paul Willis, *Learning to Labour* (New York: Columbia University Press, 1977).

27. For a discussion of various evangelical views on sexuality see Richard Quebedeaux, *The Young Evangelicals* (New York: Harper and Row, 1974), and *The Worldly Evangelicals* (New York: Harper and Row, 1978); Barbara Ehrenreich, Elizabeth Hess, and Gloria Jacobs also have a chapter on evangelical sexuality in their book, *Re-Making Love: The Feminization of Sex* (New York: Doubleday, 1986).

28. For a discussion of class and gender see Lilian Rubin, *Worlds of Pain* (New York: Basic Books, 1976); Michael W. Apple, *Education and Power* (London: Routledge and Kegan Paul, 1982); Randall Collins, "Sexual Stratification," in *Social Problems* 19, no. 1 (1971): 3–20.

29. My research did not focus on the nature or quality of relationships among boys and girls in these communities. Therefore, these data are largely impressionistic and gathered over a period of observa-

tion, and informal interviewing and conversations. More systematic work would need to be done, and much more time spent with these students in order to arrive at a more full and accurate picture of their interactions with and their perceptions of the opposite sex.

30. The Christian school samples differed from the National Youth Sample at the p = .01 significance level. The difference in sample sizes, however, limit the degree of confidence in the findings. Larger Christian school samples are needed before drawing any conclusive findings.

31. Contrast tests in ANOVA tested whether there were significant differences between all samples. The Multiple Range Test using Student-Newman-Keuls and the Scheffe Procedure tested whether there were significant differences between each of these two Christian schools and the National Youth Sample. The Academy students believed more strongly than the Covenant students (p = .03) that a "wife should submit to her husband." See Susan Rose, "Christian Schools in Secular Society" (Ph.D. dissertation, Cornell University, 1984) for greater detail.

32. Melvin Kohn, *Class and Conformity: A Reassessment* (Chicago: University of Chicago Press, 1977); David Riesman, *The Lonely Crowd* (New Haven: Yale University Press, 1977 [1950]).

33. Andrew McDearmid, "Student Achievement in Accelerated Christian Education Schools in Pennsylvania" (Ph.D. dissertation, Temple University, 1979).

34. Donald Howard, "The Strengths and Weaknesses of the A.C.E. Program" (Lewisville, TX: A.C.E., Inc., 1985), p. 34.

8 Rhetoric and Reality: Two World Views

1. Clifford Geertz, *The Interpretation of Cultures* (New York: Basic Books, 1973).

2. Robin Williams, *American Society* (New York: Alfred A. Knopf, 1970), Chap. 11.

3. For more detailed information on how the Rokeach value survey was used and analyzed for the Lakehaven and Covenant fellowships, see Susan Rose, "Christian Schools in Secular Society." Ph.D. diss., Cornell University, 1984. For more information on the survey itself, see Milton Rokeach, "Value Survey" (Sunnyvale, CA: Halgren Tests, 1967), and *Understanding Human Values* (New York: The Free Press, 1979).

4. Max Weber, *The Sociology of Religion*, trans. by Ephraim Fischoff (Boston: Beacon Press, 1963), Chap. 11.

5. N. J. Demerath, *Social Class in American Protestantism* (Chicago: Rand McNally, 1965).

6. See Basil Bernstein, *Class, Codes and Control: Theoretical Studies Towards a Sociology of Language* (New York: Schocken Books,

1975). Hereafter cited in the text as Bernstein.
7. See Michael W. Apple, "Curricular Form and the Logic of Technical Capital," in Michael W. Apple and Lois Weis, eds., *Ideology and Practice in Schooling* (Philadelphia: Temple University Press, 1983), and *Education and Power* (London: Routledge and Kegan Paul, 1982).
8. Robert Dreeben, *On What Is Learned in School* (Reading, MA: Addison-Wesley, 1968); Talcott Parsons, "The School Class as a Social System," *Harvard Educational Review* 24 (Fall, 1959): 259–318.
9. Donald Howard, "The Strengths and Weaknesses of the A.C.E. Program" (Lewisville, TX: A.C.E., Inc., 1985), p. 6.

9 Teaching Discipline: Socializing Discipline

1. See Philip Greven, *The Protestant Temperament: Patterns of Child-Rearing, Religious Experience, and the Self in Early America* (New York: Alfred A. Knopf, 1977).
2. For a discussion of how central the need to control is, see Alice Miller's discussion of child-rearing practices in *For Your Own Good: Hidden Cruelty in Child-rearing and the Roots of Violence*, trans. by Hildegarde and Hunter Hannum (New York: Farrar, Straus, and Giroux, 1984). See also Greven, *The Protestant Temperament*.
3. See .Edwin Starbuck, *The Psychology of Religion* (New York: Charles Scribner's and Sons, 1899); William James, *The Varieties of Religious Experience* (New York: The Modern Library, 1902); Joseph Kett, *The Rites of Passage* (New York: Basic Books, 1977).
4. See Kett, *Rites of Passage*; Victor Turner, *Dramas, Fields, and Metaphors* (Ithaca, NY: Cornell University Press, 1974); Arnold Gennep, *The Rites of Passage* (London: Routledge and Kegan Paul, 1960).
5. Nancy Ammerman, "The Fundamentalist Worldview." Ph.D. diss., Yale University, 1983, pp. 287–88.
6. No mention of pre-teen conversions is made in James, *The Varieties of Religious Experience*; Kett, *Rites of Passage*; Greven, *The Protestant Temperament*; Whitney Cross, *The Burned-Over District: The Social and Intellectual History of Enthusiastic Religion in Western New York, 1800–1850* (1950; reprint, NY: Ithaca, Cornell University Press, 1982); Nancy Cott, "Young Women in the Second Great Awakening in New England," *Feminist Studies* 3 (1975); Gerald F. Moran, "Conditions of Religious Conversion in the First Society of Norwich, CT: 1718–1944," *Journal of Society History* (Spring, 1972): 335–38; John Owen King III, *The Iron of Melancholy: Structures of Spiritual Conversion in America From the Puritan Conscience to Victorian Neurosis* (Middletown: Wesleyan

University Press, 1983); William McLoughlin, *Revivals, Awakenings, and Reform* (Chicago: University of Chicago Press, 1978); Bernard Weisberger, *They Gathered at the River: The Story of the Great Revivalists and Their Impact Upon Religion in America* (Chicago: University of Chicago Press, 1958). Patricia Tracy (*Jonathan Edwards* [New York: Hill and Wang, 1980], pp. 112, 242) first notes the *uniqueness* of the account of four-year old Phebe Bartlett's conversion (which Jonathan Edwards describes in his Faithful Narrative), and then questions its veracity. I have come across only four sources that mention the occurrence of early-childhood conversion in previous historical periods (Tracy, *Jonathan Edwards*; Edwin Starbuck, *The Psychology of Religion*; Jon Alexander, *American Personal Religious Accounts 1600–1980* (New York: Edwin Mellen Press, 1983); James Fowler, *The Stages of Faith* (San Francisco: Harper and Row, 1981).) In each case, they either dismiss the report of early childhood conversion, or consider such cases as few and scattered. The important point here, however, is not the single disqualifying case, but the *pattern* of conversions. A systematic and thorough search of early Sunday school records, as Nancy Ammerman has suggested, would put to good test the hypotheses that I present here.

7. The question of whether or not childhood is disappearing in late-twentieth century America is open to debate. While these authors argue that children are dressing as adults and being "exposed to adult secrets," they ignore the history of child abuse and incest, and the consequences of agencies, interest groups, laws that provide special services and protection to children. It is not so much that their evidence is wrong, but that their arguments are limited to the point of inaccuracy and their conclusions suspect because they are so selective. Nonetheless, given the currency of their ideas among many Americans, it is worth taking them seriously and critically. Neil Postman, *The Disappearance of Childhood* (New York: Delacorte, 1983); Valerie Suransky, *The Erosion of Childhood* (Chicago: University of Chicago Press, 1983); Marie Winn, *Children Without Childhood* (New York: Pantheon Books, 1982).

8. David Elkind, *All Grown Up and No Place to Go* (Reading: Addison-Wesley, 1984), and *The Hurried Child* (Reading: Addison-Wesley, 1981).

9. Starbuck, *The Psychology of Religion*.

10. James, *The Varieties of Human Experience*.

11. Cott, "Young Women in the Second Great Awakening in New England."

12. Owen King III, *The Iron of Melancholy*, p. 59.

13. Moran, "Conditions of Religious Conversion in the First Society of Norwich, CT: 1718–1944," pp. 335–38; Owen King, III, *The Iron of Melancholy*, pp. 14, 59, 355.

14. Owen King, III, *The Iron of Melancholy*, p. 355; Kett, *Rites of Passage*; Moran, "Conditions of Religious Conversion in the First

Society of Norwich, CT: 1718–1944," pp. 331–43.

15. Philip Greven quoted in Kett, *Rites of Passage*.
16. See Tracy, *Jonathan Edwards*.
17. Bennet Tyler (in Kett, *Rites of Passage*) analyzed descriptions of New England revivals from 1779–1814. He discovered that fifteen of the twenty-four revivals began among young people, with the remaining descriptions giving no indication of age structure.
18. Joan Brumberg, *Mission for Life* (New York: The Free Press, 1980), p. 20.
19. Cott, "Young Women in the Second Great Awakening in New England," Tamara Hareven, *Amoskeag* (New York: Pantheon, 1978).
20. This is not to imply that women of the Second Great Awakening gained or were close to gaining equality with men, even within the church. In fact, women's conversions can be interpreted as simultaneously representing liberating opportunities and accommodations to the socio-economic imperatives and cultural demands of the day—just as they had for men of the First Great Awakening. For those women who were marrying, the conversion prepared them for submission and more faithful service both within the church and the family; as Martha Blauvelt argues, "conversion prepared women for the radical change that accompanied marriage." Single women of the period had much more freedom than their married counterparts and "the renunciation of past sinfulness, recognition of one's powerlessness in matters of salvation, and acceptance of God's sovereignty that characterized Calvinist conversion paralleled the renunciation of youthful frivolities, acceptance of a drastic loss in independence, and recognition of man's superior authority which women experienced as they made the transition from the carefree single girl to the stolid matron" (Martha Blauvelt, "Women and Revivalism" in Rosemary Reuther and Rosemary Keller, eds., *Women and Religion in America*, vol. 1, *The Nineteenth Century* [New York: Harper and Row, 1981], p. 4.)
21. Brumberg, *Mission for Life*; Cross, *The Burned-Over District*.
22. Weisberger, *They Gathered at the River*, pp. 12, 163.
23. Weisberger, *They Gathered at the River*, p. 163.
24. Starbuck, *The Psychology of Religion*, p. 28—emphasis in the original.
25. Starbuck, *The Psychology of Religion*, p. 34.
26. Starbuck, *The Psychology of Religion*, p. 35.
27. James Hunter, *American Evangelicalism* (New Brunswick, NJ: Rutgers University Press, 1983).
28. David O. Moberg, "Fundamentalism and Evangelicalism in Society," in David Wells and John Woodbridge, *The Evangelicals* (New York: Abingdon Press, 1975), pp. 150–51.
29. See Steven Tipton, "The Moral Logic of Alternative Religions," *Daedalus* Winter, 1982; Steven Tipton, *Getting Saved from the*

Sixties (University of California Press, 1981); Dick Anthony and Thomas Robbins, "Spiritual Innovation and the Crisis of American Civil Religion," *Daedalus* Winter, 1982; J. Richardson, M. Stewart and R. Symmonds, *Organized Miracles: A Study of a Contemporary, Youth, Communal Fundamentalist Organization* (New Brunswick, NJ: Transaction Books, 1979); Milton Yinger, *Countercultures* (NY: The Free Press, 1982).

30. Thomas Luckman, *The Invisible Religion* (New York: The MacMillan Co., 1967).

31. Barbara Finkelstein, "Cultural Transmission and the Acquisition of Identity: Learners and Learning in American Educational History." Paper presented at the American Educational Research Association, March 1982.

32. The following illustrations are taken primarily from interviews with people at Covenant. While the Lakehaven Baptists likewise encouraged and legitimated conversions among children, they did not talk in as much detail about the experience.

33. Urie Bronfenbrenner, *The Ecology of Human Development* (Cambridge: Harvard University Press, 1980).

10 Re-creation or Re-production: A Critique of Christian Schools

1. C. Wright Mills, *The Sociological Imagination* (New York: Oxford University Press, 1959), p. 3.

2. See the discussion of the rhetoric of consensus by James Donald and Michael W. Apple, in Michael W. Apple, *Teachers and Texts* (New York: Routledge and Kegan Paul, 1986), pp. 122–23.

3. For a discussion of traditions in American thinking, especially the influence of biblical and republican thought and their relationship to "community," see Robert Bellah et al., *Habits of the Heart: Individualism and Commitment in American Life* (Berkeley: University of California Press, 1985).

4. Christopher Lasch, *The Culture of Narcissism* (New York: W. W. Norton, 1979), Chap. 3.

5. Samuel Bowles and Herbert Gintis, "The Long Shadow of Work: Education, the Family, and the Reproduction of the Social Division of Labor," *Insurgent Sociologist* 4 (1974).

6. Melvin Kohn, "On the Transmission of Values in the Family: A Preliminary Formulation." Unpublished manuscript, 1983, p. 8.

7. Martin Carnoy and Henry Levin, *Schooling and Work in the Democratic State* (Stanford: Stanford University Press, 1985), and *The Limits of Educational Reform* (New York: David McKay Co., 1976); Michael W. Apple, "Bringing the Economy Back into Educational Theory," *Educational Theory* (Fall, 1986), and *Education and Power* (London: Routledge and Kegan Paul, 1982); Michael W. Apple, ed., *Cultural and Economic Reproduction in*

Education (London: Routledge and Kegan Paul, 1982), and Apple, ed., *Ideology and Curriculum* (London: Routledge and Kegan Paul, 1979); Henry Giroux, *Theory and Resistance in Education* (London: Heinemann Educational Books, 1983).

8. Carnoy and Levin, *Schooling and Work in the Democratic State*; Bowles and Gintis, "The Long Shadow of Work."

9. Melvin Kohn, *Class and Conformity: A Reassessment* (Chicago: University of Chicago Press, 1977).

10. William Behn, Martin Carnoy, Michael Carter, Joyce Crain, and Henry Levin, "School is Bad; Work is Worse," in Carnoy and Levin, eds., *The Limits of Educational Reform*.

11. Behn et al., *Habits of the Heart*.

12. Kohn, *Class and Conformity*.

13. John Meyer, "The Effects of Education as an Institution," *American Journal of Sociology* 83, no. 1 (1977): 55–77; David Kamens, "Organizational and Institutional Socialization in Education," in Kerckhoff, Alan, ed., *Research in the Sociology of Education and Socialization*, Vol. 2 (Greenwich: Jai Press, 1981), p. 113.

14. Jeffrey Williams and Peter Lindert, *American Inequality: A Macroeconomic History* (New York: Academic Press, 1980).

15. Colin Greer, *The Great School Legend* (New York: Basic Books, 1972).

16. Richard Duboff, "Wealth Distribution Study," *In These Times* (December 11, 1985).

17. Christopher Lasch, " 'Excellence' in Education: Old Refrain or New Departure?" *Issues in Education* 3, no. 1 (Summer, 1985): 1–12.

18. Michael W. Apple, "Curricular Form and the Logic of Technical Control: Building the Possessive Individual," in Apple, ed., *Cultural and Economic Reproduction in Education*.

19. Michael W. Apple, "Curricular Form and the Logic of Technical Capital," in Michael W. Apple and Lois Weis, eds., *Ideology and Practice in Schooling* (Philadelphia: Temple University Press, 1983), p. 149.

20. See John Ramsay's review: "The Hunter Model: New Faces in an Old Vase," *The Review of Education*, vol. 13, no. 3 (Summer, 1987).

21. Apple, "Curricular Form and the Logic of Technical Capital," p. 151.

22. Apple, "Curricular Form and the Logic of Technical Capital,,, p. 158.

23. Paul Willis, "Cultural Production and Theories of Reproduction," in Len Barton and Stephen Walker, eds., *Race, Class, and Education* (London: Croom Helm, 1983).

24. "Facts About Accelerated Christian Education: Christian Education on the Forefront of Reformation" (Lewisville, TX: A.C.E., Inc., 1985), pp. 23–26.

25. Roger Dale, ed., *Schooling and Capitalism: A Sociological Reader* (London: Routledge and Kegan Paul, 1976), p. 3.
26. Michael W. Apple, *Teachers and Texts: A Political Economy of Class and Gender Relations in Education* (New York and London: Routledge and Kegan Paul, 1986), p. 194.
27. Apple, *Teachers and Texts*, p. 27.

Bibliography

Aidala, Angela. 1985. "Social Change, Gender Roles and New Religious Movements." *Sociological Analysis* 46, no. 3 (Fall): 287–314.

Alexander, Jon. 1983. *American Personal Religious Accounts 1600–1980*. Lewiston, NY: Edwin Mellen Press.

Ammerman, Nancy. 1983. "The Fundamentalist Worldview: Ideology and Social Structure in an Independent Fundamentalist Church." Ph.D. diss., Yale University.

Anthony, Dick, and Thomas Robins. 1982. "Spiritual Innovation and the Crisis of American Civil Religion." *Daedalus* 11, no. 1 (Winter): 215–34.

Antonovsky, Aaron. 1979. *Health, Stress, and Coping*. San Francisco: Jossey-Bass.

Anyon, Jean. 1983. "Intersections of Gender and Class: Accommodation and Resistance by Working-Class and Affluent Females to Contradictery Sex-Role Ideologies." in *Gender, Class and Education*, edited by Stepehen Walkee and Len Barton. New York: Falmer Press

Apple, Michael. 1986. "Bringing the Economy Back into Educational Theory." *Educational Theory* 36, no. 4 (Fall): 403–15.

———. 1986. *Teachers and Texts: A Political Economy of Class and Gender Relations in Education*. New York: Routledge and Kegan Paul.

———. 1982. *Cultural and Economic Reproduction*. London: Routledge and Kegan Paul.

———. 1982. *Education and Power*. London: Routledge and Kegan Paul.

Apple, Michael, ed. 1979. *Ideology and Curriculum*. London: Routledge and Kegan Paul.

Apple, Michael, and Lois Weis. 1983. "Curricular Form and the Logic of Technical Capital." In *Ideology and Practice in Schooling*, edited by Michael Apple and Lois Weis. Philadelphia: Temple University Press.

Baker, A. A. 1979. *The Successful Christian School*. Pensacola, FL: A Beka Book Publications.

Ball, William. 1981. *Constitutional Protection of Christian Schools*. Whittier, CA.

Ballweg, George. 1980. "The Growth in the Number and Population of Christian Schools Since 1966: A Profile of Parental Views Concerning Factors Which Led Them to Enroll Their Children in a Christian School." Ph.D. diss., School of Education, Boston University.

Barker. 1960. "Ecology and Maturation." In *Nebraska Symposium on Motivation*, no. 8, edited by Marshall Jones. Lincoln: University of Nebraska Press.

Barton, Len, and Stephen Walker. 1983. *Race, Class, and Education.* London: Croom Helm.

Becker, Henry. 1978. "The Impact of Racial Composition and Public School Desegregation on Changes in Non-Public School Enrollment by White Pupils," report no. 352. Center for the Organization of Schools, The Johns Hopkins University.

Beckford, James. 1983a. "Conversion and Apostasy: Antithesis or Complementary?" In *Conversion and Commitment in New Religious Movements*, edited by D. Anthony Needleman and T. Relskins. New York: Seabury.

Beckford, James, and James Richardson. 1983b. "The Bibliography of Social Scientific Studies of New Religious Movements." *Social Compass* 30: 111–35.

Behn, William, Michael Carnoy, Michael Carter, Joyce Crain, and Henry Levin. 1976. "School is Bad; Work is Worse." In *The Limits of Educational Reform*, edited by M. Carnoy and H. Levin. New York: David McKay Co.

Bellah, Robert, Richard Madsen, William Sullivan, Ann Swidler, and Stephen Tipton. 1985. *Habits of the Heart.* Berkeley: University of California Press.

Bengston, Vern. 1975. "Generation and Family Effects in Value Socialization." *American Sociology Review* 40: 358–371.

Berger, Peter. 1967. *The Sacred Canopy.* New York: Doubleday.

Berger, Peter, and Thomas Luckman. 1966. *The Social Construction of Reality.* Garden City, New York: Anchor Books.

Bernstein, Basil. 1974. *Class, Codes & Control: Theoretical Studies Towards a Sociology of Language.* New York: Schocken Books.

Blauvelt, Martha T. 1981. "Women and Revivalism." In *Women and Religion in America*, edited by Rosemary Ruether and Rosemary Keller. Vol. 1, *The Nineteenth Century.* New York: Harper and Row.

Bourdieu, Pierre, and Jacques Passeron. 1977. *Reproduction in Education, Society and Culture.* Beverly Hills, CA: Sage Publications.

Bowles, Samuel, and Herbert Gintis. 1976. *Schooling in Capitalist America.* New York: Basic Books.

———. 1974. "The Long Shadow of Work: Education, the Family, and the Reproduction of the Social Division of Labor." *Insurgent Sociologist.*

Braverman, Harry. 1975. *Labor and Monopoly Capital: The Degradation of Work in the Twentieth Century.* New York: Monthly Review.

Brim, Orville and Carol Ryff. 1980. "On the Properties of Life Events." In *Life-Span Development and Behavior*, edited by Baltes and Brim.

Vol. 3. New York: Academic Press.

Bronfenbrenner, Urie. 1979. *The Ecology of Human Development: Experiments by Nature and Design*. Cambridge: Harvard University Press.

Bronfenbrenner, Urie, and Maureen Mahoney, eds. 1975. *Influences on Human Development*. Hinsdale, IL: The Dryden Press.

Brown, Dennis. 1977. *An Investigation Into the Philosophy of Education of Christian Elementary and Secondary Schools*. Ph.D. diss., Indiana University.

Brumberg, Joan. 1980. *Mission for Life*. New York: The Free Press.

Brusselmans, Christiane, et al. 1980. *Toward Moral and Religious Maturity*. Morristown, NJ: Silver Burdette Co.

Carlson, Gerald. 1982. "Christian School Growth Continues." *American Association of Christian Schools Communicator* 2, no. 6.

Carnoy, Michael, and Henry Levin. 1976. *The Limits of Educational Reform*. New York: David McKay Co., Inc.

—————. 1985. *Schooling and Work in the Democratic State*. Stanford: Stanford University Press.

Carper, James, and Thomas Hunt, eds. 1984. *Religious Schooling in America*. Birmingham, AL: Religious Education Press.

Clausen, John, ed. 1968. *Socialization and Society*. Boston: Little, Brown and Co.

Collins, Randall. 1975. *Conflict Sociology*. New York: Academic Press.

—————. 1978. *The Credential Society: A Historical Sociology of Education and Stratification*. New York: Academy Press.

—————. 1971. "Sexual Stratification." *Social Problems* 19, no. 1: 3–21.

Cooper, Bruce. 1984. "The Changing Demography of Private Schools." *Education and Urban Society* 16, no. 4: 429–42.

Coser, Lewis. 1956. *The Functions of Social Conflict*. New York: The Free Press.

Cott, Nancy. 1975. "Young Women in the Second Great Awakening in New England." *Feminist Studies* 3: 15–29.

Cremin, Lawrence. 1977. *Traditions of American Education*. New York: Basic Books.

Cross, Whitney. 1982 (1950). *The Burned-Over District: The Social and Intellectual History of Enthusiastic Religion in Western New York, 1800–1850*. Ithaca, NY: Cornell University Press.

Dale, Roger, ed. 1976. *Schooling and Capitalism: A Sociological Reader*. London: Routledge and Kegan Paul.

D'Antonio, William, and Joan Aldous, eds. 1983. *Families and Religions: Conflict and Change in Modern Society*. Beverly Hills, CA: Sage Publishing.

DeCharms, Richard, and Gerald Moeller. 1962. "Values Expressed in American Children's Readers: 1800–1950." *Journal of Abnormal and Social Psychology* 64 (February).

Demerath, N. J. (1965). *Social Class in American Protestantism*. Chicago: Rand McNally.

Dennis, John. 1977. "An Investigation into the Philosophies of

Education of Christian Elementary and Secondary Schools." Ph.D. diss., Indiana University.

Dreeben, Robert. 1968. *On What is Learned in School*. Reading, MA: Addison-Wesley.

DuBoff, Richard. 1984. "Wealth Distribution Study Causes Change of Discomfort." *In These Times*, Dec., 11.

Durkheim, Emile. 1964. *The Rules of the Sociological Method*. Translated by Sarah Solovay and John Mueler. New York: The Free Press.

Ehrenreich, Barbara, and Deidre English. 1973. *Complaints and Disorders*. Old Westbury, NY: Feminist Press.

Ehrenreich, Barbara, Elizabeth Hess, and Gloria Jacobs. 1986. *Remaking Love: The Feminization of Sex*. New York: Doubleday.

Elder, Glen, ed. 1984. *Life Course Dynamics: From 1968 to the 1980s*. Ithaca, NY: Cornell University Press.

Elder, Glen. 1980. "Adolescence in Historical Perspective." In *Handbook of Adolescent Psychology*, edited by Joan Adelson. New York: John Wiley and Sons.

———. 1980. *Family Structure and Socialization*. New York: Arno Press.

Elkind, David. 1984. *All Grown Up and No Place To Go*. Reading, MA: Addison-Wesley.

———. 1981. *The Hurried Child*. Reading, MA: Addison-Wesley.

Elson, Rachael. 1964. *The Guardians of Tradition: American Schoolbooks of the 19th Century*. Lincoln: University of Nebraska Press.

Erickson, Donald. "Private Schools in Contemporary Perspective," report no. TTC–14. Institute for Research on Educational Finance and Governance, Stanford, CA.

Erikson, Erik. 1950. *Childhood and Society*. NY: W. W. Norton Co., Inc.

———. 1968. *Youth: Identity and Crisis*. New York: W. W. Norton.

Everhart, Robert. 1983. *Reading, Writing & Resistance*. Boston: Routledge and Kegan Paul.

Falwell, Jerry. 1980. *Listen, America!* New York: Bantam Books.

Finkelstein, Barbara. 1982. "Cultural Transmission and the Acquisition of Identity: Learners and Learning in American Educational History." Paper presented at the AERA Meetings, New York.

Fowler, James. 1981. *The Stages of Faith*. San Francisco: Harper & Row.

Geertz, Clifford. 1973. *The Interpretation of Cultures*. New York: Basic Books.

Gennep, Arnold. 1960. *The Rites of Passage*. London: Routledge and Kegan Paul.

Gilbert, Douglas, and Joseph Kahl. 1982. *The American Class Structure*. New York: Dorsey Press.

Gillespie, V. B. 1979. *Religious Conversion and Personal Identity: How and Why People Change*. Birmingham, AL: Religious Education.

Giroux, Henry. 1983. *Theory and Resistance in Education*. London:

Heinemann Educational Books.

Gleason, Daniel. 1980. "A Study of the Christian School Movement." Ph.D. diss., University of North Carolina.

Glock, Charles, and Rodney Stark. 1965. *Religion and Society in Tension*. Chicago: Rand McNally.

Gordon, David. 1984. "Dying to Self." *Sociological Analysis* 45, no. 1: 41–45.

Greeley, Andrew. 1972. *The Denominational Society: A Sociological Approach to Religion in America*. Glenview, IL: Scott, Foresman and Co.

Greer, Colin. 1972. *The Great School Legend*. New York: Basic Books.

Greven, Philip. 1977. *The Protestant Temperament: Patterns of Child-Rearing, Religious Experience, and the Self in Early America*. New York: Alfred A. Knopf.

Gusfield, Joseph. 1963. *Symbolic Crusade*. Champagne-Urbana: University of Illinois Press.

Hadden, Jeffrey. 1983. "Televangelism and the Mobilization of a New Christian Right Family Policy." In *Families and Religion: Conflict and Change in Modern Society*, edited by D'Antonio and Aldous. Beverly Hills, CA: Sage Publishing.

Hall, Richard. 1982. *Organizations: Structure and Processes*, 3rd ed. Englewood Cliffs, NJ: Prentice-Hall.

Hareven, Tamara. 1978. *Amoskeag*. New York: Pantheon Books.

Hargrove, Barbara. 1983. "Church, Family and Modernization." In *Families and Religion: Conflict and Change in Modern Society*, edited by D'Antonio and Aldous. Beverly Hills, CA: Sage Publishing.

Harris, Marvin. 1981. *America Now*. New York: Simon and Schuster.

Heirich, Max. 1977. "Change of Heart: A Test of Some Widely Held Theories About Religious Conversion." *American Journal of Sociology*, 83: 653–80.

Herberg, William. 1955. *Protestant, Catholic, and Jew: An Essay in American Religious Sociology*. New York: Doubleday.

Hess, Beth. 1984. "Protecting the American Family: Public Policy, Family and the New Right." In *Families and Change: Social Needs and Public Policy*, edited by Rosalie Genovese. South Hadley, MA: Bergin & Garvey.

Hoge, Dean, and David Roozen, eds. 1979. *Understanding Church Growth and Decline 1950–1978*. New York: Pilgrim Press.

Holt, John. 1940. "Holiness Religion: Cultural Shock and Social Reorganization." *American Sociological Review* 5 (October): 740–47.

Hostetler, John. 1963. *Amish Society*. Baltimore: The Johns Hopkins University Press.

Howard, Donald. 1985. "The Strengths and Weaknesses of the A.C.E. Program." Lewisville, TX: Accelerated Christian Education, Inc.

Hunt, Alan. 1980. *Marxism & Democracy*. Atlantic Highlands, NJ: Humanities Press.

Hunter, James. 1983. *American Evangelicalism*. New Brunswick, NJ: Rutgers University Press.

James, William. 1902. *The Varieties of Religious Experience*. New York: The Modern Library.

Kaestle, Carl. 1983. *Pillars of the Republic: Common Schools and American Society 1780–1860*. New York: Hill and Wang.

Kaestle, Carl, and Maris Vinovskis. 1978. "From Apron Strings to ABCs: Parents, Children, and Schooling in Nineteenth-Century Massachusetts." In *Turning Points*, edited by John Demos and Sarane Boocock. Chicago: University of Chicago Press.

Kamens, David. 1981. "Organizational and Institutional Socialization in Education." In *Research in the Sociology of Education and Socialization*, edited by David Kerckhoff. Vol. 2, Greenwich, CT: Jai Press.

Keim, A. 1975. *Compulsory Education and the Amish: The Right Not to be Modern*. Boston: Beacon Press.

Kett, Joseph. 1977. *Rites of Passage*. New York: Basic Books.

Kienel, Paul. 1980. *The Christian School: Why Is It Right for Your Child*. Wheaton, IL: Victor Books.

———. 1976. "Status of American Christian Schools." A Report to the National Institute of Christian School Administrators. Winona Lake, IN, July 25–30.

———. 1978. "The Teachings of Basic Academic Skills—Is It a Legitimate Function of the Religious Community?" Address prepared for the American Family Institute. Washington, D.C., May 28.

Kilbourne, Brock and James Richardson. 1984. "Psychotherapy and New Religions in a Pluralistic Society." *American Psychologist* 39, no. 3: 237–251.

King, John Owen III. 1983. *The Iron of Melancholy: Structures of Spiritual Conversion in America from the Puritan Conscience to Victorian Neurosis*. Middletown, CT: Wesleyan University Press.

Kliebard, Herbert. 1969. *Religion and Education in America: A Documentary History*. Scranton PA: International Textbook Co.

Kohn, Melvin. 1983. "On the Transmission of Values in the Family: A Preliminary Formulation." Unpublished manuscript.

———. 1977. *Class and Conformity: A Reassessment 1977*. Chicago: University of Chicago Press.

Kraushaar, Otto. 1972. *American Nonpublic Schools: Patterns in Diversity*. New York: Basic Books.

Lasch, Christopher. 1985. " 'Excellence' in Education: Old Refrain or New Departure?" *Issues in Education* 3, no. 1 (Summer): 1–12.

———. 1979. *Culture of Narcissism*. New York: W. W. Norton.

Lefcourt, Herbert, ed. 1981. *Research with the Locus of Control Construct*. Vol. 1, *Assessment Methods*. New York: Academic Press.

Levenson, Hanna. 1974. "Activism and Powerful Others: Disjunctures Within the Concept of Internal-External Control." *Journal of Personality Assessment* 38: 377–385.

Liebman, Robert, and Robert Wuthnow. 1983. *The New Christian Right*. Hawthorne, NY: Aldine Press.

Lightfoot, Sarah Lawrence. 1978. *Worlds Apart: Relationship Between Families and Schools*. New York: Basic Books.

Lofland, John, and Norman Stenoud. 1981. "Conversion Motifs." *Journal of Social Science Review* 20: 373–385.
Long, Theodore and Jeffrey Hadden. 1983. "Religious Conversion and Socialization." *Journal of Social Science Review* 22: 1–14.
Luckman, Thomas. 1967. *The Invisible Religion.* New York: The MacMillan Co.
Marsden, George. 1980. *Fundamentalism and American Culture.* New York: Oxford University Press.
Martin, William. 1981. "God's Angry Man." *Texas Monthly,* April.
Marty, Martin. 1970. *The Righteous Empire.* New York: Dial Press.
McDearmid, Andrew. 1979. "Student Achievement in Accelerated Christian Education Schools in Pennsylvania." Ph.D. diss., Temple University.
McGuire, Meredith. 1981. *Religion: The Social Context.* Belmont, CA: Wadsworth.
McLaughlin, David, and Bruce Cooper. 1982. "The Latest Word on Private School Growth." Paper presented at AERA, New York, March.
McLaughlin, Donald, and T. Burke. 1980. "Nonpublic School Pupils: How Many Are There Really? A Validation Check on the NCES Survey." Palo-Alto, CA: American Institutes for Research, SAGE, No. 9.
McLoughlin, William. 1978. *Revivals, Awakenings, and Reform.* Chicago: University of Chicago Press.
McNamara, Patrick. 1985. "The New Christian Right's View of the Family and Its Social Science Critics." *Journal of Marriage and Family* (May): 449–58.
———. 1984. "Presidential Address." *Sociological Analysis* 46, no. 2: 93–99.
Mead, Sidney. 1976. *The Lively Experiment.* New York: Harper and Row.
Meyers, John. 1977. "The Effects of Education as an Institution." *American Journal of Sociology* 83, no. 1, 55–77.
Mills, C. Wright. 1959. *The Sociological Imagination.* New York: Oxford University Press.
Moberg, David O. 1975. "Fundamentalism and Evangelicalism in Society." In *The Evangelicals,* edited by Wells and Woodbridge. New York: Abingdon Press.
Moran, Gerald F. 1972. "Conditions of Religious Conversion in the First Society of Norwich, CT: 1718–1944." *Journal of Social History* 5 (Spring): 331–43.
Morris, Arval. 1979. *The Constitution and American Education.* American Case Book Series. St. Paul, MN: West Publishing Company.
National Youth Survey. 1980. Boulder Research Institute.
Neibuhr, M. Richard. 1951. *Christ and Culture.* New York: Harper and Row.
Neugarten, Bernice and Gunhild Hagestad. 1976. "Age and the Life

Course." In *Handbook of Aging and the Social Sciences*, edited by Benstock and Shanas. New York: Van Nostrand Reinhold Co.

Neugarten, Bernice, Gunhild Hagestad, and N. Datan. 1973. "Sociological Perspectives on the Life Cycle." In *Life-Span Developmental Psychology*, edited by P. Baltes and K. Schare. New York: Academic Press.

Nevin, David and Robert Bills. 1976. *The Schools That Fear Built.* Washington, D.C.: Acropolis Books.

Nordin, Virginia and William Turner. 1980. "More Than Segregation Academies: The Growing Protestant Fundamentalist School." *Phi Delta Kappan* 61, no. 3: 391–94.

Ogbu, John. 1974. *The Next Generation: An Ethnography of Education in an Urban Neighborhood.* New York: Academic Press.

Palmer, James. "The Impact of Private Education on the Rural South." Cited in Corrine Glesne and Alan Peshkin, "The Christian Day School." In *Private Schools and Public Concerns: What the Research Says*, edited by Patricia Bauch. Greenwood Press, forthcoming.

Parsons, Talcott. 1959. "The School Class as a Social System." *Harvard Educational Review* 24 (Fall): 297–318.

Peshkin, Alan. 1986. *God's Choice: The Total World of a Fundamentalist Christian School.* Chicago: University of Chicago Press.

Peterson, Christopher. 1980. "The Sense of Control Over One's Life: A Review of Recent Literature." Prepared for the Social Science Research Council on The Self and Personal Control Over the Life Span, New York.

Pope, Liston. 1942. *Millhands and Preachers.* New Haven: Yale University Press.

Postman, Neil. 1983. *The Disappearance of Childhood.* New York: Delacorte Press.

Quebedeaux, Richard. 1978. *The Worldly Evangelicals.* New York: Harper and Row.

———. 1974. *The Young Evangelicals.* New York: Harper and Row.

Ramsay, John. 1987. "The Hunter Model: New Faces in an Old Vase." *The Review of Education* 13, no. 3 (Summer).

Ravitch, Diane. 1974. The Great School Wars: New York City 1805–1973: *A History of Schools as a Battlefield for Social Change.* New York: Basic Books.

Richardson, James. 1985. "The Active vs. Passive Convert: Paradigm Conflict in Conversion/Recruitment Research." *Journal for the Scientific Study of Religion* 24, no. 2: 119–236.

Richardson, James, Mary Stewart, and Robert Symmonds. 1979. *Organized Miracles: A Study of a Contemporary, Youth, Communal Fundamentalist Organization.* New Brunswick, NJ: Transaction Books.

Riesman, David. 1950. *The Lonely Crowd.* New Haven: Yale University Press.

Rist, Ray. 1973. *The Urban School: A Factory for Failure.* Cambridge, MA: MIT Press.

Rokeach, Milton. 1979. *Understanding Human Values: Individual and Social*. New York: Free Press.

———. 1967. *Value Survey*. Sunnyvale, CA: Halgren Tests.

Rose, Stephen. 1984. *Social Stratification in the United States*. Baltimore: Social Graphics Co.

Rose, Susan. 1987. "Women Warriors: The Negotiation of Gender Roles in an Evangelical Community." *Sociological Analysis* 48, no. 3: 245–258.

———. 1987. "Conversations of Conversion: Interviewing Evangelicals." *International Journal of Oral History* 8, no. 1: 28–40.

———. 1984. "Christian Schools in a Secular Society." Ph.D. diss., Cornell University.

———. 1984. "From Sacred to Secular Schools: The Transition as Methodological Tool." Paper presented at the Eastern Sociological Association Meetings, Philadelphia, PA.

Rothenberg, Stuart, and Frank Newport. 1984. *The Evangelical Voter*. Washington: The Institute for Government and Politics of The Free Congress Research and Education Foundation.

Rotter, Julian. 1975. "Some Problems and Misconceptions Related to the Construct of Internal Versus External to the Locus of Control of Reinforcement." *Journal of Consulting and Clinical Psychology* 43: 56–67.

Rubin, Lilian. 1976. *World of Pain*. New York: Basic Books.

Salagnik, Laura and N. Karweit. 1982. "Voluntarism and Governance in Education." *Sociology of Education* 55, no. 2/3 (April/July): 152–61.

Simmel, Georg. 1923. *On Individuality and Social Forms*. Chicago: University of Chicago Press.

Skerry, Peter. 1980. "Christian Schools, Racial Quotas, and the IRS." *Public Interest*, no. 61 (Fall): 18–41.

Sklar, Kathryn. 1973. *Catherine Beecher: A Study in American Domesticity*. New York: W. W. Norton.

Slater, Philip. 1976. *The Pursuit of Loneliness*. Boston: Beacon Press.

Smelser, Neil and Sydney Halpern. 1978. "The Historical Triangulation of Family Economy and Education." In *Turning Points: Historical and Sociological Essays on the Family*, edited by John Demos and Sarane Boocock. Chicago: University of Chicago Press.

Snow, David and Richard Machalek. 1984. "The Sociology of Conversion." *Annual Review of Sociology* 10: 167–90.

Sommerville, John. 1982. *The Rise and Fall of Childhood*. Beverly Hills, CA: Sage Publishing.

Starbuck, Edwin. 1899. *The Psychology of Religion*. New York: Charles Scribner's Sons.

Sugiyama, Takie. 1976. "Millenarian Movements and Resocialization." In *Social Movements and Social Change*, edited by Robert Lauer. Carbondale, IL: South Illinois University Press.

Suransky, Valerie. 1983. *The Erosion of Childhood*. Chicago: University of Chicago Press.

Swidler, Ann. 1979. *Organization Without Authority: Dilemmas of Social*

Control in Free Schools. Cambridge: Harvard University Press.
Tipton, Steven. 1982. "The Moral Logic of Alternative Religions." *Daedalus* (Winter).
————. 1981. *Getting Saved from the Sixties.* Berkeley, CA: University of California Press.
Tracey, Patricia. 1980. *Jonathan Edwards.* New York: Hill and Wang.
Turner, Victor. 1974. *Dramas, Fields, and Metaphors.* Ithaca, NY: Cornell University Press.
————. 1978. *Image and Pilgrimage in Christian Culture: Anthropological Perspectives.* New York: Columbia University Press.
Tyack, David. 1974. *The One Best System: A History of American Urban Education.* Cambridge, MA: Harvard University Press.
————. 1966. "The Kingdom of God and the Common School: Protestant Ministers and the Educational Awakening of the West." *Harvard Educational Review* 36 (Fall): 447–69.
Tyack, David, and Elizabeth Hansot. 1981. "Conflict and Consensus in American Public Education." Special Issue, American Schools: Public and Private. *Daedalus* (Summer): 1–25.
Waller, William. 1932. *The Sociology of Teaching.* New York: Wiley and Sons.
Ward, Patricia and Martha Scott. 1981. *Christian Women at Work.* Grand Rapids, MI: Zondervan Publishing House.
Weber, Max. 1922. *The Sociology of Religion.* Trans. by Ephrain Fischoff. Boston: Beacon Press.
Weisberger, Bernard. 1958. *They Gathered at the River: The Story of The Great Revivalists and Their Impact Upon Religion in America.* Chicago: University of Chicago Press.
Wells, David and John Woodbridge. 1975. *The Evangelicals.* New York: Abingdon Press.
Williams, Jeffrey and Peter Lindert. 1980. *American Inequality: A Macroeconomic History.* New York: Academic Press.
Williams, Robin. 1970. *American Society.* New York: Alfred A. Knopf.
————. 1968. "Values." In *International Encyclopedia of the Social Sciences*, edited by E. Shils. New York: MacMillan.
Willis, Paul. 1983. "Cultural Production and Theories of Reproduction." In *Race, Class, and Education*, edited by Len Barton and Stephen Walker. London: Croom Helm.
————. 1977. *Learning to Labor.* New York: Columbia University Press.
Wilson, Bryan, ed. 1967. *Patterns of Sectarianism: Organization and Ideology in Social and Religious Movements.* London: Heinemann.
Winn, Marie. 1982. *Children Without Childhood.* New York: Pantheon Books.
Wood, John. 1983. *Ridgewood School: An American Revitalization Effort.* Chapel Hill: New York: University of North Carolina.
Yinger, Milton. 1982. *Countercultures.* New York: The Free Press.

Index